U.S. Bureau of Labor Statistics

HOW AMERICAN BUYING HABITS CHANGE

HD
6983
A54 3
1959

↑ 935326

UNITED STATES DEPARTMENT OF LABOR
James P. Mitchell, *Secretary*

For sale by the Superintendent of Documents, U. S. Government Printing Office
Washington 25, D.C. - Price $1 (paper)

One of the millions of America's city workers—a typical consumer of the 1930's.

PHOTOGRAPHS by Ankers Photographers; Brown Brothers; E. I. du Pont de Nemours & Co., Inc.; Harper's Bazaar; Levitt & Sons, Inc.; Library of Congress; National Archives; National Capital Planning Commission; San Francisco Bay Area Rapid Transit Commission.

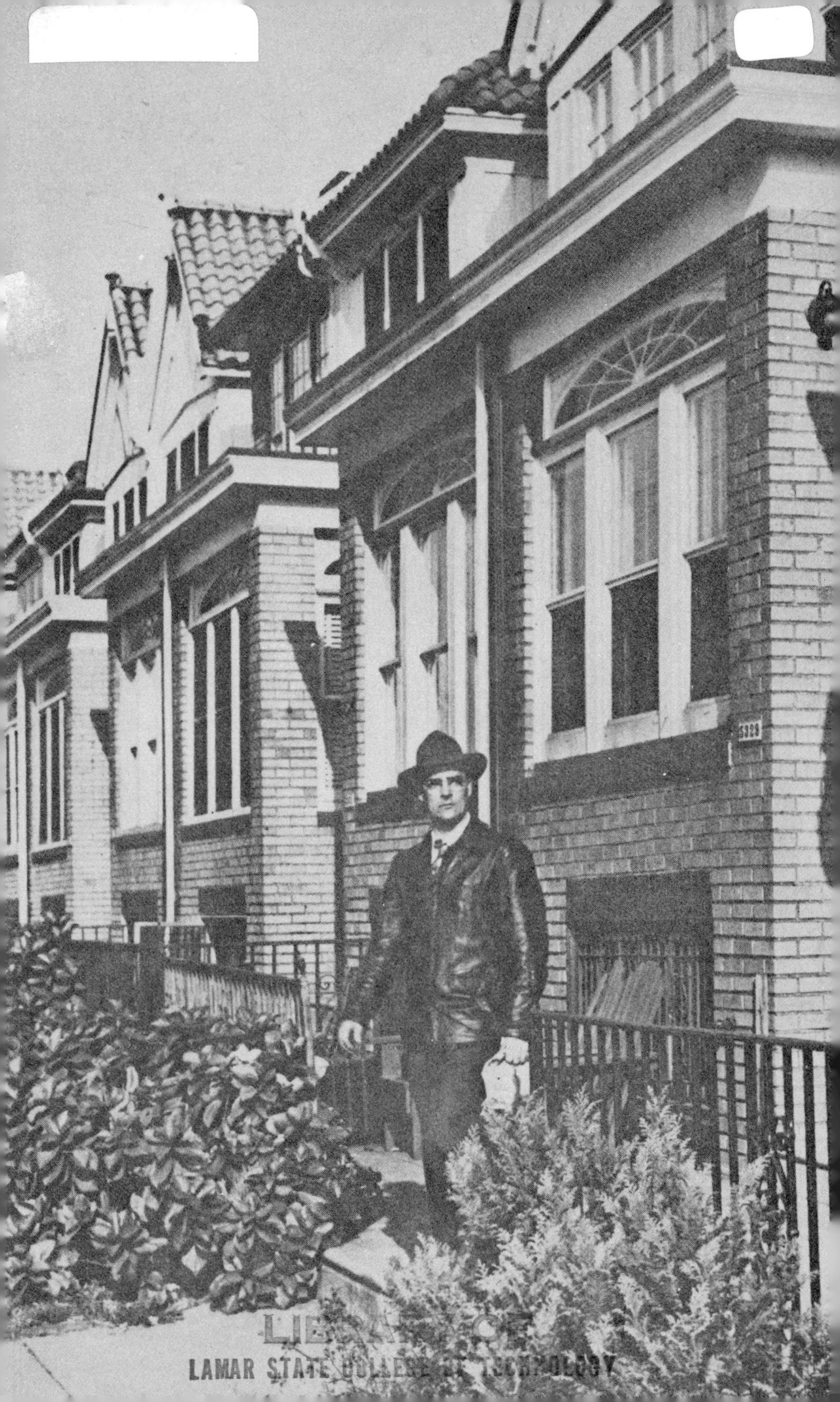

FOREWORD

This book describes the improvements in living standards which Americans have achieved since 1888.

In that year, the Commissioner of Labor initiated the Federal Government's first survey to find out how people live—what food they ate, what clothes they wore, what kinds of dwellings they lived in, what they spent on recreation and transportation.

Since that time, at fairly widespread intervals, similar studies have been made, some of national coverage. And each in turn reflected changes in the way that people live.

In this book these various studies have been dovetailed to yield a picture of changes in the consumption habits of the American people over more than half a century.

The picture is representative. Excluding the extremes of wealth and poverty, it concentrates on the middle group of consumers—the families of the millions of blue-collar and white-collar workers who make up the vast bulk of our predominantly city life. These, when all is said and done, are the American consumers, the workers who make up our society. The way they live is the way that most of us live.

As the book shows, living conditions have improved. They have improved tremendously. Not only in material things, but also in many things that might be termed spiritual. We now have not only better plumbing, better health, but also more time to read, to learn, to think, to dream, more time to restore the body and to heal the mind.

These are worthwhile accomplishments.

We are all aware, of course, that the changes here reported are taking place. The value of this book is that it brings together between covers the measured evidence of this progress. It tells not only what, but how much. It also reminds us of numerous areas of change which we might otherwise have forgotten. And it gives us some feeling, even in our own time, of the speed with which we may expect change in the future.

Having seen how far we have come, perhaps we may justifiably and with hope look forward to further improvements.

JAMES P. MITCHELL,
Secretary of Labor.

ACKNOWLEDGMENTS

This volume is the work of many members of the staff of the Department's Bureau of Labor Statistics, Ewan Clague, Commissioner. The Division of Prices and Cost of Living developed the basic framework of the book, which stems from the Bureau's studies of income and consumption.

Except as otherwise noted below, the authorship of the 10 chapters was by members of the staff of the Division of Prices and Cost of Living.

    I. Lawrence R. Klein, Office of Publications
   II. Joseph A. Clorety
  III. H. E. Riley
  IV. Faith M. Williams and Anna-Stina Ericson, Office of Labor Economics
   V. Doris P. Rothwell
  VI. Faith M. Williams, Office of Labor Economics
 VII. Helen H. Lamale
VIII. Paul R. Kerschbaum, Office of Program Planning
  IX. Abner Hurwitz
   X. Joseph A. Clorety

Mary S. Bedell, of the Bureau's Office of Publications, provided substantive editing and continuity for the contributions by the several chapter authors.

Major contributions, in the form of working papers, estimates, and tabulations, were made by a number of staff members of the Division of Prices and Cost of Living. Credit is also due to other members of the departmental staff who have assisted materially in this project.

CONTENTS

	Page
Foreword	v
Acknowledgments	vii
Chapter I. The Bell and the Bay Window	1
Bridging Two Eras	1
Ease and Status for the Worker	3
Securing of Ease	3
Life Off the Job	3
Workaday Living	4
Achievement of Status	5
Community Standing	5
Job Equity	6
The New Bent of Mind	7
The Long, Hard Row	8
The Closed Frontier	8
A New Labor Force and A New Market	8
Slum Living and the Immigrant	10
Study of the Italian Born	10
Closeup of a Slum Family	12
American and European Living Standards	13
Studies of the Era	14
The 1898 Commission	14
The Steel Story	15
The Golden Trace	17
Productivity—Prerequisite of Progress	17
Bases for Higher Productivity	18
Material Benefits	19
Social Values	19
Democracy	19
Unionism	20
Social Reform	20
Economic "Emancipation" of Women	20
Education	21
The Private Household	21
Advertising and Credit	22
Chapter II. The Broadening Base of Consumption	25
Conditions of Progress	26
Rise of Family Incomes	27
Wages and Salaries	28
Nonmonetary Income	28
Narrowing of Income Differentials	29
Taxes and Purchasing Power	30
Savings, Credit, and Economic Security	31
Shifting Patterns of Consumption	33
Expenditure Patterns in Six Surveys	34
Changes in Actual Buying Power	37
The 1950 Survey: Additional Detail	39
Patterns for Workers' Families and Other Groups	42
Redefining "Basic Necessities"	45
Role of "Sundries"	48
Collateral Measures of Consumption	53

	Page
Chapter III. From the Slums to Suburbia	57
Housing at the End of the 19th Century	57
Causes of Congestion and Poor Housing	58
Homeownership	61
Condition of the Workers' Houses	62
First 2 Decades of the 20th Century	65
Regulatory Measures	65
Urban Growth	65
War Housing	66
Housing at the End of World War I	66
Changes Between the Two Wars	68
Booming Twenties	68
Housing Expenditures During the Depression	68
Economic Recovery—Government Aid	70
Federal Housing Legislation	70
Low-Income Housing	71
World War II and Veterans' Housing	73
Workers' Housing at Midcentury	74
Extent of Homeownership	74
Cost and Choice of Housing in 1950	75
Home and Community	79
The Seamy Side	79
New Suburbs	80
Chapter IV. The Homemaker's Job and the Home Scene	83
Housekeeping in 1900	84
Condition of Houses	85
Furniture and Equipment	86
Beginnings of Mechanized Housekeeping	89
The Mid-Thirties	92
Wartime and Postwar Purchases	93
The Worker's Home in 1950	96
Technological Changes in the Home	98
The Housewife's Job Today	99
Chapter V. Meals, Menus, and Market Baskets	103
Evolution in Diets and Food Marketing	103
Variety in the Diet	103
Stores and Packages	104
Improvements in Nutrition	108
Research in Nutrition	109
Food in the Family Budget	110
Eating Out	111
Food in the Family Kitchen	112
Importance of Meats	115
Fruits and Vegetables	118
Grain Products	120
Milk and Other Dairy Products	121
Desserts and Nonalcoholic Drinks	124
Proof of the Pudding	125
Chapter VI. Clothing and Personal Care	127
Nature of the Revolution in Dress	127
Textile Fibers	129
Garment Production	129
Styling	130
Environment	131

	Page
Chapter VI. Clothing and Personal Care—Continued	
Trends in Clothing Expenditures	133
Clothing Expenses of Different Family Members	134
Types of Clothing Purchased	136
Men's Apparel	137
Women's Clothing	141
Clothing for Children	145
Trends in Expenditures for Personal Care	146
Chapter VII. Health Care: Past Gains, New Goals	149
Health Problems of Urban Workers in 1900	149
Lack of Knowledge	149
Working Conditions	150
Housing Conditions	151
Illness and Medical Care	152
Efforts Toward Improvement	153
Growth in Health Services	154
Hospitals	154
Health Service Personnel	155
Government Health Assistance	157
Voluntary Health Agencies	158
Industrial Medical Services	159
Health Advances	160
Pure Food and Drugs	160
Control of Disease	161
Lengthening the Life Span	162
Costs of Medical Care for Workers' Families	162
Medical Care Expenditures	163
Types of Medical Services Obtained	163
Differences by Occupational Group and Region	164
Influence of Family Size and Income	166
Adequacy of Expenditures	167
Variability in Medical Costs	169
Free Medical Care	169
Paying for Medical Care	171
Health of Workers Today	174
Chapter VIII. The Revolution in Transportation	177
Workers' Transportation, 1900 to 1920	179
Public Transportation	180
The Automobile	182
Changes During the Twenties and Thirties	184
Family Expenditures for Transportation	184
Transportation Facilities	185
Public Transportation	185
Automobile Travel	186
Transportation Since 1940	188
Growth in Use of Credit	189
Family Expenditures	191
New Problems of Extensive Automobile Ownership	194
Chapter IX. Time for Living	197
Changes in Working Time	197
The Workweek	197
Vacations	199
Retirement	200
Increase in Free Time	200

Chapter IX. Time for Living—Continued

	Page
Increasing Variety of Leisure-Time Activities	201
Entertainment	202
Sports	204
Travel	204
Public Recreation Facilities	205
Workers and Community Affairs	206
Radio, Television, and Music	207
Adult Education	209
Reading	213
Hobbies	213
Expenditures of Workers' Families	213

Chapter X. Consumption Statistics: A Technical Comment ... 217

Surveys of Consumer Expenditures	217
Laying the Foundation: 1875	218
Purposes of Major Surveys	218
Purposes of Other Surveys	221
Populations Represented	222
Criteria for Selection of Families	223
Survey Methods	225
Personal Consumption Expenditures	228
Adjustments for Noncomparability	228
Comparison With Expenditure Surveys	230
Estimating 1956 Family Expenditures	231
Standard Budgets as Indicators of Progress	232
Conceptual Advances	233
Budget Studies	234

References ... 243

TABLES

1. Consumption expenditures of families of wage earners in 15 cities and towns in Massachusetts, by income class, 1874–75 ... 35
2. Consumption expenditures of "normal families" of workers in 9 basic industries, by income class, 1888–91 ... 37
3. Consumption expenditures of "normal families" in principal industrial centers in 33 States, by income class, 1901 ... 40
4. Consumption expenditures of white workers' families with at least one child, in cities of all sizes, by income class, 1917–19 ... 42
5. Consumption expenditures of families of employed workers in cities of 50,000 and over, by income class, 1934–36 ... 44
6. Consumption expenditures of wage-earner and clerical-worker families in cities of 2,500 and over, by income class, 1950 ... 46
7. Average consumption expenditures of families of city wage and clerical workers of two or more persons, selected periods ... 49
8. Consumption expenditures of all families in cities of 2,500 and over, by income class, 1950 ... 50
9. Consumption expenditures of wage-earner and clerical-worker families and single consumers in cities of 2,500 and over, by region and occupational group, 1950 ... 54
10. Percent of skilled wage earners owning homes and selected items of furniture and household equipment, by region and type of city, 1950 ... 97

	Page
11. Percent distribution of expenditures for food consumed at home by urban wage-earner and clerical-worker families, selected periods, 1901-55	113
12. Average number of pounds of food purchased per week for consumption at home by urban wage-earner and clerical-worker families, estimated for 3 persons, selected periods, 1901-55	114
13. Annual clothing expenditures for members of families of employed wage and clerical workers, by age, sex, and occupation, 1934-36	135
14. Average number of garments purchased annually by men and boys over 16 years of age in families of city wage earners and clerical workers, 1917-19, 1934-36, and 1950	139
15. Average number of garments purchased annually by women and girls over 16 years of age in families of city wage earners and clerical workers, 1917-19, 1934-36, and 1950	144
16. Percent distribution of medical care expenditures by wage and clerical workers' families, 1917-19, 1934-36, and 1950	164
17. Proportion of wage-earner and clerical-worker families owning and purchasing cars in 42 cities, 1934-36	185
18. Proportion of consumer installment credit represented by automobile paper, selected dates, 1929-56	190
19. Consumers' method of financing automobile purchases, selected years, 1948-55	191
20. Percent of wage-earner and clerical-worker families reporting expenditures for automobile and other travel and transportation, by income class, 1950	192
21. Percent of wage-earner and clerical-worker families owning automobiles, by occupation of family head, 1950	193
22. Motor vehicle use in 17 States for selected occupations of principal operator, 1951-54	194
23. Wage-earner and clerical-worker family expenditures for recreation, reading, and education, selected periods, 1901-50	214
24. Distribution of total personal consumption expenditures for recreation and reading, selected years, 1929-55	215
25. Percent distribution of urban family expenditures for recreation, reading, and education, 1950	216
26. Total personal consumption expenditures per capita and average expenditures for current consumption per family member, selected years, 1901-56 (in current dollars)	226
27. Consumption expenditures of all urban consumer units, 1950 averages and 1956 estimates	232
28. Selected standard family budgets in the United States, 1903-56	236

CHARTS

1. How urban wage-earner and clerical-worker families of 2 or more divided their expenditures for current consumption at selected times	36
2. How urban wage-earner and clerical-worker families of 2 or more at selected income levels divided their expenditures for current consumption in 1950	38
3. The dumb-bell plan, 1879	63
4. Relation of the income level and expenditures for shelter by urban wage-earner and clerical-worker families, selected years, 1901, 1917-19, 1934-36, and 1950	76

xiii

		Page
5.	Importance of furnishings, equipment, and household operation in expenditures by urban wage-earner and clerical-worker families, selected years, 1917–19, 1934–36, and 1950	94
6.	Importance of food and beverages in family expenditures, selected years, 1901–50, all income classes	111
7.	The share of the family food budget going for meat, poultry, and fish, selected years, 1901–55, all income classes	117
8.	The burden of medical care expenditures among urban families in 1950	170
9.	Trends in methods of transit, selected years, 1905–54	181

CHAPTER I

The Bell and the Bay Window

> ... The front door bell and the bay window have been a boon to social conditions of the tenement dweller. The early tenements never had private entrances. When the individual began to build his own house, he had a door bell and a private entrance, even though a family lived on the floor above him. He also has a bay window on his house, and everything also has to be in keeping with that bay window—better furnishings and belongings of all types.
> —Labor Department testimony before a congressional commission, 1901.

By any material measure, city workers and their families in the United States today have remarkably higher living standards than they did at the beginning of this century. Perhaps the most evident indications are that they earn more and they buy more and have thus become the most important group of consumers of the products of the Nation's economy.

The social and economic forces which produced the upsurge of living standards in the United States between 1900 and 1950 were indeed complex. It is the purpose of this chapter first to impart some sense of the change in well-being of the American workman and his family during this time and then to discuss briefly a few of the forces which contributed to the change—the basic structure of the bridge between the two eras.

BRIDGING TWO ERAS

The 20th century American, said Henry Adams in 1904, would be a product of "incalculable coal power, chemical power, electric power, and radiating energy, as well as of new forces yet undetermined. ... At the rate of progress since 1800, every American who lived into the year 2000 would know how to control unlimited power. He would think in complexities unimaginable to an earlier mind. He would deal with problems altogether beyond the range of earlier society. To him the 19th century would stand on the same plane with the 4th ... and he would only wonder how both of them, knowing so little, and so weak in force, should have done so much."[1]

Thus Adams made a bold and broad projection of the future. Three decades later, the Presidential committee investigating social changes looked back and examined some of those unimagined complexities:

"The first third of the 20th century has been filled with epoch-making events and crowded with problems of great variety and complexity. The world war, the inflation and deflation of agriculture and business . . . the spectacular increase in efficiency and productivity and the tragic spread of unemployment and business distress . . . the stoppage of immigration . . . the struggles of the Progressive and the Farmer Labor parties . . . the sprawl of great cities . . . the expansion of education, the rise and weakening of organized labor, the growth of spectacular fortunes . . . the emphasis on sports and recreation . . . these are a few of the many happenings which have marked one of the most eventful periods of our history."

". . . Modern life," it continued, "is everywhere complicated, but especially so in the United States, where immigration from many lands, rapid mobility within the country itself, the lack of established classes or castes to act as a brake on social changes, the tendency to seize upon new types of machines, rich natural resources, and vast driving power have hurried us dizzily away from the days of the frontier into a whirl of modernisms which almost passes belief."[2]

The bridge which links the 1890's with the mid-20th century is canted broadly upward. At the lower end, it spans the war with Spain, the acquisition of territory and emergence of the Nation as a world power, the high tide of immigration, the expansion of industry in volume and in size of unit, a cascade of inventions and processes, the beginnings of a national labor movement, the broad extension of popular education, and the rumblings of social reform. These would be events aplenty for five decades, even omitting the start of the revolution in transportation and communication. But they bring us only to about 1910.

Still to be bridged are a major depression with mass unemployment, two world wars, the burgeoning of cities, the political and economic emancipation of women, the establishment of the power of unionism, and the expansion of government influence in many phases of economic and social life, especially in the role of ameliorative agent and guarantor of security.

NOTE.—Numbered footnotes are listed at end of each chapter.

In the midst of this progression of events, the improvement in the material side of American life was, as one commentator has put it, "all but convulsive."[3]

EASE AND STATUS FOR THE WORKER

In the spring of 1957, the United Steelworkers of America proudly paraded the success stories of several of the recipients of union scholarships—children of members—who share union grants totaling $40,000 yearly. Among those who had completed undergraduate or graduate work in the 10 years since the local unions had begun sponsoring the scholarships were engineers, mathematicians, psychologists, electronic technicians, and biologists. Many of them were employed as salaried experts or officials in the very plants where their fathers had served or still serve as hourly rated production workers.

The significance of this seemingly minor and limited benefit should not be overlooked. It is symptomatic of a revolution which has transformed the average American worker and his family from a precarious and sometimes comfortless production unit with a generally drab existence into a certainly more secure and possibly more relaxed household group. Reduced to a brace of words, the situation of the typical worker's family in the 1950's relative to 1900 was one of ease and status.

Homelife was easier because the material equipment of the home was more efficient and comfortable and the home itself more commodious and satisfying. Worklife required fewer hours and less physical effort, and commanded larger monetary rewards. Status in the community and in the reckoning of the employer, manifest in scores of activities and in the workaday practices of industrial relations, was firmly and widely established.

These flat assertions need elaboration.

Securing of Ease

Life Off the Job. Wholly apart from a general improvement in the quality of housing which has occurred since 1900 (see chapter III) has been the growth of homeownership itself. Farm houses aside, the proportion of all occupied dwellings which were owner occupied rose from about three-eighths in 1900 to more than half in 1950 and about three-fifths in 1956. That wage earners' families were participating extensively in this trend toward buying homes (or equities in them) is apparent from the price levels of new homes begun in 1956: more than half were planned to sell for less than $15,000.

Within the worker's home in the mid-1950's was an abundance of modern equipment. Typically, there would be no less than electricity, running hot and cold water, at least one fully equipped bathroom, central heating, a vacuum cleaner, a washing machine, a telephone, a radio and a television set, a gas or electric cooking stove, a refrigerator, and completely furnished rooms. In many instances the heating would be automatic and the kitchen would contain a dishwasher, a garbage disposal unit, and an exhaust fan. Electric air conditioners, blankets, fans, and mixers, and a multitude of other aids to housekeeping and home living, not excepting the power lawnmower, were within the range of the worker's family budget.

Of course, the personal debt outstanding on the house and on much of what was in it, as well as on the automobile parked outside, might be considerable. But the chief breadwinner's income, with increasing frequency augmented by the earnings of a working wife, plus comparatively cheap credit, carried the burden. In this respect, as in so many others, the worker's family differed little from many in higher income groups.

With the shortening of the workweek by 15 hours between 1900 and 1956, the wage earner (with exceptions and variations) now has weekend leisure. He also has several paid holidays annually and a paid vacation. His car or his outboard motor or his home workshop offers the mobility or opportunity to develop and indulge his hobbies. More important as a concomitant of this leisure is the opportunity for the wage earner to participate in the social life of the family.

Workaday Living. Increased real earnings, which have made ease of home living a commonplace to the worker, were also accompanied by an easing of physical effort on the job. One authority who has written extensively on this subject takes issue with the contention "that an hour of work now makes heavier demands upon the worker than in a simpler economy . . . ." He conceded that "the tempo of working, as of living, is faster now than formerly; and the pace or rhythm of the machine is felt by larger numbers of workers especially in the semiskilled employments." Nevertheless, he wrote, "Recent trends . . . have tended to mitigate the effects of extreme specialization, of heavy drudgery . . . . Technology has tended to mechanize and routinize production, but it has also lightened men's labors and given them an increasing role in managing machines and supervising automatic operations."[4]

The forklift truck, the mechanical handling of materials, the seemingly never-ending stream of new types of power equipment to relieve the strain of heavy labor, especially in foundry, mine, and construction work, have without doubt combined with the shorter workday and the shorter workweek and the shorter work-year to ease the physical effort involved in most jobs. Two other developments have also contributed to making work less onerous. As mechanization and automation have proceeded, many slow, tedious hand operations and heavy manual tasks have been transformed into semiskilled or even skilled work, and unskilled jobs have become less prevalent (8 percent of total employment in 1950, compared with 15 percent in 1910). At the same time, white-collar workers have come to represent a much larger proportion of the labor force (21 percent in 1950, only 10 percent in 1910).

Even such innovations as in-plant hot lunches and adequate sanitary cleanup and toilet facilities have had their beneficial effect. Moreover, with the stimulus of protective legislation, collective bargaining, and the organized safety movement, closer attention has been paid to the health and safety of the worker on the job. The extent to which this protection has contributed as well to his peace of mind is hardly capable of measurement. There is some corollary evidence that it has had a stimulating effect on production.

Achievement of Status

It would be labored and somewhat unrealistic to separate the securing of ease at home and ease at work from the achievement of status in the community and status on the job. Social conditions in a state of change do not follow neat, discrete channels; rather, many of the streams flow together at some point.

Community Standing. One of the major advantages of a shorter workday cited by the Industrial Commission established by Congress in 1898 was the time thus afforded for the development of citizenship. Conscious, perhaps, of the large proportion of foreign born in the labor force, it argued in its report: "On the side of the working population . . . they gain not only in health, but also in intelligence, morality, temperance, and preparation for citizenship . . . . Lessening of hours leaves more opportunity and more vigor for the betterment of character, the improvement of the home, and for studying the problems of citizenship. For these reasons the short workday for working people brings an advantage to the entire community."[5]

The integration of the worker with the community has always been an institutional objective of the American labor movement. As early as 1883, Adolph Strasser, close associate of Samuel Gompers, told the Senate Committee on Education and Labor that one of the principal aims of labor was to "become better citizens generally."[6]

Gompers himself, notes one keen student of labor, by 1900 had influenced American labor to "a fateful commitment: to seek a secure place within the social structure of capitalist society rather than stand outside and fight it. . . . The consequences . . . were enormous." Labor's big ambition, he continued, became the winning of "acceptance within the society as a 'legitimate' social group."[7] In pursuit of that ambition, workers and their leaders sought equity with other groups, recognition in political and governmental affairs, collective bargaining with employers, and participation in community undertakings.

By 1950, aided especially by the official recognition accorded labor during both world wars, this institutional aim of labor was established on local, national, and international levels. Organized labor had "won a respected and respectable seat at the American community table."[8]

The community status thus achieved by wage earners as a group through trade unionism is actually excelled by the changed community standing they have acquired as individuals. The enhancement of the wage earner's economic fortune by union action, whether or not he is a union member, is one contributing factor. Another is a general democratic pervasion of social life and custom. The wage earner's way of life is well-nigh indistinguishable from that of his salaried co-citizens. Their homes, their cars, their babysitters, the style of the clothes their wives and children wear, the food they eat, the bank or lending institution where they establish credit, their days off, the education of their children, their church—all of these are alike and are becoming more nearly identical.

It is not only that the typical wage earner no longer lives in an identifiably "working class" neighborhood or that his washing machine contains the same gage sheet steel and the same electric motor as that of the wealthier man; or that they both are officers of the P-TA, or are elected to public office, or may go to the same dentist. It is also that the American workingman is conscious of the fact that he has attained a position in society not even approached by his counterpart in any other part of the world. He has pride in himself and especially in the achievements of his family. He has little cause for repeating the vow often uttered through the early decades of the century, half bitterly, once hopelessly, that "no kid of mine is going to work in the shop"; his "kids" could much more freely make their own choices, and with far less cause for avoiding the "shop."

Job Equity. Work in the shop has itself acquired a new status. Directly or indirectly because of unionization, a multitude of factors have combined to give the worker a sense of equity in his job. The concept and practice of seniority, the vast development of private pension funds, and looming very important indeed, the systematic processing of grievances, freedom from arbitrary dismissal, and the right to equity through his union's representation in the assessment of discipline, are pertinent examples. Management itself has initiated or accepted programs which strengthen the job-equity feeling: stock ownership, profit sharing, and negotiations or consultations with labor on many matters until recently zealously guarded and jealously regarded as absolute management prerogatives.

The Wertheim Fellowship study of dual loyalty by Father Theodore Purcell strongly suggests that the feeling of status and satisfaction of the worker on the job flows largely from acceptance of the dual responsibilities of company and union and that the ensuing dual allegiance "is something they have, something they want, something that must not be threatened."[9]

The New Bent of Mind

Allowance for some overdrawing in our picture still leaves room for the well-based conclusion that there has been a rapid fading in the distinctive coloration of the working class. This phenomenon is strikingly apparent in comparison with 1900; it is even detectable since 1940.

The adoption of middle-class attitudes, the change in what workers have come to expect, even more than the greatly augmented real family income, points to this great revolution in class relations. "When an entire population struggles for subsistence from one day to the next," states the foreword to America's Needs and Resources, "its problems of economic philosophy are relatively few. Its choices and decisions are limited. Once this point is passed, however, each member of the population is faced with a new question; not 'Can I live?' but 'What kind of life do I wish to lead?'"[10] Certainly there is compelling evidence that the wage earner has realized formerly undreamed-of ways of working and living.

The wage earner's yearnings have long since left behind John Mitchell's quest for "better homes and education."[11] They have even broadened Philip Murray's goal of "music in the home, pictures on the wall, carpets on the floor."[12]

Some of the causes of this changed outlook on living, listed in almost the most abbreviated possible form, are the broadened scope of trade union activity and the decline of "voluntarism"; advertising and mass media of communication; education; the foreign travel of the citizen armies; accessibility and abundance of commodities and services; the working wife (increasingly working for items of "extra" living rather than to help eke out an existence); and the forward strides in real family income.

THE LONG, HARD ROW

The Closed Frontier

It was not always thus.

Theodore Roosevelt, writing in 1902 of the 5 months' strike of 150,000 anthracite coal miners, trenchantly summed up the close of an era and presaged with accuracy the essentials of a grievous labor problem:*

"A few generations ago, an American workman could have saved money, gone West, and taken up a homestead. Now the free lands were gone. In earlier days a man who began with pick and shovel might have come to own a mine. That outlet too was now closed .... The majority of the men who earned wages in the coal industry, if they wished to progress at all, were compelled to progress not by ceasing to be wage earners, but by improving the conditions under which all the wage earners in all the industries of the country lived and worked, as well, of course, as improving their own individual efficiency."[13]

By 1900, the frontier was indeed closed, and pushing against its limits was the tidal force of immigration, the source of which, by this time, had shifted markedly to southern and eastern Europe. Probably 20 million immigrants had entered the United States in the 80 preceding years. Nearly 4 million came in the 1890's; more than a million in 1905 alone. Before 1890, many of the newcomers arrived with the expectation of establishing themselves in business or as independent farmers. After 1890, most newcomers sought jobs in the cities. Usually they took manual jobs, since few had the training for professional or managerial work, and limited knowledge of English prevented them from working at office or selling jobs.

A New Labor Force and A New Market

The consequence was an increase in urban population generally, with a heavy admixture of foreign born. In 1900, the population in "urban territory" had reached 30 million, or 40 percent of the total. The proportion of foreign born in cities of 25,000 or more was 25 percent; in some of the very large cities it was 50 percent or more. Growing city populations—swollen also by migrants

---

*As President, Roosevelt had intervened in the coal strike and appointed a commission to arbitrate the issues. (See Report to the President on the Anthracite Coal Strike of May-October, 1902, by the Anthracite Coal Strike Commission, Washington, D. C., 1903.) This was a departure from previous governmental intervention in labor disputes, particularly in the railroad strikes of 1877 and the Pullman strike of 1894, when Federal troops had been employed, and its significance in social history is deserving of considerable weight.

WORKING PLACES—For its time, this was a fairly comfortable workshop. Compared with modern standards, it is crowded, poorly lighted, and cluttered with work materials. Note the clothing of the women workers.

from America's farms and small towns—simultaneously created an ample labor supply and a vast domestic market for farm products and manufactured goods. Workers, flocking to cities that were often already bursting at the seams, found in many cases that the price of survival was the development of a high degree of adaptability as workers. They achieved also a readiness to experiment with new modes of living.

The significance of immigrants in the labor force of the country was discussed at some length by the Commissioner of Labor in a 1913 report. Foreign-born workmen in 1907-8 comprised 62 percent of the soft-coal work force, 58 percent in iron and steel, 72 percent in cotton textiles, 66 percent in woolens, nearly 70 percent in oil refining and in leather, 61 percent in meatpacking, and from 50 to 60 percent in an assortment of metal manufactures.

The report noted that "the foreign born, who are in large part recent immigrants from eastern and southern Europe, constitute a majority of the labor force. The possibility of utilizing this tremendous supply of cheap though untrained labor has contributed greatly to the expansion of the iron and steel industry. The introduction of these unskilled immigrants has had a complex and important effect on the working conditions in the industry."[14]

With most of the industries where the immigrants found jobs located in cities, the resulting crowding and creation of slum areas was the subject of numerous private and official surveys and investigations. All of them revealed fragments of the life of the workingman of the period—his paycheck, his workday, his health, his eating habits, and his housing. It is difficult to realize that the level of living thus portrayed represented the highest in the world for the working class. It was meager and often squalid, but for the immigrant it was the best he had known and the money wage he received could buy many items hitherto unknown in his budget; and all the while he was buttressing the market and helping to induce a consumption-productivity relationship which, a generation hence, would so radically change his status and manner of living. (See p. 17.)

Slum Living and the Immigrant*

One of the studies of slum areas was authorized by joint resolution of Congress in 1892. The study, conducted by the Commissioner of Labor, covered Baltimore, Chicago, New York, and Philadelphia.

Almost half of the employed slum dwellers in each city earned less than $10 a week; from 10 to 24 percent earned less than $5. Average periods of unemployment over a designated year ranged from 3 to 3½ months. Weekly earnings of family groups (and multiple wage earning was common and often crucial to family survival) averaged as high as $21. (For purposes of comparison, the purchasing power of the dollar at the time of the study was equivalent to about $3.20 in 1950.)

Crowding is starkly revealed by the following figures relating to sleeping accommodations, computed from some of the basic tables of the report.

Item	Baltimore	Chicago	New York	Philadelphia
Percentage of all persons sleeping 4 or more per room	33	20	28	33
Percentage of all persons sleeping in room with only 1 or no outside window	33	70	62	25
Largest number of persons found sleeping in 1 room	9	20	[1] 92	8

[1] The dormitory sleeping 92 is listed as having 8 windows.

Study of the Italian Born. A preponderance of Italian born among the slum dwellers of Chicago disclosed by the report—1 out

---

*Not all working-class families, of course, lived in slums, but most of the foreign-born workers did, and they were a large proportion of all urban workers in the period under review.

INDUSTRIAL HOMEWORK—Late into the night at the turn of the century many a newly arrived immigrant family fought for survival by working under contract at home. Poor lighting and crowded conditions in confined living quarters were the lot of many city workers.

of every 3 of the foreign born and 1 out of 6 of all Chicago residents studied—prompted a special study in 1896 which throws further light on living conditions at about the turn of the century, particularly with respect to problems of adjustment and exploitation of immigrants. With but minor modifications to allow for ethnic differences, many of the basic findings of the study could have applied to Poles, Hungarians, Lithuanians, and a dozen other European nationalities.

Average weekly earnings were somewhat lower than those for the city's slum dwellers at large. Men's weekly earnings ranged from $2.29 to $8.25; women's, from $1.72 to $3.02. Average hours worked per week for men were 59, for women, 51. Significantly, nearly 60 percent were unemployed some part of the year, with almost half out of work for 5 or more months.

An examination of dietary habits was made, with the conclusion reached that the Italians were eating a plenitude of fat and overly starchy foods. Samples of diets generally followed by Italian laborers featured heavy quantities of lard, pork, potatoes, macaroni with beans, and beer. So loath was the Italian to adopt American food habits, the report contended, that he would often lie "sick in his own home for months while unhealthful surroundings and bad food conspire against his recovery" rather than go to a hospital where he would be compelled to eat what to him was unpalatable food.[15] The disproportionately high rate of disabling sickness among Italians (17.5 percent, compared with less than 4 percent for the city's slum inhabitants as a whole) was attributed by the report in large measure to dietary deficiencies.

Yet, the Italians were forsaking old country habits of home production of other kinds of goods. For example, although 3 out of 4 women had spun in Italy, not 1 in 100 spun in Chicago. A smaller proportion baked in Chicago than in Italy, and the percentage knitting stockings dropped from 86 to 18.

The padrone system, a particularly oppressive type of labor contracting whereby the contractor or padrone supplied a gang of men for a given job and frequently collected commissions from the laborers in the crew, affected about 22 percent of the Italian families in Chicago. Of these, nearly all paid some commission to the padrone. Moreover, the padrone commonly sold food to the gang (especially when working away from the city) at prices averaging 60 percent above the market, with macaroni up 50 percent; sausage, 72; lard, 77; and tomatoes, 65.

Closeup of a Slum Family. Very often, limited but intimate observations reveal more clearly than statistical analysis the essence of broad social problems. In 1905, a young settlement house worker published her notes on New York tenement families whom she visited over an 18-month period. She found that about half the family income went for food (which is about the proportion for this item in a 1901 nationwide survey of family expenditures), but concluded, as did the Commissioner of Labor with respect to the Italians in Chicago, that better knowledge of food values and cooking methods would result in a better diet with less waste. Half the remaining money went for rent. There were few instances of savings. The families would forego urgently needed purchases to keep up insurance payments, especially burial insurance (they would spend it and more for expensive funerals). She found little knitting or dressmaking, quoting the women as saying it was cheaper to buy than make things at home.

A typical apartment lodging a family of 8 would, she reported, have a tiny kitchen "lighted by air-shaft and window opening out into hall," a combination living and bedroom (2 windows), and a 1-window front bedroom (6' x 7'). There would be 1 closet. "There is no bath in the house. There are 4 waterclosets in the yard.

Each closet is used by 3 families, who are expected to take turns keeping it clean....

"There is a sink with 1 faucet in the kitchen and another in the hall, which is dark and unlit during the day. An open gas jet burns at night. The cook stove burns coal. Clothes washing is done in a wooden tub. Kitchen utensils and dishes are scanty. There are kerosene lamps for illumination.

"This family has 6 living children, but 3 others died at birth or in infancy. Five of the 6 suffer from chronic bronchitis. There is an earnest effort to educate the children at trade and parochial schools. The eldest daughter (16) and son (15) work in a carpet factory, earning $5 and $8 a week. The father is a derrick lifter, usually unemployed in the winter but earning up to $3 a day when on the job. Both parents had migrated from Ireland."[16]

American and European Living Standards

Despite the poverty, hardship, exploitation, and outright misery which beset large segments of the population and which were visited in the cruelest degree on the foreign born and the Negro, the relative advantage of the American worker over the European proletarian was viewed with awe by the foreign visitor. One such, whose extensive travels in various States toward the close of the 19th century resulted in a penetrating study of the American economy and its labor force, was Emile Levasseur.

Beneath all the demographic and economic data he collected, Levasseur perceived two points, which he stressed: the continual upward trends of real earnings and their influence on standards of living and minimum comfort; the relationship of productivity to high wages and low prices.

"Real wages being higher in the United States, the American workman lives more comfortably than the European.... He has acquired settled habits of consumption and enjoyment; his food is more substantial ... he dresses better; he is more comfortably lodged ... he insures his life, and is provident in his own way; he spends more for amusement and upon the societies with which he is affiliated: in other words, he has a *higher standard of life* than the European workman."[17]

He also defended the propensity of the American worker to spend all of his income, pointing out that a surplus "is not the only index of the well-being of the workingman."[18] The social position which spending creates, Levasseur claimed, was a legitimate value.

Concerning productivity and wages, he found that "the inventive genius of the American is perhaps a natural gift, but it has certainly been stimulated by the rate of wages .... The higher the price of labor, the greater will be the effort of the entrepreneur to economize in its use. Moreover, when machinery has made the laborer more productive, it is possible to pay him a higher wage . . . ."[19]

Levasseur relates the incredulity of French trade union delegates to the 1893 exposition in Chicago on witnessing the quality of equipment and the price of products available to the American worker. On shoes: "Superior to the French not only in the manufacture but also in the prices . . . 20 to 30 percent lower than in France." On machine tools: "More specialized than in France, the machinery costlier, but by its greater productivity, more conducive to low-priced products . . . ."[20]

Studies of the Era

The 1898 Commission. The period surrounding the turn of the century was a well-studied era, and much documentary evidence was assembled by Americans. Not the least of the studies—in mass as well as in scope and content—was the 19-volume report of the Industrial Commission created by joint congressional action in 1898 to investigate immigration, labor, agriculture, manufacturing, and business, and to suggest Federal and State legislation which might "harmonize conflicting interests" and also "be equitable to the laborer, the employer, the producer, and the consumer."[21]

In a summary discussion of "general social conditions and progress of working classes," the Commission abstracted testimony of witnesses, and two significant excerpts follow:[22]

> *Clare De Graffenried, member of the staff of the U. S. Commissioner of Labor:* In Massachusetts textile towns two-thirds of the employees are foreign born. The condition of native labor is steadily improving, while the foreign born are becoming Americanized. Living conditions vary greatly. Many men earn from $9 to $15 per week and are able to have 5- or 6-room cottages. Their children are able to go to school until the age of 14 or 15. Others squander their money in drink or on account of large families are kept in extreme poverty. About one-fifth of the factory population are in this class. In such cases the wife and children are driven into the mills to help family income. The front door bell and the bay window have been a boon to social conditions of the tenement dweller. The early tenements never had private entrances. When the individual began to build his own house, he had a door bell and a private entrance, even though a family lived on the floor above him. He also has a bay window on his house, and everything also has to be in keeping with that bay window—better furnishings and belongings of all types. They have a piano, carpets on the floor.
>
> *Samuel Gompers, president of the American Federation of Labor:* Workers are getting an increasingly large share of the wealth produced, especially during the past 35 years. The productivity of the American worker is far greater than that of any other.

Climatic variation makes people more active and nervous; they require more and better food, clothing, and houses and hence demand higher wages. Only the southern Negro is akin to the European worker in terms of exploitation. A shorter workday does not lessen production, and the hours saved become hours of opportunity for thought and improvement. Shortening of hours is always followed by improvement of machinery.

Two of the ultimate recommendations of the Commission warrant attention in relation to present-day attitudes on the subjects. On minimum wages and maximum hours, the Commission argued that while there was equity in a demand for such limitations, and limits might in some cases be set by statute for hours of work, "legislation fixing a minimum scale of wages is obviously impracticable. There does not appear to be any possible device whereby a minimum can be established . . . ."[23]

So far as Government contract work was concerned, the Commission took much the same position, condoning limitation of hours but deeming it "inadvisable that the Government should go so far as to fix rates of wages to be paid by contractors on public work . . . ."[24]

The Commission was quick to set a firm limit to any reduction in hours, lest "the increased cost of production would overbalance [the] gains." For example, the Commission cautioned, if hours were to be reduced "to absurdly low limits," there would be no merit in the action. Absurdly low limits were conceived of in terms of a "5- or 6-hour day."[25]

The Steel Story. As a final item in this series of social vignettes, a 1913 report of the Commissioner of Labor on working conditions in the steel industry supplies a comprehensive picture. The coverage of the study was extensive: more than 300 plants employing 173,000 employees (82 percent of total industry employment in the branches covered) in 26 States.

Almost 30 percent of the entire work force in 1910 were on a 7-day week; on shift transfers (from nightwork to daywork or vice versa), which usually occurred each week or fortnight, a man would work from 18 to 24 consecutive hours. More than 2 out of every 5 employees in steelworks and rolling mills had weekly hours of 72 or more; the ratio was almost 7 out of 10 in blast furnaces, where 63 percent had a weekly schedule of 84 or more hours. (By contrast, the average workweek in nonfarm industries as a whole was about 51 hours.)

In 1910, 42 percent of the steelworks and rolling-mill employees were earning less than 18 cents an hour. The potential full-time weekly earnings of nearly half of the workers were under $12.50. In plants which operated 6 months or more in 1910, the median of possible annual earnings was $630. And the dollar would buy only about 2½ times as much in 1910 as in 1950.

The punishing hours and low real income were only part of the woes of the steelworkers. Overtime, which affected 30 percent of the work force, averaged about 6 hours a week above the normal 72. Generally no premium was paid for overtime or Sunday work.

There were various deductions from paychecks, with practices ranging widely. Some of these were for ice water, disablement funds, medical fees, credit advanced by company stores, rent for company houses, and identification badges. There were only two pension plans in effect. In that of the major company, the benefit was based on 1 percent of the average regular monthly pay received during the last 10 years of service multiplied by total years of service. Voluntary retirement commenced at age 60 after 20 years of service. Thus, a man who worked 25 years and averaged $60 a month for the last 10 years would receive $15 a month. Pensions could be terminated by the trustees.

Company ownership of houses constituted a real grievance of the workers in those communities in which few other facilities were available and in which there was little or no interest in maintenance or sanitation. The report describes one such company-owned community thus: "The company owns every dwelling in the community, and also owns every acre of land in the immediate vicinity . . . . It also owns the only railroad entering the community [and a financial interest in] the only store in the community . . . ."[26] The report pointed out that there was no municipal government; governing powers were vested in the company and in a justice of the peace who was also the superintendent of schools and the coroner who held inquests into accidental deaths in the plant. This individual was quoted as considering himself a company employee.

The housing of officials and skilled workers was described as good. "A very different condition exists in the housing of the large force of unskilled laborers, composed mainly of Negroes, Russians, and Hungarians. The steel company properly designates the abodes it provides for these men as 'shanties.' "[27]

Workers were generally handicapped in protesting conditions in the industry because large numbers of them could not speak English (in 1908 nearly a fourth overall, but in the Midwest nearly a third) and because "they are almost entirely without organization . . . . The Amalgamated Association of Iron, Steel, and Tin Workers, it is true, still exists, but . . . it possesses little strength, except in a very narrow field."[28]

A return to the world of the 1950's reveals amazing contrasts. The more than 1 million members of the United Steelworkers of

America include many of the offspring of the 1910 work force. The steelworker in mid-1958 has as a minimum a basic hourly rate in the neighborhood of $2 an hour. He receives a 50 percent premium for hours in excess of 8 a day or 40 a week. Sunday work—so resented by his forebears—earns a premium of 25 percent; holiday work warrants a 125 percent bonus. His pension is contractual, and, after 30 years' service, it would be at least $72 a month plus Federal social security benefits. A company-paid supplement to unemployment insurance benefits helps tide him over periods of unemployment. He enjoys an annual paid vacation—as much as 3 weeks if he has long service. His union contract provides a formal grievance procedure for him. If the cost of living rises, his wage rates rise in proportion under a union-negotiated escalator plan. He is also provided with insurance and welfare benefits.

THE GOLDEN TRACE

Productivity—Prerequisite of Progress

What alchemy enabled the steelworker to change his status so surprisingly in half a century? What forces made possible the rise in buying power of the weekly earnings of factory workers—25 percent in the first 3 decades of the century and more than 25 percent in the fourth decade—while the shorter workweek was adding more and more free time? Or the increase in weekly spendable earnings (after deducting income and social security taxes and in constant buying-power dollars) of a factory worker with 3 dependents from $42 in 1940 to $63 in 1956?

There is first of all the golden trace of productivity. As technological changes have made it possible to produce more and more goods (frequently of better quality) with the same number of workers, or to produce the same amount with fewer workers, industry has been able to reduce unit costs of production and at the same time shorten work schedules and raise wages. The workers, in turn, have used their increased buying power to purchase more and more goods of a larger variety and their added leisure has created demand for new goods and services.* These increased demands have supported rising production levels for which the necessary manpower has been available partly because some workers in industries with rapidly rising productivity could be released for other employment.

---
*There is some debate among economists as to which created demand first, the productivity or consumption stimulus—the productivity chicken or the consumption egg. One can only marvel at the capacity of each.

AUTOMATION—As a result of technological advances, in many modern mass-production factories one worker controls an entire bank of highly complex and costly machinery.

Bases for Higher Productivity

The productivity rate and the volume of production in the United States are unmatched. With but 6 percent of the world's population and 7 percent of the land area, the Nation produces more than one-third of the world's goods. The individual American worker's output today in a 40-hour week is 3 times that of his grandfather in a 70-hour work span.

The high rate of power application and the development of tools and techniques have, of course, been basic causes of this production record. Other pertinent reasons are: (1) the experimental bent of the American businessman in a free enterprise economy, his surprising freedom from tradition and custom; (2) a mobile and adaptable work force; (3) inventive genius in production methods and devices (more than 40,000 patents are usually issued annually); and (4) the vast stores of accessible raw materials (supplemented by synthetics).

The forces of culture development are cumulative, and the invention of one item to serve a specific use may stimulate new uses and the need for additional inventions. Americans have been quick to make invention the mother of necessity.*

Material Benefits

Perhaps the best way to sum up the immediate and tangible results of a high rate of productivity is to refer to a concrete budget. A given factory worker's budget for 1948 cost $49.51 a week at that time. A worker in 1914 would have had to work about 100 hours a week to buy the things it included; the 1948 worker, less than 34 hours. Moreover, automobiles, radios, television sets, most of the household electrical appliances, frozen foods, and many other products were nonexistent or beyond the reach of workers earlier in the century.

Nonfarm workers have perhaps benefited more from rising productivity than other groups in the population. Certainly, low-income workers have benefited immeasurably since the beginning of the 20th century. In 1901, a U. S. Bureau of Labor survey shows, 42 percent of the workers' families in principal industrial centers had incomes which were equivalent to less than $2,000 in 1954 purchasing power. The comparable proportion in 1954 was 7 percent, and only one-fifth of all families with income of less than $2,000 were headed by nonfarm workers.

Social Values

Rising levels of productivity also have important social values for individuals in the society. A population with advancing techniques and an expanding economy has a wider and more secure margin for such values as education, social reform, unions and other free associations, and the use of credit based upon the assurance of growth.

Democracy. Truly, the growth of democracy has been nurtured by productivity. "The democratic spirit of the American people has assisted materially in preserving the custom of high wages," Levasseur observed in 1900. "The testimony of de Tocqueville upon this point, given some 60 years ago, before the development of the labor union, is still worthy of citation: 'I think that, upon

---

*In this connection one of Levasseur's notes of 1893 is amusing: "Some time ago I found myself at Berne in the company of Mr. Hollerith, the American inventor of an ingenious machine for tabulating statistical returns. The tabulating machine of Mr. Hollerith . . . was used with economy and success in . . . the Eleventh Census at Washington. . . . In Vienna and Rome, where wages are much lower, the experience . . . was not so favorable. *It seems, however, that there is a future for this kind of machine.*" [Italics supplied.] (The American Workman, translated by Thomas S. Adams, Baltimore, The Johns Hopkins Press, 1900, pp. 71, 73.)

the whole, it may be asserted that a slow and gradual rise of wages is one of the general laws of democratic communities. In proportion as social conditions become more equal, wages rise; and as wages are higher, social conditions becomes more equal.' " [29]

The tough fiber of the American worker's democratic spirit is manifest in a healthy skepticism, a fierce predilection to defend his rights, and a willingness to defer to accepted, democratic procedures in his defense.* These qualities take verbal expression in familiar phrases of working class vernacular, such as:

   Hire a hall.
   You and who else?
   I'll take it up with the union.

Unionism. The foregoing phrases reflect something of the philosophy of American trade unionism, which rejected a socialist orientation and the theory of class conflict nearly a half century ago and helped to bring capitalist production to full fruition. Trade union growth was in part a response to expanding productivity and the workers' desire to share in it. Trade union strength is an essential of democratic capitalism, especially in times of stress.

Social Reform. Some of the distressing conditions described in this chapter were inevitable in an era when the economy was rapidly expanding and comparatively undisciplined. But its expansion enabled the Nation to afford reform consistent with the strong democratic taproots of the social order. The surveys cited demonstrate the force of free inquiry, for they exposed the worst problems of the industrial expansion, to which the pioneering reforms of the decade and a half before World War I were largely a response. Later reforms have, of course, differed in direction, since, as Justice Cardozo observed in 1937, "What is critical or urgent changes with the times." [30] They have all, however, enhanced prevailing consumption standards and thus leave the Nation in better position to afford needed future reforms.

Economic "Emancipation" of Women. The "emancipation" of women, in itself a "reform," freed them for more extensive labor-market participation. The proportion of all workers who are women rose from less than a fifth to about a third between 1900 and 1956. In the latter year, nearly three-fifths were married,

---

*James Russell Lowell recognized the significance of these attributes when he said that democracy through the common man had the habit of making itself "generally disagreeable by asking the Powers That Be at the most inconvenient moment whether they are the powers that ought to be." (From his address on "Democracy," October 1864, as quoted in Democracy Today, edited by Christian Gauss, New York, Scott, Foresman and Company, 1917, p. 31.) And Levasseur: "Except in Switzerland the sentiment of equality is nowhere so general as in the United States. This feeling emboldens the laborer in the defense of his rights and at the same time preserves him against revolutionary excess. It has also been favorable to the formation of labor unions which in turn have served to keep wages high." (Op. cit., pp. 390-391.)

and of these, nine-tenths had working husbands. Even when the incomes of husbands were substantial, many wives also held paying jobs. The participation rate of wives with husbands making between $7,000 and $10,000 a year was 21 percent, a tripling in 5 years.

The extra income of the working wife, by helping to expand the worker-family consumption pattern, has doubtless hastened the narrowing of class distinctions in consumption habits. That women have largely replaced children as secondary workers in the labor force has obviously also significantly changed the consumption habits of workers' families. The needs of a working wife are obviously somewhat different—with respect to clothing and personal care, in particular—from those of a housewife. And, despite the shorter workday and even part-time work, the working wife must often buy time—in the form of part-time household help, laundry service, prepared meals, and the like, which the housewife may dispense with for the sake of economy or as a matter of personal preference. Equally obvious are the differences in the needs of a child in school from those of a child toiling in a sweatshop.

Education. Another boon to the purchasing power of the worker family has been the opportunity for schooling, which in turn helps to sustain the productive system. Free public school education was a goal of the American wage earner from the beginning.

In 1910, only 43 percent of the 16- and 17-year-olds were in school; by 1950, 74 percent of that age group were in classrooms. Of the 25–29 year group in 1950, half had completed at least 12 years of school. In 1956, college enrollment totaled 2.9 million—over 8 times the 1910 level. The percentage of the 22-year-old population with a college degree in 1955 was 7 times greater than in 1910; the percentage of 18-year-olds who were high school graduates was 10 times greater.

Education for their children has become so firmly established as part of their level of living that American parents of all income classes take a lively and democratic interest in school standards and curriculums. Parent-teacher associations of the United States, with more than 11 million members, constitute one of the largest dues-paying organizations in the world.

The Private Household. Another benefit of the rise in productivity is that the worker's household today is likely to consist only of himself, his wife, and their younger children, whereas in 1900 it typically included a boarder, a lodger, or a dependent relative as well. The formation of households has proceeded at a more rapid rate than the growth of the population; the number of households increased about 205 percent between 1900 and 1956, compared with a 120 percent rise in the population, and the average size of the household dropped from nearly 5 persons to about 3⅓.

Higher earnings and expanding job opportunities made it easier for single workers to have their own quarters. Furthermore, with social security payments and private pensions, most parents and other elderly relatives who are no longer at work can afford to live in their own household or to go to a home for the aged. About one-eighth of all households in 1956 were headed by persons living alone or with people not related to them.

Advertising and Credit. Two further influences on productivity and demand and levels of living should be briefly mentioned. These are advertising and credit.

One observer recently wrote: "The 'social function' of advertising is to stimulate wants, to make people work harder and earn more. In that sense, advertising, and its helpmate the installment plan, are the two most fearsome social inventions of man since the discovery of gunpowder."[31]

Advertising has vastly stimulated, and often directed, consumer demand, particularly in the markets most dependent upon the expanding incomes of workers' families—the major group of the Nation's consumers. To these the producers appeal for consumption of the vast output—not just the electric blanket, but the electric blanket with dual control. And, while the consumer may purchase injudiciously as a result of such advertising, he nevertheless has the protection of laws requiring accurate labeling of many products and preventing false advertising claims as to their merits.

How does the American worker satisfy the desires created by advertising for an avalanche of commodities and services? For the more expensive items—his house, his car, his furniture, even his travel—he may dip into his savings, although he is much more apt to buy on time.

The worker's propensity to buy on time is demonstrated by the extent of credit used by all United States consumers. In 1956, installment credit totaled nearly $32 billion and mortgage debt on nonfarm houses $99 billion—respectively about 30 and 12 times the 1920 totals. Nearly $14.5 billion of the 1956 installment debt was for automobiles, and another $8.5 billion was for consumer goods (mostly such durable items as furniture, which 45 percent of the families in a 1956 Federal Reserve survey bought on the installment plan).

Extensive consumer credit is a function of our productive system and has been an increasingly potent force in establishment of the worker's consumption pattern.

Perhaps the greatest product of productivity itself—the simplest explanation of the cause and effect of this cornucopia—has been the stimulation of desire. In America there has been a combination of circumstances, events, and genius to permit the fullest realization yet of the yearnings of men—what the felicitous-tongued lady from the Labor Department meant, 57-odd years ago, when she spoke of the bell and the bay window.

Footnotes

[1] *The Education of Henry Adams, An Autobiography* (New York, Book League Edition, 1928), pp. 496-497.

[2] *Recent Social Trends in the United States*, Report of the President's Research Committee on Social Trends, Vol. 1. (New York, McGraw-Hill Book Company, Inc., 1933), pp. xi-xii.

[3] Henry Steele Commager, *The American Mind, An Interpretation of American Thought and Character Since the 1880's* (New Haven, Yale University Press, 1950), p. 406.

[4] Witt Bowden, Changes in Modes of Living (in *Monthly Labor Review*, July 1950, p. 29).

[5] U. S. Bureau of Labor, *Final Report of the Industrial Commission on the Relations of Capital and Labor Employed in Manufactures and General Business*, Vol. XIX of the Commissioner's Report (Washington, Government Printing Office, 1902), p. 772.

[6] Quoted by Witt Bowden in *American Labor and the American Spirit*, U.S. Bureau of Labor Statistics Bulletin 1145 (Washington, Government Printing Office, 1954), p. 3.

[7] Daniel Bell, The Worker and His Civic Functions (in *Monthly Labor Review*, July 1950, pp. 62-63).

[8] Bell, *op. cit.*, p. 69.

[9] Theodore V. Purcell, S. J., *The Worker Speaks His Mind on Company and Union* (Cambridge, Mass., Harvard University Press, 1953), p. 280.

[10] By J. Frederick Dewhurst and Associates (New York, The Twentieth Century Fund, 1955), p. vii.

[11] Commission on Industrial Relations, *Final Report and Testimony Submitted to Congress*, Vol. I (Washington, Government Printing Office, 1916), pp. 413–414.

[12] Congress of Industrial Organizations, *Proceedings, 8th Constitutional Convention* (Washington, 1946), p. 252.

[13] Quoted in Charles and Mary Beard, *A Basic History of the United States* (New York, The New Home Library, 1944), p. 411.

[14] U.S. Bureau of Labor, *Report on Conditions of Employment in the Iron and Steel Industry in the United States*. Vol. III: *Working Conditions and the Relations of Employers and Employees* (Washington, Government Printing Office, 1913), p. 84.

[15] *The Italians in Chicago, A Social and Economic Study*, Ninth Special Report of the Commissioner of Labor (Washington, Government Printing Office, 1897).

[16] Elsa G. Herzfeld, *Family Monographs, The History of Twenty-Four Families Living in the Middle West Side of New York City* (New York, The James Kemper Printing Co., 1905), pp. 44-46, 89-94.

[17] Emile Levasseur, *The American Workman*, translated by Thomas S. Adams (Baltimore, The Johns Hopkins Press, 1900), pp. 450–451.

[18] *Ibid.*, pp. 430-431.
[19] *Ibid.*, p. 72.
[20] *Ibid.*, pp. 60-61.
[21] U.S. Bureau of Labor, *Report of the Industrial Commission on the Relations of Capital and Labor Employed in Manufactures and General Business*, Vol. VII of the Commissioner's Report (Washington, Government Printing Office, 1901), p. 2.
[22] *Ibid.*, pp. 27ff.
[23] *Ibid.*, Vol. XIX, p. 737.
[24] *Ibid.*, p. 746.
[25] *Ibid.*, p. 773.
[26] U.S. Bureau of Labor, *Report on Conditions of Employment in the Iron and Steel Industry in the United States, op. cit.*, p. 420.
[27] *Ibid.*, p. 424.
[28] *Ibid.*, p. 15.
[29] Levasseur, *op. cit.*, pp. 365–366.
[30] Quoted by Arthur J. Altmeyer in The Worker's Quest for Security (in *Monthly Labor Review*, July 1950, p. 33).
[31] Daniel Bell, The Impact of Advertising (in *The New Leader*, Feb. 11, 1957, p. 9).

CHAPTER II

The Broadening Base of Consumption

> *All of the acts which constitute the existence of a working family sooner or later tend to influence its income and its expenses.*
> —Frederic Le Play.

As the 20th century dawned, the relatively advantageous position of city workers in the United States was strongly attested by the large and rapidly accelerating inflow of people, even from nations most nearly resembling our own in the opportunities and status of workers. American workers' levels of living have continued to be enviably high. Comparisons of the buying power of an hour's work in the United States and 16 other countries in 1949 in respect to basic items of food showed only one nation, Australia, ahead of the United States. "If nonfood items were included," observed an outstanding student of productivity, "the comparisons would undoubtedly be even more favorable to the United States."[1]

The rise in the American workers' levels of living, outlined in broad terms in this chapter, is described in detail in subsequent chapters. Similarly, only the most fundamental and pervasive causes of the rise are touched upon here.

The broad analytical approach used here, and indeed, the remarkable progress shown in workers' levels of living, may predispose us to view too much in the shadow the worker of 1900 and to see too much of the present's rosy tints. This is particularly true in a volume dealing with workers as consumers, which must rely heavily on materialistic measures of the well-being of the typical or average worker. These measures show such great advances since the beginning of the 20th century that the analyst tends to lose sight of the problems which accompanied the change and to look only for its explanations.

Even when an explanation is sought for the comparatively unfavorable current situation of such groups as racial minorities, the unskilled, some groups of white-collar employees, and retired workers, one is overwhelmed by the improvements that have occurred in their status—much more remarkable in many cases than those reflected in the measures of the average worker's level of living. Thus, the groups at the lower end of the income scale are somewhat nearer the average today than formerly. Nevertheless, a word of caution is in order. Even though the authors of the various chapters have pointed to substandard levels of living, where they exist, the need to rely primarily on averages may have resulted in an unintentional overdrawing of the contrast between today and 1900.

CONDITIONS OF PROGRESS

The standards of living of workers' families in the United States have been progressively higher than their actual levels of living.* This traditional bent of American wage earners, as well as other Americans, to think in terms of rising standards and to devise methods for translating their ambitions into actual levels of living, has been an important reason for the continual betterment of their way of living. Moreover, it has been instrumental in reforms of such bad conditions as slums, child labor, sweatshops, excessive work schedules, and many others.

The workers' gains as consumers were and are primarily contingent, however, on their command of purchasing power to translate their ambitions for betterment into effective demand. Such demand means money; and for city workers, wages and salaries account for all but a small fraction of their incomes. But real incomes can rise substantially only if people are able to buy more of the things they want. This, in turn, is dependent on rises in the volume of goods produced in the same unit of working time.

Estimates made by the Bureau of Labor Statistics in early 1958 indicated that the increase in the total private product per man-hour, in terms of monetary values adjusted to eliminate the effects of price changes, totaled 164 percent between 1909 and 1956. Those estimates indicate an average increase of more than 2 percent per year.

Hardly less important than the rise in productivity is recognition of the fact that volume of production may fall even when productivity is rising, as when unemployment is increasing or when, from any cause, there is a considerable reduction in man-hours of productive labor in relation to the total population. It is also important to recall that the total volume of production is not the same, by any means, as the production available for current consumption; war requirements, for example, or deferred invest-

---

*The term "levels of living" in professional parlance relates to how we actually live; "standards of living" to the conditions we think fitting and proper for ourselves to enjoy. This useful distinction—more elegantly stated—has been recommended for international use by the United Nations.

ment needs, or assistance to other nations, may reduce for a time the proportion of output available for current consumption.

In the long run, however, the average of the actual purchasing power or real income of the consumers as a whole, and even of a large group such as city workers and their families, sustains a fairly stable relationship to productivity or to the average output of workers. The average per worker has, of course, risen less rapidly than the average of man-hour output because hours per worker have been greatly reduced.

RISE OF FAMILY INCOMES

Fortunately for the purposes of long-run comparisons of income, the Commissioner of Labor's survey of the incomes and expenditures of city workers' families for the year 1901 provides a comparable start. Furthermore, the Bureau of Labor had by then developed the collecting of retail price data, especially for foods, to such an extent as to make feasible a comparison not merely of monetary income but also of equivalent buying power over the period since 1901. The various official surveys of the spending and saving of workers' families provide our primary sources of information on changes in levels of living. (See chapter X.)

The last general survey of city workers' family income and expenditures by the Bureau of Labor Statistics was made for the year 1950. However, a reasonably accurate projection for 1956 can be made by using trends shown in family income data collected by the Bureau of the Census. The following tabulation shows income per family and per family member for 1901, 1950, and 1956, converted into dollars of 1950 buying power and expressed as percentages of 1950 income.* The gain per family member has been substantially larger, primarily because the family of the 1950's consists of an average of slightly more than 3 persons, compared with 4 persons in 1901. Another reason for the larger gain per family member is that only about 1 of every 20 married

Item	Average net income as a percent of 1950 buying power		
	1901	1950	1956
Per family	48	100	123
Per family member	39	100	119

*1901 data are from U. S. Department of Commerce and Labor, Eighteenth Annual Report of the Commissioner of Labor, Cost of Living and Retail Prices of Food; 1950 data from Monthly Labor Review, September 1956, Standards and Levels of Living of City-Worker Families, by Faith M. Williams; 1956 data based on trend in urban family income, 1950 to 1956, reported in U. S. Bureau of the Census, Current Population Reports, Series P-60, Nos. 9 and 26.

women worked outside the home in 1901, but by 1956 the ratio had risen to about 3 of every 10. Apparently the wife's added contributions to the family income had more than offset the loss of earnings due to the later entrance of children into the labor force.

Wages and Salaries

Family incomes naturally differ somewhat in trend from the wages or salaries of individuals. There is a varying number of wage earners per family; and nonwage income, though rarely significant, is not a constant proportion of the incomes of workers. The trends, nevertheless, should be similar.

The tracing of the trend of "composite" wages and salaries for the entire period since 1901 has been undertaken by the ingenious putting together of a variety of official but fragmentary data. There are available also two other indexes covering more limited areas in a much more precise manner, namely, union hourly wages in the building trades and average weekly earnings in manufacturing. For comparison with the family income series, these three series are presented for the same years, again in terms of income in constant buying-power dollars.*

Item	Income as a percent of 1950 buying power		
	1901	1950	1956
Composite of wages and salaries	42	100	119
Union hourly rates in building trades	38	100	117
Average weekly earnings in manufacturing	43	100	119

The computations given above tend to validate each other as evidence not only of the general trend but also of the approximate extent of the gains in real income. Because of the reductions in hours of work, the weekly earnings series affords a particularly significant comparison with the trend of income per family.

Nonmonetary Income

The increase in family incomes, reflecting mainly the rise in wages and salaries, is by no means the whole story of the expanded basis of material well-being. At the beginning of the century,

---

*The three series, with notes on sources, are given to 1947 in Employment and Wages in the United States, by W. S. Woytinsky and Associates, pp. 584-586. The building trades series and that of factory weekly earnings were extended to 1956 by use of Bureau of Labor Statistics data; the "composite" index is regularly computed and published by the Federal Reserve Bank of New York. Adjustments for price changes in the estimates for 1950 and 1956 are of course made by use of the official Consumer Price Index.

women, it is true, contributed more largely than nowadays to family living by household work and rendering some of the services—baking bread, for example—that now commonly exact a part of the family income.

Of greater significance, however, is the fact that workers in 1900 obtained from employers virtually nothing but wages and from governments little save such elementary items as police protection and basic schooling and some extremely limited community facilities. Present-day workers obtain from their employers, in addition to their wages, a wide range of "fringe" benefits and, as a rule, a priceless asset of mutuality—union recognition, collective bargaining, grievance procedures—a "humanizing" of labor-management relationships. From governments they receive—albeit not without some cost to themselves—the complex of benefits associated with the term social security, not otherwise obtainable and now regarded as indispensable. Governments also provide a vastly wider range of community facilities and of recreational as well as educational advantages.

Narrowing of Income Differentials

Fringe benefits such as sick leave, paid vacations, group insurance funds, hospitalization, and medical care (some of the more important benefits) usually constitute, for workers with relatively small wages or salaries, a comparatively larger supplement to basic wages than for better paid workers. Even more significant in the equalizing trends are the advantages accruing from workmen's compensation and other social security measures and from other highly varied advances such as improved safety, sanitation, lunch facilities, reduced hours of work. Public schools, community facilities, parks, highways, are available to all. In a word, such supplements, although varying in some degree with differences in direct monetary compensation, have become nevertheless a highly significant equalizing force.

Since the beginning of the century there has also been a substantial narrowing of occupational differentials in rates of pay. In 1907, skilled workers in manufacturing received more than double the pay of unskilled workers, by midcentury, less than 50 percent more. Similar trends occurred outside of manufacturing; the estimated union hourly wage rates of laborers in the building trades, for example, averaged 21 cents in 1907 and the journeymen's average was 42 cents; in 1957, the laborers' average had risen to $2.45, or 72 percent of the journeymen's rate of $3.39.

Various other differentials have been significantly narrowed. Exacting and detailed researches summarized in a Twentieth Century Fund volume [2] have led to the conclusion that, in addition to skill differentials, the following kinds of disparities have been greatly reduced:

1. Geographical differentials—the contrast between primarily agrarian, low-wage regions and industrialized, high-wage areas.
2. Industrial differentials—the contrast between low-wage and high-wage pursuits, particularly between agriculture and urban industries and between manual and white-collar workers.
3. Racial differentials—differentials against Negro workers.

Some of the causes of the narrowing of differentials are apparent; others are intricate and elusive. Technological changes (the mechanizing of railroad trackwork, for example, and even of the building custodian's jobs) progressively reduced the demand for heavy unskilled manual work, while concurrently better educational opportunities were raising the levels of competence. More recently, the routinized, semiskilled jobs, so prominent in the earlier stages of mechanization, have declined in relative numbers with the perfecting of mechanical devices and automatic controls. The restricting of immigration and consequent easing of the competitive struggle for jobs would also seem to be an evident cause. In addition, differentials by industry, by region, and by size of firm have been reduced by collective bargaining, by minimum wage laws (notably the Fair Labor Standards Act of 1938, as amended), and by the increased mobility and wider range of choice on the part of jobseekers.*

Taxes and Purchasing Power

Most of the surveys of family incomes and expenditures take account of personal taxes. Those taxes are deducted because they reduce the amount of income the recipient, as an individual, is free to use as he sees fit. The Federal income tax and State and local income or payroll taxes, are, of course, direct personal taxes reflected in the "income after taxes" concept but only partially in "net spendable earnings."

Much more significant is a recognition of "value received" for tax dollars. To the extent that governments provide services of value to citizens, taxes may be viewed as measures of improved welfare. Public education, clinics and other public health facilities,

---

*Harry M. Douty, in his discussion of differentials and their causes in the 1957 edition of the Occupational Outlook Handbook, cautions against oversimplification. Some differentials, he notes (p. 43), comprise "an extraordinarily complex subject." The complexity extends, indeed, to a distinction between those differentials which, in our system, are intrinsically equitable and those that are merely traditional survivals.

water systems, parks and playgrounds, libraries, sanitation, maintenance of minimum standards of safety and other standards, the administration of social security programs, the expanding complex of endowments and nongovernmental agencies for social betterment exempted from taxes—these are some of the facilities and services (aside from national defense) that have come into being or have been vastly expanded on a tax-supported or tax-free basis during the present century. By and large, they are services which private industry has not historically provided or could furnish much less economically.

There are additional payments to government in many localities, representing direct charges for goods and services furnished to individual consumers, such as water, garbage disposal, electric power, gas, local transportation, and postal facilities. These items should be considered in the same light as payments for any other goods and services, rather than as a cost of government.

Indirect taxes, those not levied directly on persons, account for much of the tax burden. At the Federal level, they are represented by tariffs, manufacturers' and processors' taxes, and corporation income taxes. State and local governments rely primarily on property taxes and sales and use taxes.

The impact of indirect taxes on consumers generally, and especially on a particular group such as city workers, is beyond precise analysis; a major difficulty is the highly variable extent of passing the taxes on to consumers. One recent rough estimate sets nonpersonal taxes at about 15 percent of income for people in the $3,000–$7,500 income range, which includes the great majority of city wage earners' families.

For 1950, the Bureau of Labor Statistics survey indicates that personal taxes accounted for about 7 percent of city workers' family income, compared with 0.09 percent in 1917-19, the earliest date for which a comparable figure is available. The incidence of personal taxes varied considerably in 1950, depending on income. Thus, it was 4.7 percent for families in the $2,000 and under $3,000 income class, 8 percent for the $5,000 and under $6,000 class, and 9.1 percent for the group in the $6,000 and under $7,500 bracket.

Savings, Credit, and Economic Security

There have been important changes, over the decades, in the extent to which workers set aside part of their incomes as savings to meet future needs, or use consumer credit to buy things they might not have purchased out of current income. Early in the 20th century, there were many incentives for the city worker's family to accumulate a cash reserve, since its only resources in emergencies such as unemployment were either savings or the earnings of other family members.

Workers' families in 1901 put into direct cash savings larger portions of their earnings than most families save today. About half of all families reported a significant surplus, and only 1 family in 6 a deficit. The average surplus, for families which had one, was about $121—quite a large amount in comparison with the family head's wages; almost 10 weeks' pay.

The current situation is quite different. In 1950, the city worker family's average expenditure of $3,925 for current consumption was almost exactly equal to its income of $3,923 after taxes. In early 1957, a survey covering a representative group of families in all occupational categories showed that about 3 out of 5 had some personal or installment debt, not counting mortgages and charge accounts; about 1 in 3 had debts of more than $500. About 2 out of every 3 families in the typical wage-earner income range ($3,000–$5,000) had some personal debts. Liquid assets (savings accounts, Government bonds, etc.) were less than debts in about half the families, but one-third had liquid savings with no debts.

The greater readiness of today's worker to incur debt reflects several changes. The fear of unemployment, which reached its peak in the depression of the 1930's, has been mitigated by the inauguration of public policies providing protection against economic insecurity, collective agreements for easing the impacts of layoffs and discharges, and the increased mobility of workers with a widened range of choice of jobs.

Public policies include a nationwide employment service and a closely related system of unemployment insurance. In 1955, the employment service made over 6 million nonfarm job placements. Employment in jobs covered by unemployment insurance averaged over 36.5 million.

Provisions covering layoff and worksharing procedures applied to about three-fourths of the workers covered by major collective bargaining agreements in effect in late 1954 and 1955. In addition, over 2 million workers are currently employed under agreements which provide supplemental unemployment benefits designed to maintain the unemployed worker's income at 60 to 65 percent of his usual earnings for as long as 6 months or a year.

Moreover, by temperament, Americans are a mobile people. This characteristic, together with a wide ownership of automobiles, enables workers to seek employment wherever prospects seem good. About one-fifth of the population of the United States moved to a different dwelling in each of the 9 years following 1947.

Defenses against economic insecurity are provided also by other phases of the social security system, notably the old age and survivors' insurance program. In 1955, a total of 66 million workers worked at some time during the year on jobs covered by the program, which in that year paid benefits to nearly 5.5 million retired workers and dependents of such workers and more than 2 million survivors. Workmen's compensation, under State laws, assures most wage earners of benefits, limited and lacking in uniformity but nevertheless highly important. Also worthy of mention are the temporary disability insurance programs for workers on railroads and in 4 States and the provision of paid sick leave for Federal civilian and military personnel as well as for the employees of some State and city governments. Other security bulwarks are private insurance and pension plans, usually under collective bargaining agreements. Basically, the reliance of workers on these defenses against disability, unemployment, and dependent old age, and on additional measures when needed, springs from the public policy embodied in the Employment Act of 1946 and in the reiterated bipartisan pledges of national action consistent with the policy of that act.

The social security programs and the vast expansion of insurance, especially group insurance, provide in themselves a form of workers' saving that has been described as "automatic." Furthermore, the greatly increased buying of homes and substantial types of durable goods requires a highly significant kind of saving. In earlier generations, most workers had to do without homes of their own and found it necessary to put off the buying of durable goods for long periods while they were trying to accumulate the necessary savings. Present-day workers, by means of amortization and gradual payment, are able to "save" while actually living in the homes and using the automobiles for which they are paying.

SHIFTING PATTERNS OF CONSUMPTION

Ability to obtain goods and services in addition to the basic necessities is probably the most widely accepted criterion of consumer well-being. A corollary proposition, however, has been a more convenient analytical tool: As buying power (real income) rises, the proportion of income devoted to necessities declines. Conversely, of course, consumers are able to increase the share of income spent for other goods and services (variously designated as secondary necessities, conveniences, and luxuries) as their command of purchasing power increases. These propositions had an early and lasting effect on analysis of data from the consumer expenditure surveys.*

Expenditure Patterns in Six Surveys

The influence of these ideas was particularly evident in the surveys of family incomes and expenditures for 1874–75, 1888–91, and 1901, which were directed by Carroll D. Wright, a contemporary of Ernest Engel, the Prussian statistical official who formulated the ideas. Tables 1, 2, and 3 show the effect of this clearly, having been constructed on lines suggested by the classification of consumption expenditures originally used in these 3 studies. The 3 other surveys used liberally in this volume, those for 1917–19, 1934–36, and 1950 (tables 4, 5, and 6), were not explicitly concerned with Engel's propositions. They were influenced, however, by the same spirit of inquiry; in procedures, they resembled Wright's earlier surveys; and in content, they cast a revealing light on the basic question studied by Engel and Wright, namely, the importance of a margin for spending beyond the subsistence level.

The immense detail of those six surveys has limited their use except by specialists. The accompanying tables embody efforts to make readily visible the main outlines of the several surveys. The analysis deals chiefly with the surveys shown in tables 3 through 6, because they are more nearly representative and more indicative of continuity, and all within the present century.**

The city workers for whom family income and expenditure data are presented in these four tables are wage earners and lower salaried clerical or sales employees.† Together with their families, these workers currently make up about three-fourths of the population and labor force in urban areas. They comprise two-thirds of all employed family heads in the Nation as a whole.

---

*One of the stated purposes of an 1875 Massachusetts expenditure survey was a testing of the validity of consumption "laws" formulated by Christian Lorenz Ernest Engel, director of the Prussian Bureau of Statistics and an eminent 19th century consumption economist, who was noted, as a Prussian, for a liberal interest in labor's problems. Based on European studies during the 1860's and reflecting the expenditure patterns thus revealed, these "laws" as stated by Carroll D. Wright (then head of the Massachusetts Bureau of Statistics of Labor and subsequently U. S. Commissioner of Labor) held that as income increased, the proportion devoted to: (1) food decreased; (2) shelter and fuel remained invariably the same; (3) clothing stayed about the same; and (4) sundries (all other categories of consumption) increased. Like all succeeding studies in the United States, the Massachusetts survey confirmed the first and fourth of these propositions and demonstrated that the second and third were not valid—at least in our economy.

**Information is given in the final chapter regarding the origins, purposes, procedures used, and limitations of comparability affecting the several surveys, standard budgets, and the continuing series of estimates of total personal consumption expenditures.

†About a quarter of the persons in the urban labor force today are not "city workers" as the term is used in this chapter. This quarter consists mainly of professional and technical workers or managers, proprietors, and self-employed persons. Also excluded are the relatively small numbers of domestic servants, farmworkers, and inexperienced workers who live in urban areas.

A graphic view of the successively higher levels of living for city workers is given in chart 1. The chart relies on group averages, which comprise, of course, significant differences. It nevertheless reveals real progress; for the average or typical family represents, at the several periods, substantially comparable groups of urban workers. In view of the narrowing of wage differentials in a variety of ways, previously described, the "average" worker of today is more significantly typical of his group than was the average in the earlier surveys.

The tables demonstrate the ever-widening margin of resources available for conveniences and luxuries that wage earners and clerical workers were able to command after obtaining the basic necessities. Chart 1 "pictures" the advance. In terms of "sundries" as defined in 1875, workers have been able to increase the proportion allocable to this category from a bare 6 cents of each dollar to 43 cents in 1950. Between 1901 and 1950, the proportion more than doubled (from 20.1 percent to 43.0 percent)—in itself a revolutionary rise in living levels. Moreover, the 1901 study was the first which can be considered representative of city workers generally.

TABLE 1.—*Consumption expenditures of families of wage earners in 15 cities and towns in Massachusetts, by income class, 1874–75*

Item	All income classes	$300 and under $450	$450 and under $600	$600 and under $750	$750 and under $1,200	$1,200 and over
Number of families	397	6	52	143	188	8
Average family size	5.1	5.0	5.2	4.8	5.3	6.9
Average annual money income [1]	$763	$395	$549	$679	$871	$1,383
Total expenditures for current consumption	$738	$410	$555	$668	$832	$1,212
Subsistence [2]	427	262	350	401	466	618
Clothing	106	29	58	94	125	230
Rent	117	82	86	94	141	182
Fuel	44	25	33	40	50	60
Sundry expenses	44	12	28	40	50	121
Percent of expenditures for current consumption	100.0	100.0	100.0	100.0	100.0	100.0
Subsistence [2]	58.0	64.0	63.0	60.0	56.0	51.0
Clothing	14.0	7.0	10.5	14.0	15.0	19.0
Rent	16.0	20.0	15.5	14.0	17.0	15.0
Fuel	6.0	6.0	6.0	6.0	6.0	5.0
Sundry expenses	6.0	3.0	5.0	6.0	6.0	10.0

[1] At this period, Massachusetts was among the States where wage earners and clerical workers received incomes which were high relative to most States.
[2] Includes food, kerosene oil, and provisions commonly purchased in grocery stores.

NOTE: Items may not add to totals because of rounding. Average expenditures for all categories except fuel by all income classes combined differ by a few dollars from those shown elsewhere in the source.

SOURCE: Derived from the Sixth Annual Report on the Statistics of Labor, Commonwealth of Massachusetts, Public Document No. 31 (Boston, 1875), Part IV, pp. 221–354, 441.

Chart I.

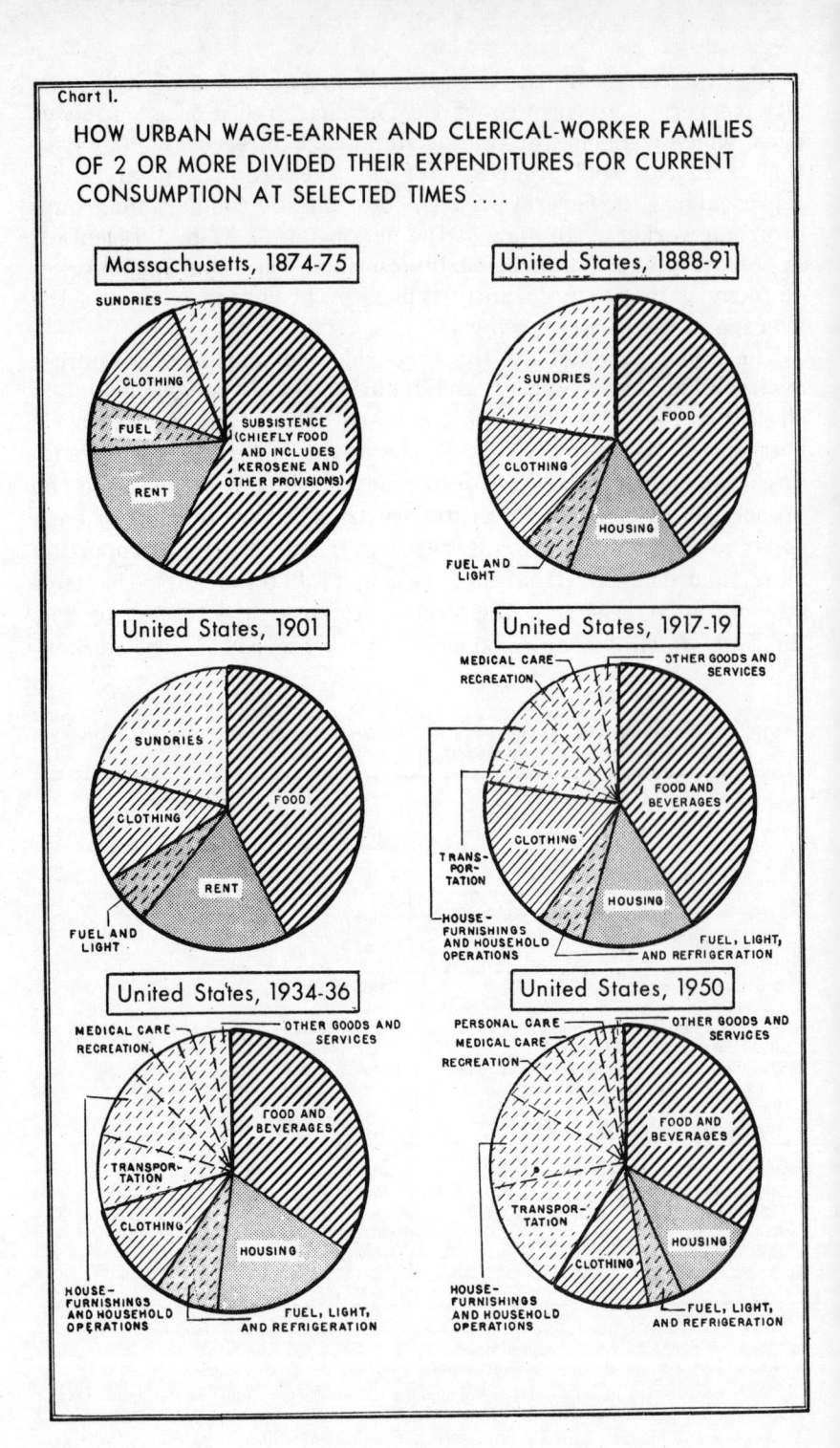

HOW URBAN WAGE-EARNER AND CLERICAL-WORKER FAMILIES OF 2 OR MORE DIVIDED THEIR EXPENDITURES FOR CURRENT CONSUMPTION AT SELECTED TIMES....

Differences by income class are of course considerable. The tables provide information on the distribution of worker families in the sample by income as well as insight into the effects of income differentials on expenditure patterns. They also show the number of families or consumer units included in the sample for each class. In addition to the light the figures shed on family income distributions, they provide a basis for appraising the reliability of the averages shown.

TABLE 2.—*Consumption expenditures of "normal families" [1] of workers in 9 basic industries,[2] by income class, 1888–91*

Item	All income classes	Under $200	$200 and under $400	$400 and under $600	$600 and under $800	$800 and under $1,000	$1,000 and under $1,200	$1,200 and over
Number of families	2,562	24	500	1,168	492	206	86	86
Average family size	3.9	3.4	3.7	3.9	3.9	4.1	4.2	4.3
Average annual money income	$573	$156	$335	$486	$674	$883	$1,064	$1,450
Total expenditures for current consumption	$534	$233	$363	$476	$608	$746	$878	$1,128
Food	219	116	165	212	245	271	295	323
Housing	80	36	54	73	95	116	126	142
Fuel and light	32	18	26	31	34	37	38	34
Clothing	82	30	51	70	97	119	151	177
Sundries	121	33	67	90	137	203	268	452
Percent of expenditures for current consumption	100.0	100.0	100.0	100.0	100.0	100.0	100.0	100.0
Food	41.0	49.8	45.5	44.5	40.3	36.3	33.6	28.6
Housing	15.0	15.5	14.9	15.3	15.6	15.5	14.4	12.6
Fuel and light	6.0	7.7	7.2	6.5	5.6	5.0	4.3	3.0
Clothing	15.4	12.9	14.0	14.7	16.0	16.0	17.2	15.7
Sundries	22.7	14.2	18.5	18.9	22.5	27.2	30.5	40.1

[1] As defined for the survey, a "normal family" had a husband and wife, no more than five children and none over age 14, no boarders or dependents; did not own its dwelling place; and reported expenditures for rent, fuel, lighting, clothing, and food.

[2] Pig iron; bar iron; steel; bituminous coal; coke; iron ore; cotton; woolen; and glass.

NOTE: Items may not add to totals because of rounding.

SOURCE: Derived from Sixth and Seventh Annual Reports of the Commissioner of Labor, Cost of Production: Iron, Steel, Coal, etc. (Washington, 1891, 1892), Part III.

Changes in Actual Buying Power

The division of expenditures among the several kinds of goods and services, for which the dollar figures reported in the original sources suffice, is the main emphasis in this chapter. However, any realistic evaluation of workers' welfare must also take into account the effect of price changes on their purchasing power. Therefore, figures on average income and outlays for current consumption have been converted into dollars of 1950 purchasing power for each of the surveys since 1888–91, and these are shown

Chart 2.

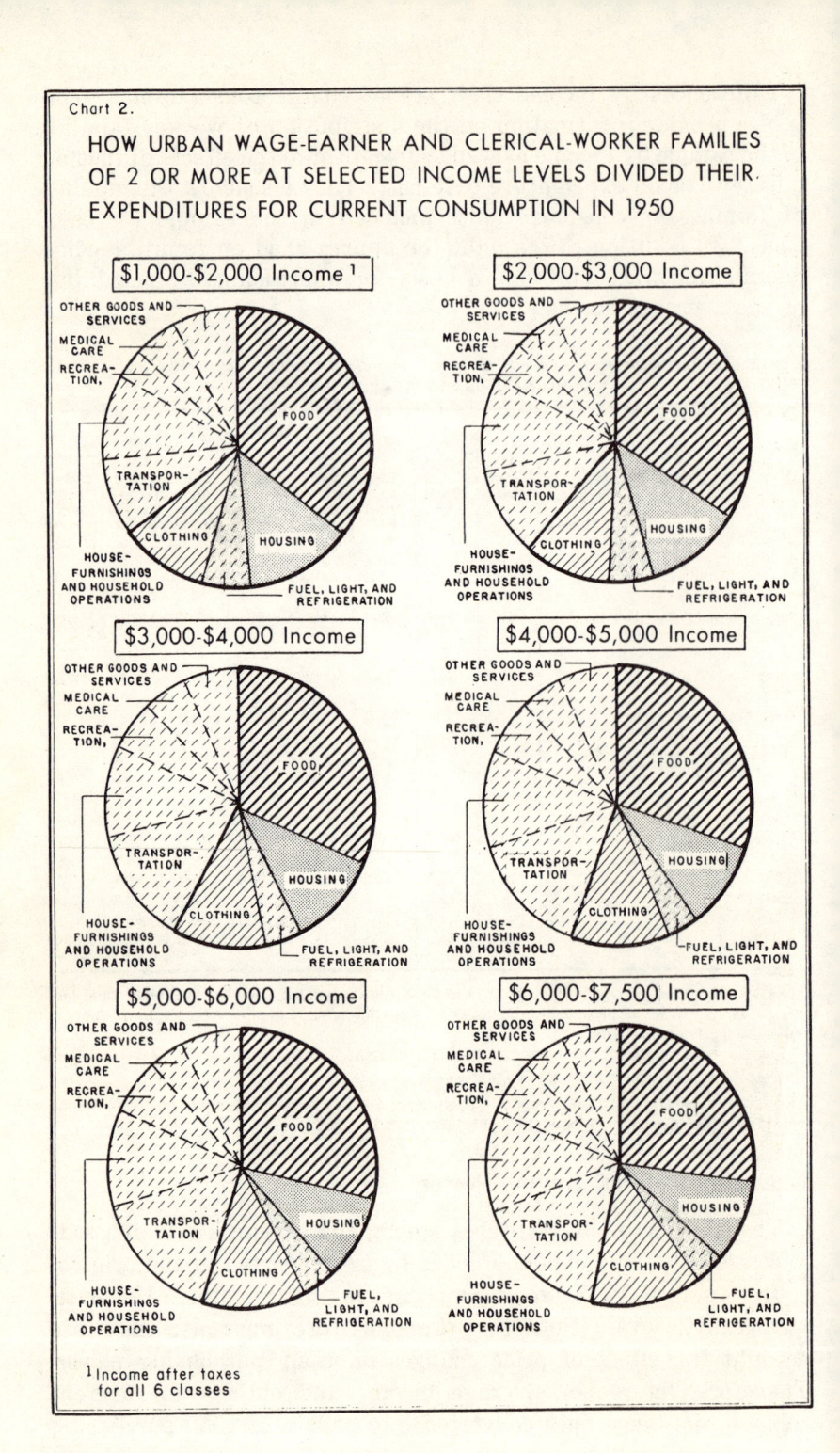

HOW URBAN WAGE-EARNER AND CLERICAL-WORKER FAMILIES OF 2 OR MORE AT SELECTED INCOME LEVELS DIVIDED THEIR EXPENDITURES FOR CURRENT CONSUMPTION IN 1950

[1] Income after taxes for all 6 classes

in table 7. Only total expenditures and food could be converted in the two earliest surveys because official price indexes for other major categories of expenditures are not available before 1913. Data relate to wage and clerical workers' families in large cities; for this reason, those for 1950 do not correspond to those shown in table 6, which also include such families in suburbs and small cities.

Comparison of the figures in 1950 dollars with current income and expenditures reported at the time of the earlier surveys (tables 2 through 5) indicates significant improvements. Although the rise in prices cut the purchasing power of each dollar by 66 percent between 1901 and 1950, for example, incomes rose enough to support the purchase of 2¼ times as many goods and services in physical quantity terms. And the volume of purchases commanded by the workers' buying power had almost doubled, even since the end of World War I. Thus, although the proportion of total expenditures going for necessities had decreased, the smaller share would buy larger quantities or better qualities of these required items. Similarly, the fact that the share of outlays going for other items (the "sundries" of earlier surveys) has more than doubled assumes added significance when it is considered that the number of dollars allocated to such purchases now commands nearly 3 times the quantity it did in 1917–19.

The 1950 Survey: Additional Detail

For each survey, the appropriate table is designed to provide a summary view of key data relating to city workers at the time of the survey. Perhaps a special value attaches to the 1950 survey data relating to expenditure distributions at different levels or ranges of income. Those distributions (table 6) provide the basis for chart 2, which excludes three of the less numerous income classes, primarily for convenience.

The 3 groups not represented in the chart are the lowest income class (less than $1,000 income after personal taxes) and the 2 highest ($7,500 and under $10,000 and $10,000 and over). Corresponding classes are often omitted in such analyses of the wage-earner and clerical-worker groups, because the families sampled represent a small proportion of all such consumer units. In this case, less than 4 percent of the sample are eliminated. Each of the remaining 6 classes includes not less than 5 percent of the total sample and ranges up to almost a third (31.1 percent) falling in the $3,000 and under $4,000 bracket in 1950.

The graphic analysis of the allocations of expenditures by each of these 6 income classes in 1950 in chart 2 is analogous to that shown for the 6 different surveys in chart 1. The similarities of

TABLE 3.—*Consumption expenditures of "normal families"[1] in principal industrial centers in 33 States, by income class, 1901*

Item	All income classes	Under $200	$200 and under $300	$300 and under $400	$400 and under $500	$500 and under $600	$600 and under $700	$700 and under $800	$800 and under $900	$900 and under $1,000	$1,000 and under $1,100	$1,100 and under $1,200	$1,200 and over
Number of families	11,156	32	115	545	1,676	2,264	2,336	2,094	806	684	340	96	168
Average family size	4.0	3.2	3.4	3.8	3.8	3.9	3.9	4.0	4.2	4.1	4.3	4.0	3.8
Average money income	$651	(²)	(²)	(²)	(²)	(²)	(²)	(²)	(²)	(²)	(²)	(²)	(²)
Total expenditures for current consumption	$618	$196	$312	$389	$466	$540	$612	$693	$771	$816	$900	$973	$1,052
Food	266	100	148	187	218	249	266	287	319	326	349	367	384
Rent	112	33	56	73	87	100	113	126	132	144	158	161	183
Fuel	28	13	19	23	26	27	28	29	30	31	34	35	41
Light	7	2	4	4	5	6	7	8	8	9	10	11	12
Clothing	80	17	27	39	53	65	79	94	105	117	136	145	165
Sundries	124	31	59	63	77	93	119	150	177	189	213	254	267
Percent of expenditures for current consumption	100.0	100.0	100.0	100.0	100.0	100.0	100.0	100.0	100.0	100.0	100.0	100.0	100.0
Food	43.1	50.8	47.3	48.1	46.9	46.2	43.5	41.4	41.4	39.9	38.8	37.7	36.4
Rent	18.1	16.9	18.0	18.7	18.6	18.4	18.5	18.2	17.1	17.6	17.5	16.6	17.4
Fuel	4.6	6.7	6.1	6.0	5.5	5.1	4.6	4.1	3.9	3.8	3.8	3.6	3.8
Light	1.1	1.3	1.1	1.1	1.1	1.1	1.1	1.1	1.1	1.1	1.2	1.1	1.2
Clothing	13.0	8.7	8.7	10.0	11.4	12.0	12.9	13.5	13.6	14.4	15.1	14.9	15.7
Sundries	20.1	15.6	18.8	16.1	16.5	17.2	19.4	21.6	23.0	23.2	23.7	26.1	25.4

[1] As defined for the survey, a "normal family" had a husband at work, a wife, not more than 5 children and none over age 14, no dependent, boarder, lodger, or servant; and had expenditures for rent, fuel, lighting, food, clothing, and sundries.
[2] Not available.

NOTE: Items may not add to totals because of rounding.

SOURCE: Cost of Living and Retail Prices of Food, Eighteenth Annual Report of the Commissioner of Labor (Washington, 1903), pp. 581, 592, 593.

these charts are immediately evident: the proportion of total expenditures available for "sundries" rises steadily as income rises; conversely, the proportion spent for food declines—in 1950, from 35.8 percent in the $1,000 and under $2,000 class to 27.3 percent in the $6,000 and under $7,500 group.

Food and shelter (housing plus fuel, light, and refrigeration), which may be regarded as basic necessities, in 1950 took about 55 cents per dollar in the lowest income class shown and just over 40 cents in the highest. Moreover, the decline progressed smoothly and steadily.

Certain consumption groups exhibit a similar progressive percentage decline with rising levels of income. Among them are medical care, tobacco, and personal care. The evidence of the 1950 and earlier surveys is that tobacco showed just this pattern, which may mean that tobacco users regard it as a necessity, but as income increases they are able to satisfy this requirement for a smaller share of their total expenditures. Medical and personal care traditionally have absorbed approximately constant proportions of income (or expenditures) at each income level. The change in their patterns in 1950 probably was due in part to the rise in real incomes and the consequently greater margins available beyond basic needs. The sharp increase in medical care insurance, too, may have played a part in enabling families to devote smaller shares of income to medical care.

Except for the two lowest income classes shown (where the same percentage held), clothing expenditures in 1950 took an increasing share of the total expenditures as income rose. In this respect, it "behaved" like a convenience or luxury. This steady rise also characterized such consumption groups as automobile ownership and operation, recreation, and alcoholic beverages.

The differences in spending patterns among income groups in 1950 were smaller, it will be noted, than the differences from time to time for the entire group. One obvious, tangible cause is the entry into the market, over the decades, of new items of consumption—the automobile, for example. Workers 50 years ago may now and then have dreamed of buying cars; workers today throughout the ranges of income actually buy them. The buying of cars today makes no great difference in the expenditure patterns of workers in the different ranges of income. The group as a whole in 1950 used 11.5 percent of expenditures for automobile transportation (more than 6 percent in even the lowest income range) in contrast to a no doubt almost negligible proportion for all kinds of transportation in 1901, hidden in "sundries" in the report of that year's survey. The spending for automobiles in 1950 was of course at the cost, percentagewise, of spending for other items. Thus, aside from other causes, the automobile in itself brought about, in the half century, readily visible changes in the expenditure patterns.

Patterns for Workers' Families and Other Groups. The data thus far sumarized for 1950 relate to city workers' families having

TABLE 4.—*Consumption expenditures of white workers' families with at least one child, in cities of all sizes, by income class, 1917–19*

Item	All income classes	Income class						
		Under $900	$900 and under $1,200	$1,200 and under $1,500	$1,500 and under $1,800	$1,800 and under $2,100	$2,100 and under $2,500	$2,500 and over
Number of families	12,096	332	2,423	3,959	2,730	1,594	705	353
Average family size	4.9	4.3	4.5	4.7	5.0	5.1	5.7	6.4
Average money income [1]	$1,505	$810	$1,070	$1,336	$1,622	$1,914	$2,261	$2,777
Total expenditures for current consumption [1]	$1,352	$804	$1,016	$1,234	$1,452	$1,656	$1,937	$2,331
Food	549	372	456	516	572	627	712	860
Alcoholic beverages	7	4	7	7	7	7	9	16
Tobacco	17	12	14	15	17	20	21	28
Housing [2]	187	122	150	180	207	232	248	260
Fuel, light, and refrigeration	74	57	64	73	79	87	93	102
Household operation	37	18	14	32	41	51	61	63
Furnishings and equipment	62	28	43	54	71	79	93	105
Clothing	238	112	156	206	257	307	384	503
Automobile	16	1	4	9	18	31	50	58
Other transportation	26	11	18	23	29	32	43	54
Medical care	64	36	46	58	71	78	87	102
Personal care	14	9	11	13	15	17	19	24
Recreation	33	8	15	25	38	52	69	97
Reading	11	6	8	10	11	13	15	16
Education	7	4	3	5	8	11	16	22
Miscellaneous	10	4	7	8	11	12	17	21
Percent of expenditures for current consumption [1]	100.0	100.0	100.0	100.0	100.0	100.0	100.0	100.0
Food	40.7	46.3	44.8	41.8	39.3	37.9	36.7	36.8
Alcoholic beverages	.5	.5	.7	.6	.5	.4	.5	.7
Tobacco	1.3	1.5	1.4	1.2	1.2	1.2	1.1	1.2
Housing [2]	13.8	15.2	14.8	14.6	14.3	14.0	12.8	11.2
Fuel, light, and refrigeration	5.5	7.1	6.3	5.9	5.4	5.3	4.8	4.4
Household operation	2.7	2.2	1.4	2.6	2.8	3.1	3.1	2.7
Furnishings and equipment	4.6	3.5	4.2	4.4	4.9	4.8	4.8	4.5
Clothing	17.7	13.9	15.3	16.7	17.7	18.5	19.8	21.6
Automobile	1.2	.1	.4	.7	1.2	1.9	2.6	2.5
Other transportation	1.9	1.4	1.8	1.9	2.0	1.9	2.2	2.3
Medical care	4.7	4.5	4.5	4.7	4.9	4.7	4.5	4.4
Personal care	1.0	1.1	1.1	1.1	1.0	1.0	1.0	1.0
Recreation	2.4	1.0	1.5	2.0	2.6	3.1	3.6	4.2
Reading	.8	.7	.8	.8	.8	.8	.8	.7
Education	.5	.5	.3	.4	.6	.7	.8	.9
Miscellaneous	.7	.5	.7	.6	.8	.7	.9	.9

[1] Income and expenditure data have been regrouped to conform with the 1950 classification.
[2] Excludes 301 families whose rent included the cost of either heat or light or both.
NOTE: Items may not add to totals because of rounding.
SOURCE: Cost of Living in the United States, U.S. Bureau of Labor Statistics Bulletin 357 (Washington, 1924).

two or more persons. That segment of the 1950 coverage is most nearly comparable to the coverage of earlier surveys. The inclusion in the 1950 survey of a sampling of all city consumers makes feasible certain desirable comparisons of the group of city workers' families with certain other urban groups and with all urban consumers.

Income after taxes, as well as expenditures and apparent savings,* naturally averaged higher for all urban families (table 8) than for the families of wage earners and clerical workers (table 6). The difference in average income, however, was only about $300, and in expenditures, only about $200. The patterns of spending of all urban families were not markedly different from those of workers' families—evidence that urban worker families' consumption habits resemble those of other urban family groups.

One other tabulation has distinctive interest: it presents data for all wage-earner and clerical-worker consumers, both families and individuals, by region and occupational group (table 9). Single workers accounted for 1 in 9 of all city worker consumer units surveyed. The inclusion of single consumers reduced average income and expenditures somewhat below the average for urban workers' families shown in table 6.

Single workers typically were younger or older than the family man, and their income was slightly less than half of family income. And, because many of the single workers maintained their own households, they spent nearly two-thirds as many dollars for housing, fuel, and light. The single workers also apparently often ate in restaurants, as food and beverages represented about the same share of their budget as of families' expenditures. Since only minor differences were noted in other expenditure categories, it may be assumed that the single workers had either more or somewhat better clothing, medical care, recreation, personal care, etc., since they were spending about half as many dollars for these purposes, yet their expenditures covered purchases for 1 person, compared with an average of 3.4 in families.

The regional data reveal a substantial difference between average incomes in the South ($3,225) versus those in the North ($3,838) and in the West ($3,768). Average expenditures for various categories of goods and services show approximately the same regional relations. Expenditure patterns, however, were remarkably similar among the 3 regions. In all cases, the differences were either so minute they could easily have resulted from sampling error or were readily explicable. Moreover, income dif-

---

*Adequate treatment of savings as reflected by family expenditures surveys is beyond the scope of this volume. See the study by Dorothy S. Brady in A Study of Saving in the United States by R. W. Goldsmith, Dorothy S. Brady, and Horst Mendershausen (Princeton University Press, 1956), Volume III, Part II, pp. 139-276.

TABLE 5.—*Consumption expenditures of families of employed workers in cities of 50,000 and over, by income class, 1934–36*

Item	All income classes	\$500 and under \$600	\$600 and under \$900	\$900 and under \$1,200	\$1,200 and under \$1,500	\$1,500 and under \$1,800	\$1,800 and under \$2,100	\$2,100 and under \$2,400	\$2,400 and under \$2,700	\$2,700 and under \$3,000	\$3,000 and over
Number of families	14,469	116	1,215	2,952	3,444	2,937	2,185	810	391	188	231
Average family size	3.6	3.1	3.2	3.4	3.5	3.6	3.8	4.0	4.3	4.4	4.8
Average annual money income after personal taxes [1]	\$1,518	\$550	\$775	\$1,062	\$1,348	\$1,634	\$1,928	\$2,241	\$2,507	\$2,867	\$3,450
Total expenditures for current consumption	\$1,463	\$637	\$832	\$1,081	\$1,332	\$1,576	\$1,804	\$2,075	\$2,305	\$2,590	\$3,093
Food and alcoholic beverages	508	250	315	398	472	540	597	683	756	837	1,021
Housing	259	132	169	215	246	281	300	324	346	370	411
Fuel, light, and refrigeration	108	64	76	94	106	114	123	136	131	131	148
Household operation	58	20	30	38	49	63	77	92	102	119	142
Furnishings and equipment	60	13	28	39	55	70	77	90	96	83	112
Clothing	160	49	74	102	136	173	211	258	309	388	471
Automobile	87	9	20	40	73	99	137	162	161	197	212
Other transportation	38	17	25	29	33	40	43	52	65	78	115
Medical care	59	22	33	42	53	64	78	81	97	109	115
Personal care	30	13	17	22	27	32	37	43	51	59	71
Recreation, reading, and tobacco	82	28	38	54	72	87	104	129	152	177	232
Education	7	2	2	4	5	7	11	14	19	17	22
Miscellaneous	7	18	5	4	5	6	9	11	20	25	21
Percent of expenditures for current consumption	100.0	100.0	100.0	100.0	100.0	100.0	100.0	100.0	100.0	100.0	100.0
Food and alcoholic beverages	34.7	39.4	37.9	36.8	35.4	34.3	33.1	33.0	32.8	32.2	33.0
Housing	17.7	20.7	20.3	19.9	18.4	17.9	16.6	15.6	15.0	14.3	13.3
Fuel, light, and refrigeration	7.4	10.0	9.1	8.7	8.0	7.2	6.8	6.6	5.7	5.1	4.8
Household operation	4.0	3.1	3.6	3.5	3.7	4.0	4.3	4.4	4.4	4.6	4.6
Furnishings and equipment	4.1	2.0	3.4	3.6	4.1	4.4	4.3	4.3	4.2	3.2	3.6
Clothing	10.9	7.7	8.9	9.4	10.2	11.0	11.7	12.4	13.4	15.0	15.2
Automobile	5.9	1.4	2.4	3.7	5.5	6.3	7.6	7.8	7.0	7.6	6.9
Other transportation	2.6	2.7	3.0	2.7	2.5	2.5	2.4	2.5	2.8	3.0	3.7
Medical care	4.0	3.5	4.0	3.9	4.0	4.1	4.3	3.9	4.2	4.2	3.7
Personal care	2.1	2.0	2.0	2.0	2.0	2.0	2.0	2.1	2.2	2.3	2.3
Recreation, reading, and tobacco	5.6	4.4	4.6	5.0	5.4	5.5	4.8	6.2	6.6	6.8	7.5
Education	.5	.3	.2	.4	.4	.4	.6	.7	.8	.7	.7
Miscellaneous	.5	2.8	.6	.4	.4	.4	.5	.5	.9	1.0	.7

[1] Taxes deducted were poll, income, and personal property, which averaged \$5 per family.

SOURCE: *Money Disbursements of Wage Earners and Clerical Workers, 1934–36, Summary Volume*, U.S. Bureau of Labor Statistics Bulletin 638 (Washington, 1941), pp. 12, 22.

NOTE: Items may not add to totals because of rounding.

ferentials among workers have narrowed appreciably since earlier studies, as indicated previously.

The relationships of average incomes and expenditures among the broad occupational groups of wage and clerical workers—clerical and sales workers and, among wage earners, the skilled, the semiskilled, and the unskilled*—appear consistent with conclusions derived from other sources. So also the expenditure patterns seem to reveal no surprises. The most apparent differences were that the white-collar workers had smaller families but uniformly spent more of their income on housing and clothing than skilled workers, although the incomes of the two groups were not far apart. Skilled workers, on the other hand, spent relatively more than clerical workers on food, transportation, and tobacco. And both groups were better off than the semiskilled and unskilled workers.

Redefining "Basic Necessities"

The traditional classification of basic necessities has come to mean merely that even the simplest manner of living requires a modicum of food, clothing, and shelter. Early consumption studies abroad, primarily among the poor in European countries, elaborated what must have been more or less apparent, namely, that ordinary workers had little, often nothing, left for spending beyond the meeting of rather primitive requirements for food and clothing and shelter. Nor was it widely assumed in other circles that workers should aspire to more. Indeed, a widely held doctrine of "the utility of poverty" gave rise to countless frank expressions of views, even among liberty-loving Englishmen, that a "state bordering on want" must prevail among the "lower orders" if they were to be kept at work.[3]

Even in 19th century America, if the satisfying of food needs required only 50 instead of 75 percent of expenditures, that was a significant indicator of well-being. Today, in contrast, we cannot say with assurance that the use of 40 percent for food as compared with 30 percent proves the existence of a real difference in degree of well-being, although there is a strong presumption that it does so. The uncertainty arises from the fact that workers' food expenditures nowadays are divided between foods as luxuries and foods as necessities. As the income of the individual worker (class of workers) rises above what is needed for maintenance of his current way of living, he has three choices regarding food (or other expenditure categories). He can maintain his past

---
*Occupations were classified in accordance with the U. S. Bureau of the Census occupational classification system.

TABLE 6.—*Consumption expenditures of wage-earner and clerical-worker families in cities of 2,500 and over, by income class, 1950*

Item	All income classes	Under $1,000	$1,000 and under $2,000	$2,000 and under $3,000	$3,000 and under $4,000	$4,000 and under $5,000	$5,000 and under $6,000	$6,000 and under $7,500	$7,500 and under $10,000	$10,000 and over
Number of families	7,007	64	498	1,423	2,180	1,453	749	427	164	49
Average family size	3.4	2.3	2.9	3.1	3.4	3.5	3.7	3.9	4.2	4.5
Average money income after personal taxes	$3,923	$651	$1,629	$2,564	$3,487	$4,454	$5,434	$6,606	$8,394	$13,292
Total expenditures for current consumption	$3,925	$1,683	$1,924	$2,795	$3,573	$4,408	$5,262	$6,187	$7,161	$10,342
Food	1,205	540	690	946	1,139	1,324	1,514	1,691	1,992	2,656
Alcoholic beverages	70	8	25	41	58	82	102	134	158	289
Tobacco	79	29	50	66	73	88	96	107	130	126
Housing	415	283	249	336	390	454	511	590	606	976
Fuel, light, and refrigeration	163	122	111	140	158	174	194	208	228	287
Household operation	155	77	71	108	135	169	213	245	304	814
Furnishings and equipment	278	86	117	193	242	331	388	462	435	805
Clothing	453	131	197	286	385	508	648	822	1,026	1,588
Automobile	472	107	131	248	421	561	737	887	1,052	1,002
Other transportation	69	25	37	53	56	73	98	113	158	202
Medical care	200	112	102	150	194	221	246	294	333	411
Personal care	91	35	51	69	84	99	118	132	161	212
Recreation	177	33	46	93	155	219	256	324	397	605
Reading	34	14	17	26	33	38	44	50	55	80
Education	17	1	6	7	14	20	29	39	43	84
Miscellaneous	47	81	25	34	37	49	70	89	84	206
Percent of expenditures for current consumption	100.0	100.0	100.0	100.0	100.0	100.0	100.0	100.0	100.0	100.0
Food	30.7	32.0	35.8	33.8	31.9	30.0	28.8	27.3	27.8	25.6
Alcoholic beverages	1.8	.5	1.3	1.5	1.6	1.9	1.9	2.2	2.2	2.8
Tobacco	2.0	1.7	2.6	2.4	2.0	2.0	1.8	1.7	1.8	1.2
Housing	10.6	16.8	12.9	12.0	10.9	10.3	9.7	9.5	8.5	9.4
Fuel, light, and refrigeration	4.2	7.2	5.8	5.0	4.4	3.9	3.7	3.4	3.2	2.8
Household operation	3.9	4.6	3.7	3.9	3.8	3.8	4.0	4.0	4.2	7.9
Furnishings and equipment	7.1	5.1	6.1	6.9	6.8	7.5	7.4	7.5	6.1	7.8
Clothing	11.5	7.7	10.2	10.2	10.8	11.5	12.3	13.3	14.3	15.4
Automobile	12.1	6.4	6.8	8.8	11.8	12.7	14.0	14.4	14.7	9.7

Other transportation	1.7	1.5	1.9	1.9	1.6	1.7	1.9	1.8	2.2	2.0
Medical care	5.1	6.7	5.3	5.4	5.4	5.0	4.7	4.8	4.7	4.0
Personal care	2.3	2.1	2.7	2.5	2.4	2.2	2.2	2.1	2.2	2.0
Recreation	4.5	2.0	2.4	3.3	4.3	5.0	4.9	5.2	5.5	5.8
Reading	.9	.8	.9	.9	.9	.9	.8	.8	.8	.8
Education	.4	.1	.3	.3	.4	.5	.6	.6	.6	.8
Miscellaneous	1.2	4.8	1.3	1.2	1.0	1.1	1.3	1.4	1.2	2.0

[1] Taxes deducted were Federal, State, and local income tax, poll tax, and personal property tax.

NOTE: Items may not add to totals because of rounding.

SOURCE: Study of Consumer Expenditures, Incomes and Savings: Statistical Tables, Urban U. S.—1950 (University of Pennsylvania, 1956), Volumes I, II, III, IX, X, table 16 in each volume.

level of food consumption and spend more for other categories; he can devote a higher proportion of income to food, buying greater quantities or better qualities or eating in restaurants instead of at home; or he can use part of the additional income for food and part of it for other items or for savings. In fact, there have been substantial increases in consumption of items of food formerly regarded universally as "luxuries."*

Actually, of course, as workers have obtained added buying power they have usually decided to raise their food consumption level in some degree, to improve their housing facilities somewhat, to add a bit to their savings, and in other ways to make a complex series of adjustments. This is especially true in periods of rapidly rising real income. It is the very complexity of such choices and resultants in terms of consumption that make periodic expenditure surveys necessary for keeping up with changes in patterns of consumption.

The chapters on housing, housekeeping, and food which follow leave no doubt that the food and shelter procured for successively smaller shares of the dollar provided steadily increasing consumer values and, presumably, satisfactions. Thus, our century has created the phenomenon of more than half of the workers attaining homeownership. Both homeowners and tenants commonly have comforts and facilities unknown or rarely available to their counterparts in 1901. So, too, the 31 cents of each dollar devoted to food in 1950 provided much more than the 43 cents per dollar in 1901. If the sole improvement had been the better balanced diet, the gain would be noteworthy. Similar conclusions are valid for clothing, the other group of traditional basic necessities. Although allocating a somewhat smaller part of their expenditures to clothing than in 1901, present-day workers and their families wear apparel far more smartly styled and more efficiently functional. (See chapter VI.) Their clothing, generally conforming in off-the-job uses to prevailing fashions, is evidence of the dimming of class distinctions.

Role of "Sundries"

The transformation of the three traditional categories of "basic necessities" into composites of primary essentials, secondary needs, conveniences, and luxuries impairs their significance, as envisaged by consumption economists of earlier generations, as

---

*This analysis assumes a substantially stable relationship among the prices of the main items in the family budget. Actually, the percentages of family expenditures allocated to the various groups are at times significantly influenced by divergent price trends but this does not invalidate the analysis of basic changes.

bases for appraising advances in well-being beyond subsistence levels. Nevertheless, the expenditures for food and clothing and shelter, although they rise with additions to buying power, remain relatively stable because of the large "hard core" elements of necessary spending for those categories. In comparison with various items for which expenditures are much more elastic in response to changes in buying power, food and clothing and shelter thus retain much significance as a point of departure for appraising advances in well-being.

The comparatively elastic items were formerly often classified as "sundries." The 1875 survey in Massachusetts thus described groups of items designated in more recent surveys as medical care, transportation, housefurnishings, household operation, and leisure activities.

TABLE 7.—*Average consumption expenditures of families of city wage and clerical workers of two or more persons, selected periods*

[In dollars of 1950 purchasing power [1]]

Item	1888–91 survey	1901 survey	1917–19 survey	1934–36 survey	1950 survey
Number of families covered	2,562	11,156	12,096	14,469	5,994
Average family size (persons)	3.9	4.0	4.9	3.6	3.3
Average money receipts			In 1950 dollars		
Money income before personal taxes				$2,661	$4,299
Money income after personal taxes	$1,793	$1,914	$2,408	2,659	4,005
Other receipts				4	33
Total receipts (after taxes)				2,663	4,038
Average outlays					
Current outlays for goods and services (total)	1,671	1,817	2,163	2,564	4,076
Food and drink	797	952	854	1,030	1,335
Clothing			343	309	473
Shelter (current expense)			252	356	448
Fuel, light, refrigeration and water			126	158	153
Housefurnishings and equipment			109	119	281
Household operation				80	167
Automobile purchase and operation				150	457
Other transportation				57	81
Medical care				88	213
Personal care			479	55	93
Recreation				67	191
Reading				27	36
Education				11	19
Tobacco				46	80
Miscellaneous goods and services				11	49

[1] The cost of living index developed by Paul Douglas (see American Economic Review, Supplement, March 1926, p. 22) was used to convert the 1888–91 and 1901 expenditures into 1950 dollars. The Consumer Price Index of the Bureau of Labor Statistics was used for the surveys of 1917–19, 1934–36, and 1950.

SOURCE: For 1888–91, 1901, and 1917–19, see tables 2, 3, and 4, respectively; 1934–36 and 1950 data are from Faith M. Williams, Standards and Levels of Living of City-Worker Families (in Monthly Labor Review, September 1956, p. 1018).

TABLE 8.—*Consumption expenditures of all families in cities of 2,500 and over, by income class, 1950*

Item	All income classes	Under $1,000	$1,000 and under $2,000	$2,000 and under $3,000	$3,000 and under $4,000	$4,000 and under $5,000	$5,000 and under $6,000	$6,000 and under $7,500	$7,500 and under $10,000	$10,000 and over
Number of families	10,791	284	982	1,962	2,807	2,058	1,191	793	425	289
Average family size	3.3	2.4	2.7	3.1	3.3	3.5	3.7	3.7	4.0	3.7
Average money income after personal taxes [1]	$4,224	$622	$1,556	$2,549	$3,492	$4,464	$5,449	$6,638	$8,432	$15,932
Total expenditures for current consumption	$4,119	$1,863	$1,892	$2,809	$3,613	$4,469	$5,277	$6,062	$7,160	$10,808
Food	1,221	605	679	944	1,135	1,313	1,498	1,648	1,995	2,423
Alcoholic beverages	67	15	20	37	55	74	96	112	140	223
Tobacco	74	25	41	60	71	85	88	95	103	112
Housing	455	278	262	343	408	485	536	620	704	1,146
Fuel, light, and refrigeration	172	137	126	146	161	179	196	211	242	306
Household operation	191	89	79	114	144	184	235	281	389	968
Furnishings and equipment	290	105	103	190	242	334	383	438	456	906
Clothing	476	131	168	282	388	511	649	776	971	1,535
Automobile	490	133	120	252	422	572	728	841	973	1,172
Other transportation	69	22	35	51	57	70	89	103	140	199
Medical care	215	142	111	154	202	227	256	302	378	453
Personal care	92	37	46	68	84	99	116	129	150	203
Recreation	185	40	45	92	155	217	251	317	365	598
Reading	37	19	18	27	34	40	45	52	59	83
Education	26	9	4	9	15	26	35	48	70	166
Miscellaneous	60	76	34	41	39	53	76	88	95	316
Percent of expenditures for current consumption	100.0	100.0	100.0	100.0	100.0	100.0	100.0	100.0	100.0	100.0
Food	29.7	32.6	35.9	33.5	31.4	29.2	28.2	27.2	26.8	22.5
Alcoholic beverages	1.6	.8	1.1	1.3	1.5	1.7	1.8	1.8	2.0	2.1
Tobacco	1.8	1.3	2.2	2.1	2.0	1.9	1.7	1.6	1.4	1.0
Housing	11.0	14.9	13.8	12.2	11.3	10.9	10.2	10.2	9.8	10.6
Fuel, light, and refrigeration	4.2	7.4	6.7	5.2	4.5	4.0	3.7	3.5	3.4	2.8
Household operation	4.6	4.8	4.2	4.1	4.0	4.1	4.5	4.6	5.4	9.0
Furnishings and equipment	7.0	5.6	5.4	6.8	6.7	7.5	7.3	7.2	6.4	8.4
Clothing	11.6	7.0	8.9	10.0	10.7	11.4	12.3	12.8	13.6	14.2
Automobile	11.9	7.1	6.3	9.0	11.7	12.8	13.7	13.9	13.6	10.8
Other transportation	1.7	1.2	1.8	1.8	1.6	1.6	1.7	1.7	2.0	1.8

Medical care	5.2	7.6	5.9	5.5	5.6	5.1	4.9	5.0	5.3	4.2
Personal care	2.2	2.0	2.4	2.4	2.3	2.2	2.2	2.1	2.1	1.9
Recreation	4.5	2.1	2.4	3.3	4.3	4.9	4.8	5.2	5.1	5.5
Reading	.9	1.0	1.0	1.0	.9	.9	.9	.9	.8	.8
Education	.6	.5	.2	.3	.4	.6	.7	.8	1.0	1.5
Miscellaneous	1.5	4.1	1.8	1.5	1.1	1.2	1.4	1.5	1.3	2.9

[1] Taxes deducted were Federal, State, and local income tax, poll tax, and personal property tax.

NOTE: Items may not add to totals because of rounding.

SOURCE: Derived from Study of Consumer Expenditures, Incomes and Savings: Statistical Tables, Urban U. S.—1950 (University of Pennsylvania, 1957), Volume XVIII, table 2.

Medical care reached 4.7 percent of total expenditures in 1917-19 and remained near 5 percent in subsequent surveys. The level of medical care has probably risen much more, as is pointed out in the chapter on that subject, than the expenditure surveys reveal. The quality of care has risen perhaps more than the quantity. On the other hand, averages of medical care expenditures are peculiarly inadequate: families afflicted by catastrophic illness contribute much more than their share to the average and yet may fail to command adequate medical care.

In the expenditure surveys, leisure activities commonly comprise recreation, education, and reading. By 1950, those expenditures had reached 5.8 percent for all wage-earner and clerical-worker families. More than three-fourths of those expenditures were classified as recreation, 15 percent as reading, and less than 10 percent as education. In the last category, of course, the costs are mainly met through taxation. Many leisure activities require no money disbursement; others cannot be isolated from average expenditures for other consumption groups. Automobile transportation costs, for example, include not only the expense of driving to and from work but also of a motor vacation, trips to movies and ball games, and the "Sunday afternoon drive."

The metamorphosis in transportation most nearly deserves to be termed revolutionary. (See chapter VIII.) As recently as 1917-19, wage earners and clerical workers were allocating only 3.1 percent of their spending to transportation; in less than 20 years the proportion had almost trebled; it rose, according to the 1934-36 survey, to 8.5 percent. By midcentury it had become one of the largest items in the worker's family budget, accounting for nearly 14 percent of all spending. Half a century ago, none but the wealthiest families commanded their own private nonlocal transportation facilities. There is no more remarkable evidence of rising levels of living than the fact that today's worker and his wife and often their son or daughter commonly take car ownership for granted.

The increasing proportion of expenditures that workers have been able to devote to secondary needs, conveniences, and luxuries is only a pale reflection of the actual advance. A 5 percent allocation of a worker's buying power to recreation, for example, in 1888, or even in 1934, represented only a fraction of 5 percent of the worker's buying power in recent years. Even more significant is the widening of the range of choice—the enlarging of the area of freedom—with the widening margin of power to select the varied goods and services that lie beyond the basic necessities and the secondary needs.

COLLATERAL MEASURES OF CONSUMPTION

The six major surveys of the incomes and expenditures of city workers' families, and especially the four in the first half of the present century, suffice for many significant conclusions, notably as to the remarkable advances in material well-being. Additional sources of information, however, call for summary evaluation here as data collateral to our subject. (For further description and evaluation, see chapter X.) Those sources are the estimates of total personal consumption expenditure compiled by the Department of Commerce and the standard budgets from various sources, which deal primarily with specified standards rather than actual levels of living.

The four chief family expenditure surveys, it will be recalled, covered 1901, 1917-19, 1934-36, and 1950. Those surveys, made at considerable intervals, cannot reflect the intervening economic ups and downs—the boom years of the twenties, the sharp downturn of the early thirties, the recovery trend and temporary setback of 1937-38, the feverish wartime activity with restricted consumption, the inflationary postwar spending, and the recession of 1948-49.

As a reflection of those changes, the Commerce personal consumption expenditure series provides a useful supplement. Per capita expenditures for food, for example, fell from $145 in 1929 to $78 in 1933 (table 26, p. 226), a decline of not far from half; when the drop in retail food prices is considered, the decline was still about 15 percent.*

These expenditure data are chiefly significant, for our present purpose, as a substantial confirmation of rising levels of living over the period covered and of workers' family spending as more closely approximating the spending by other groups as the century advanced.

The standard budgets (table 28, p. 236), broadly speaking, have represented standards desirable in the view of their authors or objectively determined standards of adequacy. Both approaches have usually resulted in standards somewhat above levels of living actually attained by sizable economic groups. The remarkable advances in standards thus formulated comprise highly significant evidences of the advances actually made as families surpassed one standard after another.

The earlier budgets defined adequacy for self-sustaining families at the minimum which would enable them to subsist without resort to charity. Later, the focus turned to whether such families were receiving a "living wage" decidedly above the subsistence

---

*It is not unlikely that depression resort to home gardening, canning and preserving, and subsistence farming held the decline in actual food consumption to less than 15 percent.

TABLE 9.—*Consumption expenditures of wage-earner and clerical-worker families and single consumers in cities of 2,500 and over, by region and occupational group, 1950*

Item	U.S. total	North Total	North Clerical and sales workers	North Wage earners Skilled	North Wage earners Semi-skilled	North Wage earners Un-skilled	South Total	South Clerical and sales workers	South Wage earners Skilled	South Wage earners Semi-skilled	South Wage earners Un-skilled	West Total	West Clerical and sales workers	West Wage earners Skilled	West Wage earners Semi-skilled	West Wage earners Un-skilled
Number of consumer units	7,895	3,675	742	1,045	1,099	789	1,885	382	516	456	531	2,335	561	693	508	573
Average family size	3.1	3.2	2.9	3.4	3.4	2.8	3.2	2.9	3.4	3.4	3.2	3.0	2.8	3.3	3.2	2.8
Average money income after personal taxes [1]	$3,714	$3,838	$4,100	$4,324	$3,789	$3,021	$3,225	$3,937	$3,854	$3,140	$2,295	$3,768	$4,107	$4,209	$3,750	$2,924
Total expenditures for current consumption	$3,695	$3,816	$4,028	$4,279	$3,789	$3,046	$3,204	$3,868	$3,873	$3,082	$2,302	$3,757	$4,033	$4,207	$3,748	$2,954
Food and beverages	1,206	1,271	1,286	1,377	1,290	1,094	1,041	1,146	1,195	1,066	816	1,172	1,182	1,274	1,205	1,011
Tobacco	74	78	73	85	80	69	70	74	86	69	56	70	62	74	79	64
Housing	405	424	512	447	396	350	337	473	399	299	231	409	485	417	389	342
Fuel, light, and refrigeration	151	163	158	181	164	146	140	140	159	137	126	128	132	144	127	108
Household operation	147	148	199	156	127	121	139	222	155	122	89	151	202	154	136	109
Furnishings and equipment	254	254	263	292	269	177	229	246	280	227	173	271	307	322	262	182
Clothing	426	446	492	492	438	354	383	487	441	359	287	409	484	438	400	308
Transportation	501	482	454	628	477	322	422	503	622	385	229	599	567	772	625	398
Medical care	186	189	203	213	193	141	152	200	187	144	99	200	221	221	192	161
Personal care	86	88	95	94	87	74	81	99	88	79	64	84	93	91	84	69
Recreation, reading, and education	214	227	247	265	228	157	165	215	213	162	95	216	245	248	207	157
Miscellaneous	45	44	46	48	42	40	44	63	47	37	35	48	54	51	41	41
Percent of expenditures for current consumption	100.0	100.0	100.0	100.0	100.0	100.0	100.0	100.0	100.0	100.0	100.0	100.0	100.0	100.0	100.0	100.0
Food and beverages	32.6	33.3	32.0	32.2	34.0	35.9	32.5	29.6	30.9	34.5	35.5	31.2	29.3	30.2	32.2	34.2
Tobacco	2.0	2.0	1.8	2.0	2.1	2.3	2.2	1.9	2.2	2.2	2.4	1.9	1.5	1.8	2.1	2.2
Housing	11.0	11.1	12.8	10.5	10.4	11.5	10.6	12.2	10.3	9.7	10.1	10.9	12.0	9.9	10.4	11.6
Fuel, light, and refrigeration	4.1	4.3	3.9	4.2	4.3	4.8	4.4	3.6	4.1	4.4	5.5	3.4	3.3	3.4	3.4	3.7
Household operation	4.0	3.9	4.9	3.6	3.4	4.0	4.3	5.7	4.0	4.0	3.9	4.0	5.0	3.7	3.6	3.7
Furnishings and equipment	6.9	6.7	6.5	6.8	7.1	5.8	7.1	6.4	7.2	7.4	7.5	7.2	7.6	7.7	7.0	6.2

Clothing	11.5	11.7	12.2	11.5	11.6	11.6	12.0	12.6	11.4	11.6	12.5	10.9	12.0	10.4	10.7	10.4
Transportation	13.6	12.6	11.3	14.7	12.6	10.6	13.2	13.0	16.1	12.4	9.9	16.0	14.1	18.3	16.7	13.4
Medical care	5.0	5.0	5.0	5.0	5.1	4.6	4.7	5.2	4.8	4.7	4.3	5.3	5.5	5.3	5.1	5.5
Personal care	2.3	2.3	2.4	2.2	2.3	2.4	2.5	2.6	2.3	2.6	2.8	2.2	2.3	2.2	2.2	2.3
Recreation, reading, and education	5.8	5.9	6.1	6.2	6.0	5.2	5.1	5.6	5.5	5.3	4.1	5.7	6.1	5.9	5.5	5.3
Miscellaneous	1.2	1.2	1.1	1.1	1.1	1.3	1.4	1.6	1.2	1.2	1.5	1.3	1.3	1.2	1.1	1.5

[1] Taxes deducted were Federal, State, and local income tax, poll tax, and personal property tax.

NOTE: Items may not add to totals because of rounding.

SOURCE: Derived from Study of Consumer Expenditures, Incomes and Savings: Statistical Tables, Urban U. S.—1950 (University of Pennsylvania, 1956), Volumes I and II, table 8.

level. Later still, the budgets presented standards which satisfied current "social" concepts. The progression is obscured to some extent by the special requirements of two world wars and a major depression.

The rapidly advancing concept in the standard budgets of what constituted "adequacy" mirrored, in some respects, the progress of our society somewhat more significantly than did the surveys of actual conditions. The advancing concept reflected changes in basic attitudes and therefore, at length, registered the feasibility of translating the advancing concept into reality.

Footnotes

[1] W. Duane Evans, in *Employment and Wages in the United States* by W. S. Woytinsky and Associates (New York, Twentieth Century Fund, 1953), p. 81 (citing Work Time Required to Buy Food, by Irving B. Kravis, in *Monthly Labor Review*, November 1949).

[2] *Op. cit.*, p. 510.

[3] Many similar views are cited by E. S. Furness in *The Position of the Laborer in a System of Nationalism* (Boston, Houghton Mifflin, 1920), pp. 118ff.

CHAPTER III

From the Slums to Suburbia

> ... *the first thing a man does when he obtains a considerable increase of income and sets about spending it, generally is to look for a better house.*
> —N. G. Pierson.

Among the significant achievements of the United States economy in the 20th century are the improvements in housing and the growth in homeownership. For wage earners, as well as other members of our society, the home has come to embody a multitude of new goods and services which lighten the burden of housekeeping, make it better suited as a center of family life, and symbolize economic and cultural advantages available in the United States today.

The story of workers' housing since 1900 is compounded of growth in purchasing power, the development of a mass-production housing industry and low-cost amortized financing, and changing social attitudes. Perhaps the key to this changing pattern is the fact that the approach to the housing problem is no longer primarily that of "workers' housing," as in early years of the century. Thus, United States delegates at conferences of the International Labor Organization on workers' housing talk of all housing.

This chapter traces the major changes in housing since the turn of the century, and stresses the current factors which suggest continued improvements in housing, not only for wage earners but for all Americans.

HOUSING AT THE END OF THE 19TH CENTURY

In every country at some period in its history, the worker's need for shelter has been related to the requirements of his occupation or the location of his job. Before the industrial revolution, the home was often also the place of employment. With the development of the factory system, industrial workers sought housing near the factory and the factory town grew up.

Early industrial development in America followed the same course. The typical pattern of crowded urban housing had been established before the end of the 19th century. Descriptions of housing conditions of the time revealed the effects of rapid and planless city growth.

Causes of Congestion and Poor Housing

The rapid growth of industry and population in the United States in the 1800's led to extreme congestion in some areas, notably in New York City. In 1894, there were 143 persons per acre on the island of Manhattan, for example, as compared with 125 in the city of Paris; in the 10th ward of New York City, the density was 626 per acre. Prague, one of the most crowded of European cities, had 485 persons per acre. Overcrowding, poor housing, and unsanitary conditions were by no means confined to New York City; slums housed an estimated 10 percent of all persons living in the 16 United States cities with populations of 200,000 or more. Even in the comparatively small mill towns of New England and the South and in mining villages and logging camps, workers and their families often lived under conditions little to be preferred to those of the more congested parts of Manhattan Island.

There were several general causes, economic, social, technological, for the crowded, unsanitary, and uncomfortable housing in most of the factory areas at the turn of the century. Low wages provided income for little more than subsistence for workers' families. By today's standards, the wage earner had to spend a disproportionately large share of his income for food, and consequently had insufficient funds for other purposes, such as good housing. Other factors tended to force him into crowded quarters near his job. One of these was the long workday. In 1900, 6 days of 9 or 10 hours each were still considered a normal working week in the United States. After spending so much time at his job, the workman could not face the prospect of a long ride home. Marcus T. Reynolds, writing in 1893, observed:

> A cottage in the suburbs is certainly more attractive. . . . Unfortunately the peculiar location of many of our cities prohibits this solution of the problem. . . . The hour lost in going and coming to his work more than counterbalances the advantages gained by suburban residence, in the mind of the average workman. At whatever cost of comfort and health, and even of money, the workman will live near his work, and unless the factories are moved into the suburbs, he will continue to reside in the most crowded portion of our cities.[1]

Not only time but also transportation problems prevented the workers from spreading out into the suburban areas. Transpor-

CITY DWELLING—Today's apartment blocks, with their lawns, their all-round exposure to daylight, and their obvious dwelling purpose, are a great improvement on the crowded streets and tenement dwellings of earlier days, cheek by jowl with industrial and commercial enterprises.

tation was a factor also in limiting decentralization of industry. Not until the development of the motortruck and a paved highway system was it possible to cut the ties between the factory and the railroad and move both the plant and the workers' homes out of the central city.

In other respects, also, the easing of city crowding waited for technological advances. Early in the century, the height of apartment houses was limited by the materials used in the structural framework and the tenants' stair-climbing ability—6 or 7 stories was the upper limit. Not until the initiation of public low-cost housing programs and their acceleration in the 1930's did elevator apartments become available in any quantity for low- and middle-income families. In recent years, the evils of overcrowding have been greatly alleviated in many high-density areas by replacing the 5- or 6-story tenements with 20- and even 25-story elevator-type structures, set in large areas of open space.

Long before the turn of the century, land had become scarce in the big cities and the New England factory towns. As the working population increased, additional buildings were crowded onto lots formerly considered no more than adequate for a single-family house. In a study of Chicago slum conditions in 1900, 23 percent of the 3,117 structures surveyed were found to be located on the rear of lots occupied by other structures. The added buildings were usually "walk-up" apartment houses, containing as many living units as could be crowded into 5 or 6 stories.

Except in the large cities and some of the mill towns, workers' homes were usually single-family structures, whether owned or rented. In what eventually became densely crowded slum areas of the cities, much of the housing was provided by subdividing old family residences and converting them into apartments and lodging houses. Many families, already badly overcrowded in small makeshift apartments, supplemented their meager incomes by taking in lodgers. In the mill towns of New England and later in the South, the factory owners commonly found it necessary to provide housing for their workers. This led to the construction of company-owned housing, rented by the employees.

Immigration, of course, created many urban problems in the early years of the century. The incoming jobseekers, mostly unskilled and unable to speak English, tended to cluster together. With limited resources and earning power, thrown into a strange social environment, the newcomers sought housing near members of their own ethnic group. These foreign communities crowded in upon already overcrowded slum areas. An 1894 study by the U. S. Commissioner of Labor showed the following distribution of foreign-born population in four large cities:

City	Percent of foreign-born population—	
	In city as a whole	In slums
Baltimore	16	40
Chicago	41	58
New York	42	63
Philadelphia	26	60

Special circumstances aggravated the housing problems of New York City. In the decade of the nineties its population grew by nearly a million; its geographical limits were putting extreme pressure on space available; and, as the major port of entry, it was becoming a more and more constricted bottleneck for immigrants coming increasingly from overcrowded European countries of low living standards and levels.

Homeownership

The first census report on homeownership (1890) showed that nearly 37 percent of the families in the United States owned their homes. The data did not relate homeownership to occupation or income, but the geographical variations suggest that the incidence of owner-occupancy among factory workers was very low. In fact, a 1901 survey of income and expenditures by the Commissioner of Labor found that, among a sample of 25,440 worker families in "principal industrial centers," only 19 percent owned their homes. Ownership was especially low in the New England and Middle Atlantic regions and in Georgia and Louisiana.

Limited income was the chief, but by no means the only, deterrent to homeownership. Lack of job security was prevalent; the 1901 survey showed that nearly half of the heads of families were idle at some time during the year—9 weeks, on the average. The difficulty of borrowing money and the high cost of financing presented an almost insuperable obstacle to most workers. The long-term amortized mortgage loan was rarely used. The maximum loan offered was typically about half of the appraised value, on a 1- to 5-year note, payable in full at maturity, and bearing interest at from 6 to over 10 percent. Renewal of the note involved heavy refinancing charges. The result was that only the relatively well-off could own their homes.

That limited income also prevented many renters from meeting their housing standards is apparent from an examination of the importance of rents in the expenditures of families at different income levels. The 1901 survey showed that rent expenditures, as a percent of total spending, did not decline significantly as family income rose—they represented 16.6 percent among families with incomes of $1,100–$1,200, compared with 18.7 percent among the $300–$400 group. (See table 3.) Thus, even the higher income families apparently had not satisfied their housing wants to an extent that permitted them to devote a substantially larger share of their expenditures to other less necessary items.

This inference is borne out by the Eighth Special Report (1895) of the Commissioner of Labor, which stated: "Investigation shows indubitably that the percentage of earnings of heads of tenant families which is absorbed in payment of rent in all large cities is far too high." [2] In that report also, the tenements built after 1880 were described as representing "wonderful progress," but they lacked most of the basic facilities available to most of the urban workers even during the depression of the 1930's.

Condition of the Workers' Houses

Not only did financial considerations prevent most urban wage earners from obtaining better homes, but also much of the workers' housing was badly designed and built and poorly maintained. It provided few of the comforts which we take for granted today.

In New York, the Tenement House Act of 1879 required outside windows for all rooms in newly constructed residential buildings. Each floor of these "dumb-bell" tenements typically contained 4 apartments with 2 centrally located bathroom facilities. (See chart 3, p. 63.) An especially noxious feature of these structures was the air shaft, formed by the space between any 2 adjoining buildings, which widened from as little as 6 inches or a foot at the front and back to perhaps 5 feet in the center. This was the device used to satisfy the legal requirement of outside windows. These shafts were entirely enclosed and extended from top to bottom of the building. Small windows opening on the shaft provided the only direct light and air for most of the rooms in the apartment. Often the bottom of the shaft became covered with a nauseating collection of garbage and debris. Rather than light and air, as the law had envisaged, the shaft provided foul odors and discordant sounds and, like a chimney, a ready means of spreading fire throughout the structure.

Early studies of public health problems called attention to the hazards of overcrowding, not only to the inhabitants of the slums but also to the entire community. The Seventh Special Report of the Commissioner of Labor revealed that in 1893 the slum dwellings of New York housed an average of 1.9 persons per

Chart 3.

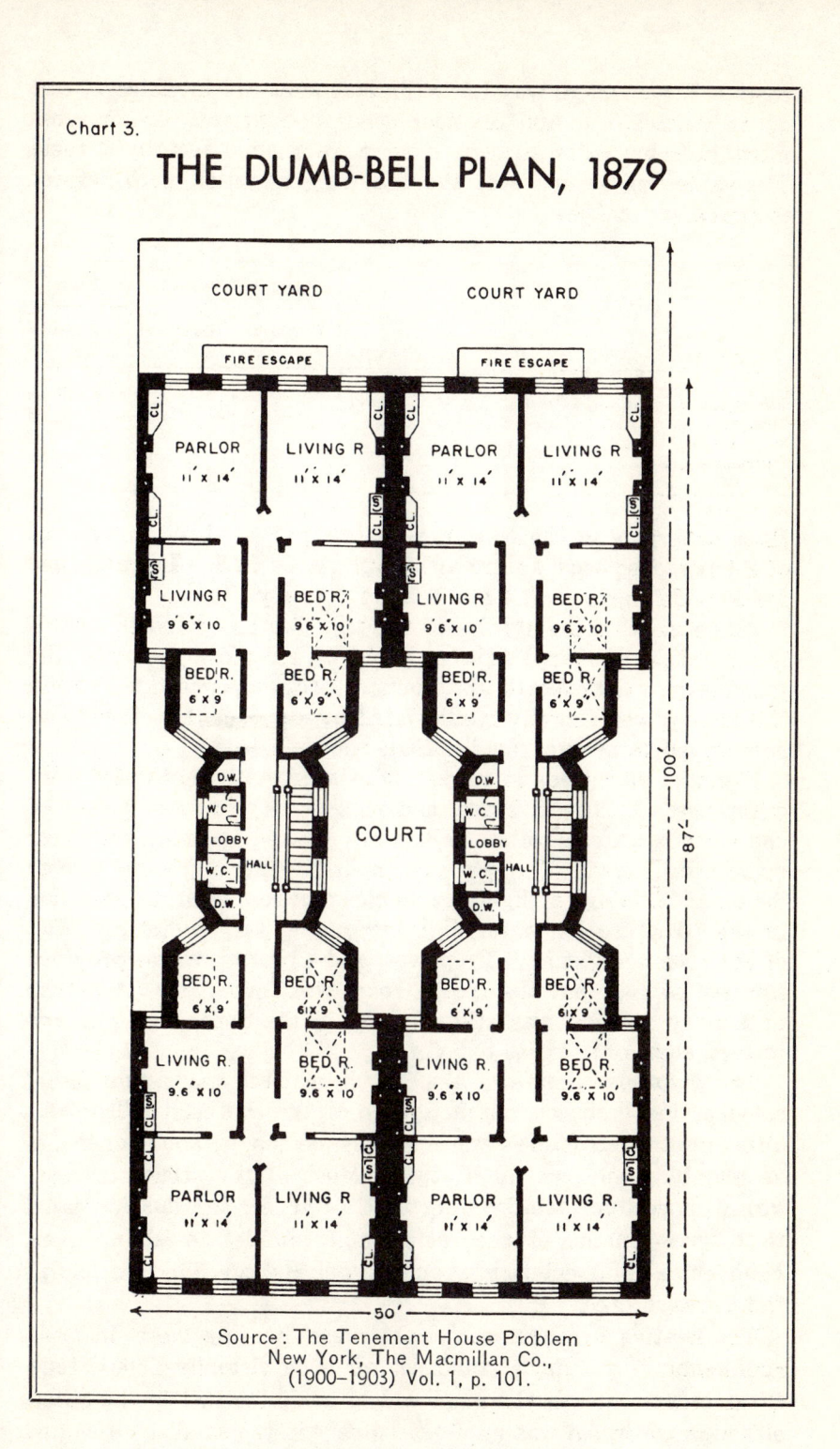

THE DUMB-BELL PLAN, 1879

Source: The Tenement House Problem
New York, The Macmillan Co.,
(1900–1903) Vol. 1, p. 101.

room. The average was 1.5 in Philadelphia, 1.4 in Chicago, and 1.2 in Baltimore. And the floor space in a typical old-law tenement bedroom often measured no more than 6 feet by 7 feet! The same report indicates the following situation with respect to sanitary facilities:

City	Percentage of families having access to—		
	Bathroom	Watercloset only	Outside privy only
Baltimore	7	5	88
Chicago	3	24	73
New York	2	45	53
Philadelphia	17	13	70

Each bathroom in the New York slums was used by an average of 8.1 persons; each watercloset or privy, by 10.5. The averages for Philadelphia were 7.4 and 6.9, respectively.

While most of the studies of the time were devoted to crowding in cities, similar conditions probably existed in many of the mill villages, both North and South. Crowded conditions within the houses were, however, alleviated by the fact that there was some freedom of movement outside them.

Regional variations in worker housing resulted naturally from differences in climate, space, and rate of city growth. Most of the early southern cotton mills were located in small towns or even rural areas. The workers' houses generally were 4-room detached buildings of light frame construction, with no provision in the structure for water, lighting, or sanitary facilities. Two of the rooms might have fireplaces, and a cookstove was provided for the kitchen, but the fourth room was unheated. This type of factory housing was still common in the South in 1900, and in fact, some of it exists today.

The rigorous climate of the North required more substantial construction than was characteristic of the southern mill towns, although the structures were equally devoid of such amenities as plumbing and central heating. Most of the structures contained more than one dwelling unit. Surveys in 1908 indicated that three-fourths of the cotton mill families in Maine, New Hampshire, Massachusetts, and Rhode Island lived in multi-family structures.

The heating arrangements in workers' housing were, in 1900, rudimentary by today's standards, or even virtually nonexistent. Bituminous coal was the most widely available fuel in the cities, although cordwood was used extensively in the smaller cities and towns, especially in the South and West. Central heating systems were practically unknown, even in the largest and most "modern" tenement buildings. Typical of the period were the Riverside Buildings in Brooklyn, described by the U. S. Commissioner of Labor in 1895 as a worthy "philanthropy" which had nevertheless proved to be a financial success:

> There are no fireplaces. Slate slabs are fixed in the floors for stoves, which are used for heating, to rest upon. There are no heating registers. . . . Gas on the stairs, in the public hallways, bathrooms, and office is furnished by the proprietor, but the tenants, as a rule, burn oil in their rooms. . . . A cooking range is not furnished by the company, but there is a coalbox in each kitchen which holds a quarter of a ton.[3]

FIRST 2 DECADES OF THE 20TH CENTURY

This was the condition of workers' housing in 1900. But economic, legal, technical, and social forces were already in motion to bring about changes. Appeals to public conscience regarding slum housing problems had been made as early as 1834.

Regulatory Measures

New York City, as the Nation's largest center of immigration and industry, exhibited almost the gamut of housing problems, and it became the proving ground for housing legislation. The first tenement house law was adopted for New York City in 1867, forbidding dwellings in a cellar unless its ceiling was at least a foot above ground, and setting a few sanitation standards. Next came the tenement act of 1879, already mentioned, and Pennsylvania passed a tenement house law in 1895.

It was, however, the radically revised New York act of 1901 which stimulated housing legislation in other States. The new law set higher standards for new construction of all types of houses, requiring more nearly adequate light, air, open space, and fire protection. Laws patterned after the New York act of 1901 were enacted between 1904 and 1919 in New Jersey, Connecticut, Wisconsin, Indiana, California, Kentucky, Massachusetts, Michigan, Minnesota, and Iowa.

Urban Growth

Early in the century the first signs of suburban expansion began to appear. By 1912, the expansion of electric street railways made it possible in many communities for at least the higher paid workers to escape from the shadow of the factory walls and the confinement of the slums. In this period also, the struggle for the shorter workday somewhat reduced work schedules.

Moreover, with the growing popularity of the motor vehicle and improvements in highways, industries began to move out of the cities, seeking more space, cheaper land, and a better environment for the workers. This movement made it possible for even some of the unskilled factory workers to live in somewhat better surroundings than the city slums.

War Housing

The first world war introduced a new phase in the development of workers' housing. Private building was virtually suspended during 1917 and 1918 as a result of Government restrictions, high building costs, and the transfer of capital to other activities. At the same time, serious housing shortages developed in the war-production and shipbuilding centers. For the first time, the Federal Government went into housing construction on a large scale. In this enterprise the Department of Labor played a major role, through its administration of the United States Housing Corporation. The Housing Division of the Shipping Board also was responsible for a large volume of housing built for shipyard workers. Both agencies have been credited with setting improved standards for small house design and community development through these programs.

Government housing notwithstanding, the restriction on normal building activity in the war years inevitably brought about conditions which led to doubling up of families, occupancy of makeshift quarters and dwellings unfit for habitation, and relaxation of housing code enforcement by city authorities. Although their earnings from wartime employment were high, workers found it difficult to improve their housing conditions.

Housing at the End of World War I

It is difficult, looking back 40 years, to assess the status of workers' housing in the period of the first world war. The only comprehensive data available come from the family expenditure survey of 1917–19, which provided some information on the economic status of wage earners and salaried workers in 92 shipbuilding and industrial centers. That study, however, was made in the midst of wartime conditions, when prices were rising rapidly, and it excluded slum families.

The families in the 1917–19 survey allocated about 19 percent of their expenditures for housing, fuel, and light, compared with 24 percent for the families in the 1901 survey. (See tables 3 and 4.) The reduction was due in large measure to an increase of about one-fourth in their income, in dollars of equivalent pur-

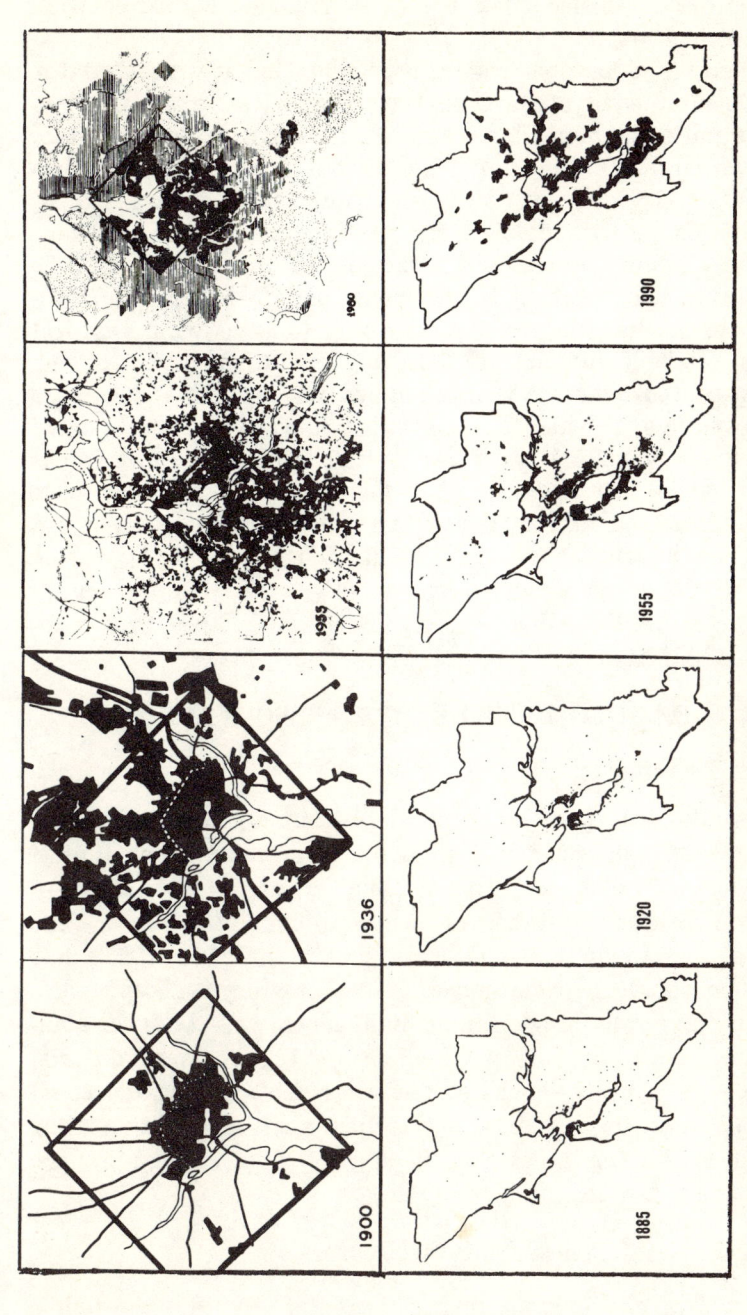

SUBURBAN GROWTH—Automobiles and public transportation have made it possible for workers to inhabit suburban areas remote from their places of work. These maps show how far flung has been the extension of occupied areas in two major cities of the United States.

chasing power. Homeownership by wage earners had increased substantially since the beginning of the century—27 percent of the city workers owned their homes in 1917–19, compared with 19 percent in 1901.

Electricity had become widely available, and it was used for lighting even in some of the older tenements. Gas was still, however, the most common illuminant in the urban workers' homes. Forty-five percent of the families used gas for lighting, whereas 41 percent used electricity. Because manufactured gas was expensive, gas was rarely employed for heating except in areas near gas fields. Twenty percent of the families included in the 1917–19 study used gas for heating, but it should be noted that a substantial number of the 92 cities surveyed were in areas where natural gas was available in quantity. In any event, only half of the rooms in rented quarters were equipped for heating.

The dwellings in which these families lived typically consisted of 5 rooms, or about 1 room per person, virtually the same as in 1901. This fact suggests that the effect of excluding slum dwellings from the 1917–19 survey may have been partially offset by wartime housing shortages. And among the nearly three-fourths of the families who were renters, more than 7 in every 10 lived in a dwelling which had an inside watercloset, and somewhat over half had a full bathroom.

CHANGES BETWEEN THE TWO WARS

Booming Twenties

By 1921, private homebuilding was beginning to recover from the effects of war restrictions. This recovery continued until 1925, when 937,000 nonfarm dwelling units were started—a record which was to stand for nearly a quarter-century. The volume of apartment house construction in the early 1920's has never been equaled. Row houses, 2- and 3-story walkup apartment buildings, and single-family bungalows were built in sufficient quantities to provide new housing for higher paid industrial workers. Perhaps the mass of low-wage factory workers could not afford these new homes, but it has been argued that they benefited by having access to the old housing vacated by the higher income families.

Housing Expenditures During the Depression

Not until after the stock market crash of 1929 did the public realize that homebuilding had been showing a continuous decline since 1925, and was then more than 45 percent below the record high. In 1933, only 93,000 new nonfarm dwelling units were placed under construction. This was the nadir.

As the depression focused attention on changes in consumer spending, the Bureau of Labor Statistics in 1934 launched a new survey of expenditures by wage-earner and clerical-worker families which provides another check-point on progress in workers' housing. The study did not include detailed data for families on relief and included no cities with populations of less than 50,000. Nevertheless, the information it provides on housing casts a revealing light on the progress achieved during the twenties. Among the families surveyed, 30 percent were homeowners, as compared with 27 percent of those surveyed in 1917–19, when small cities were included in the study. In many of the qualities of the housing available to workers, the gains were more impressive than in homeownership.

The annual income of the families surveyed averaged $1,518. (See table 5.) Of their total expenditures, over 25 percent was devoted to housing, fuel, light, and refrigeration, a significantly higher proportion than was found in the 1917–19 survey. Since the incomes of the 1934–36 families, in constant dollars, averaged about 10 percent higher, while rents were at about the same level, the increased proportion spent for housing may have been due in part to the rise in homeownership. Other factors which probably exerted influence included improvement in the quality of housing, higher fuel bills resulting from central heating, and increased utilization of electricity, not only for lighting but also for electrical appliances. The fact that the percentage going for housing declined from about 31 percent in the lowest income group to 18 in the highest also suggests that substantial numbers of families had attained a level of housing sufficiently satisfactory that they preferred to devote increases in income to procuring other goods and services.

"The home of the typical wage earner or clerical family with an income above $500 had," according to the 1934–36 study, "a bathroom with inside flush toilet and hot running water. It had electric lights and gas or electricity for cooking." [4] Among all of the tenant families interviewed in 42 large cities, 98 percent were living in dwellings supplied with running water, 90 percent had bathrooms, and 96 percent had inside flush toilets. Owner-occupied housing was even better equipped with these basic essentials. Homeowners also had larger dwellings—an average of 6.4 rooms, compared with about 4 rooms for rented houses and about 4½ for apartments.

The improvement in New York City was especially striking: Over nine-tenths of the families occupied dwelling units equipped with running hot water, inside flush toilet, electric light, and gas or electricity for cooking. Of the dwelling units in New York occupied by white families, 99 percent had inside flush toilets, while all of those occupied by Negro families were provided with such facilities.

Improvements were apparent; but in many facilities important for health as well as comfort, large numbers of dwelling units throughout the country, especially among those occupied by Negro families, were gravely deficient.

The omission from the 1934-36 study of relief families and of families with incomes below $500 leaves unanswered the question as to how many seriously substandard dwelling units may have been occupied by families not within the scope of the survey. About one-fourth of the white wage-earner families in the $500–$750 income class in New York City had living quarters which were not equipped with running hot and cold water, inside flush toilet, and electric lights. Presumably even less adequate housing could be obtained by families with smaller income. Estimates prepared by the National Resources Committee at that time showed 4.5 percent of the nonrelief families in large metropolitan areas receiving under $500 in annual income. Certainly, the plight of the unemployed workers and families on relief was in many instances desperate. Nevertheless, most workers had been able to achieve far better housing than had been possible in the early years of the century, or even during World War I.

Economic Recovery—Government Aid

Federal Housing Legislation. The depression crisis of the early 1930's brought demands for Federal action to rescue the lending institutions, prevent widespread foreclosures of home mortgages, and provide a stimulant to the economy. The first move occurred in 1932 with the passage of the Federal Home Loan Bank Act, which established a nationwide system patterned after the Federal Reserve System, to provide a credit reserve for savings and loan associations. This was followed in 1933 by the establishment of the Home Owners' Loan Corporation, to finance long-term loans at low interest rates for distressed homeowners who were unable to refinance their delinquent loans through normal channels.

Further legislation in 1934 completed a basic system of home financing which set the stage for a new era in homebuilding, bringing homeownership within reach of a vastly larger proportion of wage earners throughout the country. The National Housing Act of June 1934 created the Federal Housing Administration, "to encourage improvement in housing standards and conditions, and to provide a system of mutual mortgage insurance." The new agency was authorized to insure housing loans, upon application by the lender, provided the structure, the amount and conditions of the loan, and the borrower's financial status met its standards. Modern standards for construction, lot size, services, and facilities were also required. Insurance on each dwelling was extended only on a single, long-term mortgage, not exceeding a stipulated maximum and repayable in monthly installments. The law initially limited interest to not more than 5 percent on the loan balance. The agency set the rate at 4½ percent, plus a one-half of 1 percent mortgage insurance fee, and required that taxes and fire insurance premiums be included in the monthly payment.

Such was the power of Federal assistance in the uncertain financial situation of that time that residential loan practices were substantially changed almost overnight. The prevalent method of home financing involved two mortgages. The first-trust loan, covering up to 60 percent of the appraised value of the property, typically was due in full in 3 to 10 years, with interest at 6 percent or more. If the house buyer required more credit, which was usually the case among the middle-income groups, he had to obtain a second-trust loan, repayable in semiannual or annual installments over a period of 3 to 4 years, with interest at a considerably higher rate. Under the new program, a first-mortgage monthly amortization loan for upwards of 80 percent of the purchase price of a low-cost home could be obtained. The long-term amortized loan quickly became almost universal, for both insured and noninsured housing loans. Thus, the National Housing Act stimulated the construction of medium-priced housing indirectly as well as directly, although a majority of the new nonfarm housing units built in most years since its inception have not been covered by FHA-insured mortgage loans.

Low-Income Housing. The act was not, however, intended as a device for attacking the problem of housing the lowest income families or for eliminating slums. The trade unions, concerned with their members' need for both jobs and homes, became actively interested in the housing problem in the 1930's. By 1934, the American Federation of Labor had formulated a housing program, the main features of which were incorporated in the United States Housing Act of 1937. The American Federation of Labor, the Congress of Industrial Organizations, and now the combined organization, have fought vigorously and continuously for programs to provide more and better housing for the low- and middle-income groups, slum clearance and urban rehabilitation, low interest loans for nonprofit housing cooperatives, and special housing programs to meet the needs of elderly persons.

Labor organizations have also sponsored a few notable housing projects financed by private lenders or with union funds (particularly, in recent years, pension and welfare funds). The first major development of this type, the Amalgamated Clothing Workers' project, built in 1927 in New York City under provisions of the New York Limited Dividend Housing Companies Act, now provides housing for 2,486 families. Others include the Carl Mackley homes in Philadelphia, built by the American Federation of Hosiery Workers in 1934, a Flushing, Long Island, development for 2,200 families sponsored by Local 3 of the International Brotherhood of Electrical Workers in 1950-54, and the Cooperative Village of the International Ladies' Garment Workers' Union, consisting of four 20- or 21-story apartment buildings, which opened in New York City in 1955.

The United States Housing Act of 1937 authorized Federal financial assistance to local communities "to remedy the unsafe and insanitary housing conditions and the acute shortage of decent, safe, and sanitary dwellings for families of low income." To this end, local authorities sponsoring low-rent housing projects were to receive Federal construction loans as well as annual cash contributions to help meet operating deficits. Occupancy of the public housing units is limited to families adjudged eligible by the local housing authority. One of the major criteria for tenancy is income—the family's net income may not exceed limits set by the local authority. In addition, preference is given to families living in substandard housing and those being displaced by slum clearance programs.

In quantity terms, publicly owned housing is a minor factor in the housing supply. From 1934, when the first public housing projects were built under the Public Works Administration program, through 1956, about 650,000 new permanent nonfarm dwelling units were constructed for government ownership. Private builders, using private funds, have built, for all groups, over 15 million units in the same period.

The real significance of public housing lies in its influence on housing design and community development, especially in the very large cities. With the construction of the "First Houses" in New York City in 1937, the skyline began to change. Those public housing buildings were relatively small—4 stories in height—but they were surrounded by open spaces. Structures in later developments grew higher, to accommodate more low-income families, but each project was planned as a complete community, with parks, playgrounds, and community services. A prominent trade magazine, although opposed to it in principle, in 1952 conceded that "public housing since the war has done more to improve design and planning of apartments at lower rentals than all private enterprise in the same period." [5]

These developments have replaced some of the worst slums and decayed industrial properties, not only in the largest cities but in a number of smaller communities throughout the country. More recent public housing legislation has emphasized urban rehabilitation, requiring the adoption of broad local programs for redevelopment as a condition of Federal assistance. This, together with the low-cost financing provided under various Government loan insurance programs, has stimulated private construction of large, modern apartment buildings, many of which are within the rent range of higher paid wage earners.

WORLD WAR II AND VETERANS' HOUSING

Stimulated by general economic recovery and the support of the Government loan insurance programs, the housing industry began to recover rapidly after the depression. In 1941, the volume of new nonfarm dwelling units placed under construction reached 706,100. With the onset of World War II, new housing starts fell far below the volume needed to keep pace with population increases. Again the critical need for workers' housing in the rapidly growing war production centers led to the adoption of a variety of expedients. Rent controls were established to protect the workers and to help prevent inflation. Thousands of temporary and demountable dwelling units were erected. For the first time, the house trailer became an important factor in worker housing, gaining a degree of acceptance which it has apparently retained. (Spokesmen for the trailer manufacturers claim that upwards of 1 million house trailers are now in use, with over 60 percent owned by workers.)

With demobilization after the war and the return to private life of millions of young men, the housing crisis became acute and there were insistent demands for Government action. The most effective action taken, and one which made it possible for hundreds of thousands of wage earners to buy homes, was the Veterans Readjustment Act of 1944, which provided, among other things, for Government guarantee of loans to veterans for home purchase. By the end of 1957, over 5 million "GI" home loans had been made—almost 3 million of these for new homes. The veterans' loan guaranty program has emphasized low interest

73

rates, low downpayments or none at all, and repayment periods extending to 30 years. On this basis, almost any employed veteran could qualify for a modest home.

The cumulative effect of the veterans' guaranty program, FHA insurance, and constantly increasing housing demand generated by population growth and higher incomes, brought an unprecedented volume of new housing activity. Huge suburban developments have been created to meet the housing demand supported by the GI loan and the FHA insurance programs. The annual number of new nonfarm dwelling units placed under construction exceeded 1 million for the first time in 1949, and remained above that level through 1957. Despite increasing costs of land and construction, a large share of these new houses have been bought by wage earners and salaried workers.

WORKERS' HOUSING AT MIDCENTURY

Extent of Homeownership

The main trends in housing since the turn of the century suggest the extent to which the American worker has shared in housing improvements. Although homeowning is still beyond the reach of many wage earners and salaried employees, our social and economic system has succeeded in providing the ways and means by which a majority of the workers can obtain homes of their own if they wish. Homeownership is not denied them, although they may choose to use their resources in other ways.

In 1950, 53 percent of the occupied nonfarm dwelling units were owned by their occupants, and indications are that the proportion has continued to rise. The proportion of ownership by urban workers was almost as high—nearly 51 percent, or more than 2½ times the percentage in 1901. Homeownership among worker families was lowest in the North, 47 percent, and highest in the West, 58 percent; in the South, it was 54 percent. The lower percentage in the North is explained by the larger and older cities, the greater availability of multiple-family dwelling units, the higher costs of housing associated with the climate, and the lack of land conveniently located for low-cost single-family housing. In the West, where population growth has been extremely rapid in recent years, cities have been built on a broader scale, and have not developed the dense urban core typical of the older cities which grew large before the automobile age.

Despite the enormous increase in homeownership, a large proportion of wage earners are and probably will continue to be renters. Many homeowners may have bought houses in recent years because of their inability to rent satisfactory quarters. Certainly the proportion of new residential building intended for rental has been declining since the beginning of the thirties. In the decade 1920-29, about 30 percent of the new nonfarm dwelling units built were in two-family and multifamily structures; in the period 1930-56, all but 16 percent of the total were in single-family houses. Moreover, most of the additions to the single-family housing supply in recent years have been built for sale, whereas in the 1920's many investors found it profitable to build such housing and hold it for the rental income.

Cost and Choice of Housing in 1950

Whether they owned or rented their homes, city workers' families in 1950, with more than twice the income, in dollars of equivalent purchasing power, of their 1901 counterparts, were able to devote a substantially smaller share of their expenditures to housing, fuel, and light—15 instead of 24 percent. (See tables 3 and 6, pp. 40 and 46.) Moreover, the relative importance of expenditures for shelter declined more rapidly in 1950 as family income rose. (See chart 4, p. 76.)

The proportion spent on housing, heat, and light also varied with the occupation of the chief earner and the climate in which the family lived. Clerical and sales workers spent the most and unskilled workers the least in all regions—in terms of actual amounts expended. (See table 9, p. 54.) And for all groups of workers—white-collar, skilled, semiskilled, and unskilled—expenditures for housing were highest in the North and lowest in the South. Skilled workers, for example, reported average expenditures for housing, fuel, light, and refrigeration of $628 in the North, as against $558 in the South and $561 in the West.

These figures represent the annual cost of housing, whether owned or rented. The relative cost of ownership and renting was the subject of a study of buyers and renters of new housing in 9 large metropolitan areas, made in 1949 and 1950 by the Bureau of Labor Statistics. In the market situation of that time, the homeseeker in most of the areas could buy more cheaply than he could rent new quarters providing approximately equivalent living space. Other considerations in the choice between buying and renting are suggested in a report on interviews with new home buyers, conducted by the Survey Research Center of the University of Michigan in 1949-50. That study revealed that more than half of those interviewed had never previously owned a home. Some were heads of newly formed families, but most had been

Chart 4.

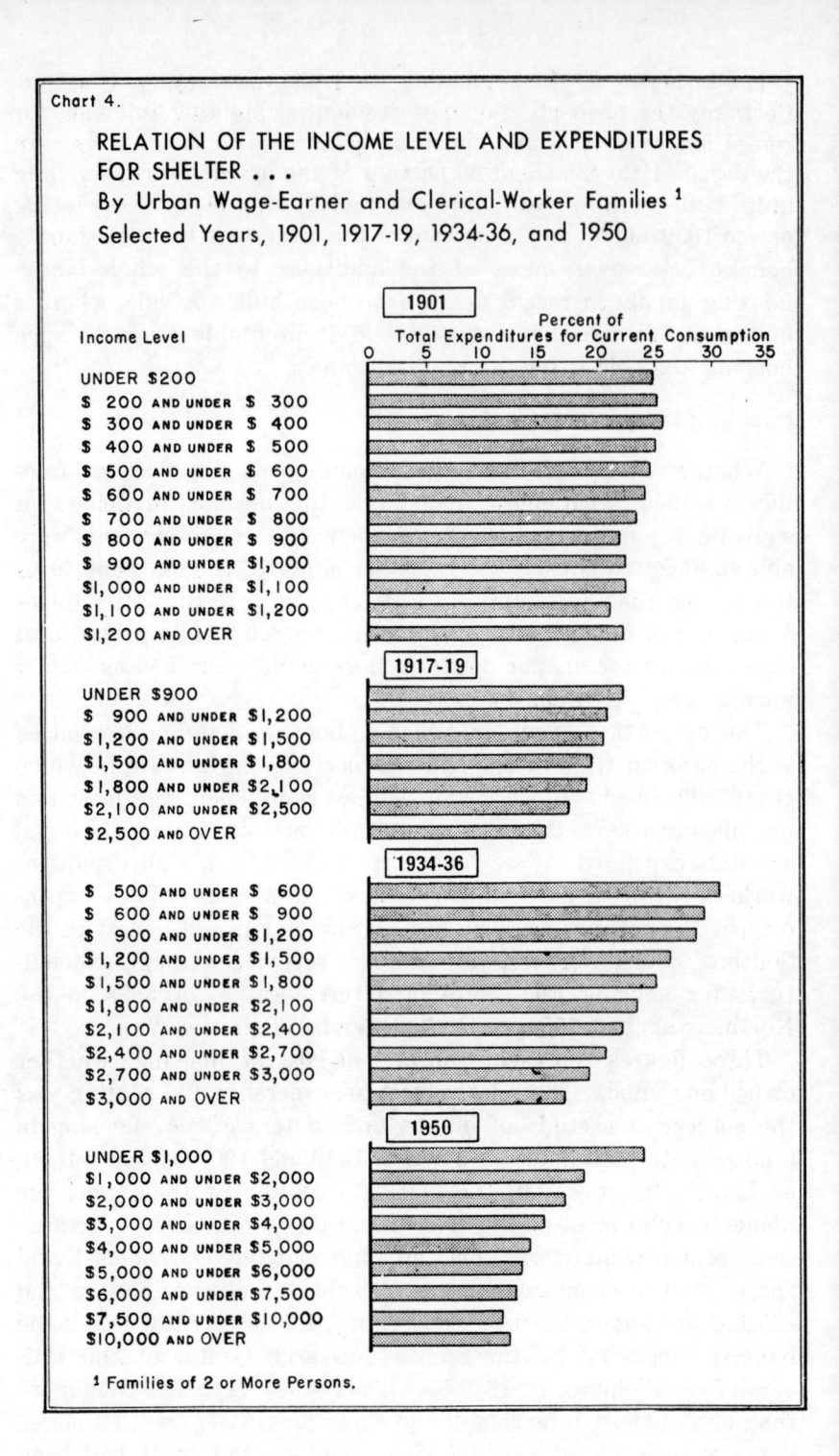

RELATION OF THE INCOME LEVEL AND EXPENDITURES FOR SHELTER ...
By Urban Wage-Earner and Clerical-Worker Families [1]
Selected Years, 1901, 1917-19, 1934-36, and 1950

[1] Families of 2 or More Persons.

renters. Their chief reasons for buying were summarized as follows:

	Percent reporting
Rent too high; ownership cheaper	24
Buying is an investment	24
Ideal of homeownership	22
Forced to buy; could find no place to rent	19
Desire for independence; security	11

SOURCE: Housing Research, Housing and Home Finance Agency, October 1952.

The average employed worker's family seeking a home today in a large city has as a rule only three choices: to rent an apartment in a fairly old building; to buy an older house; or to buy a new house. New apartment house projects are rarely designed to meet the worker's needs at rent he can afford to pay. The number of single-family rental houses, except in some of the small towns and medium-size cities, is relatively insignificant. If he buys an older house, the worker may have a fairly wide choice, but he may find it difficult to obtain advantageous financing. In increasing numbers, therefore, wage-earner and clerical-worker families have been buying homes in the rapidly growing suburban housing developments.

Renting, however, appeals to large numbers of workers with families; for personal reasons, they prefer to rent even when buying an equity in a home is feasible. Others may be deterred from buying by fear that they will lose their jobs for such reasons as an unfavorable economic outlook in their occupation, industry, or community, the introduction of new methods or processes, or a business recession.

Some indication of the relative desirability of owned and rented housing is found in housing surveys conducted by the Bureau of Labor Statistics in 1950–52. The homeowner typically lived in a single-family house. The renter, by contrast, was apt to live in a single-family house only if he lived in the South or West. This type of dwelling comprised more than half of all rental dwellings in 8 of the 19 small cities, in 6 of the 27 medium-size cities, but in only 2 of the 29 large cities—all in the South or West. Two- to four-family structures predominated in 13 of the 29 large cities and in several of the medium-size and small cities. Half or more of the rented units were apartments in 5 large cities only.

The homeowner usually had more spacious quarters. In no city did more than half the owner-occupied dwellings have less than 5 rooms. On the other hand, half the rented dwellings had as many as 5 rooms in only 4 of the large cities; in 23 large and medium-size cities, the median room count was 3, and in 29 cities, 4. It was 3 in 8 of the 19 small cities and 4 in the other 11.

Owners had dwellings of substantially better quality than renters, the report on the surveys indicated, to the extent that having a complete private bath indicates quality. The proportion of owner-occupied units with a bathroom exceeded 90 percent in 33 of the 56 large and medium-size cities. It was less than 80 percent only in Birmingham, Memphis, and Mobile. On the other hand, 1 out of 3 rented units lacked a complete private bath in 34 of the 75 cities—small, medium-size, and large cities scattered throughout the country.

Similarly, a higher proportion of owned than of rented units had gas or electricity for cooking, mechanical refrigerator, and central heating equipment in nearly all cities.

The foregoing comparisons, of course, relate to all housing—new and old. For workers who chose to buy a new house, some clues to its description and cost are found in a Bureau of Labor Statistics study of representative new nonfarm 1-family houses on which construction was started in 1956. Half of the houses were designed to sell for $14,500 or less, including land; 4 percent had a selling price of less than $7,000; 10 percent, of $7,000–$9,999; and 13 percent, $10,000–$11,999. (The average factory worker earned $80 a week in 1956, so most lending institutions would consider him a sound loan risk on houses in these price ranges.)

The average floor area of the new houses of 1956 was 1,230 square feet, with 5 percent of the units having less than 800 square feet, 17 percent from 800 to 999, and 31 percent from 1,000 to 1,199. Only 1 percent were 1-bedroom houses; 20 percent had 2, and 70 percent had 3 bedrooms. For the family of average size, a 3-bedroom house would provide at least 1½ rooms per person. This is a vivid contrast to the ratio of about 1½ persons per room which prevailed in the city slums in 1893 and a marked improvement over the average of 1.04 persons per room observed in the broader 1901 survey of city workers.

Most of the houses were supplied with electricity, running water, and bathrooms, and had water heaters and some type of central heating system. The few exceptions occurred in the warm southern States and in the small, low-priced structures. In over one-third of the houses, the sales price included the cost of a kitchen range. One-third also included an electric garbage disposal unit; 11 percent had dishwashers; and 55 percent were equipped with kitchen exhaust fans. All of these items were included in the selling price, and the buyer could spread his cost over a long period at a low interest rate.

The growing popularity of homeownership raises again the often-debated question whether workers who own homes lack the mobility needed for optimum distribution of the labor force and for best utilization of their skills. It has been argued that a homeowner may be reluctant to seek or accept a better paying job in another neighborhood or city, because of the risk of loss if he sells his house. There is some evidence, however, that the worker can buy or sell a house with relative ease and a minimum of risk, as a result of the countrywide growth of a liberal system of financing and a large volume of modern housing at various prices in most cities. Moreover, the general ownership of automobiles, in conjunction with the increasing dispersal of industry and employment within a given metropolitan area, has enabled the worker more readily to change jobs without changing his place of residence. Finally, the rise in homeownership may have restrained but it does not seem to have reduced population mobility. Census data show that the movement of population varied little, in percentage terms, during the 9 years 1948–56. In 1948, and again in 1955, 19.9 percent of the population moved. The high point of the period was 21.0 percent in 1951, and the low point was 18.6 in 1954.

Home and Community

Population movements within the United States during the present century have been of two major kinds: from the farm to the city, and from the city to the suburbs. The first was relatively more important in urban growth during the first decades of the century. Between 1940 and 1950, however, the population of metropolitan areas living outside the central cities grew 2½ times as fast as that in the cities. Slightly more than half of the Nation's increase in population in that decade occurred in the portions of metropolitan areas outside the central cities.

It is in these new suburbs that most of the tremendous volume of postwar house building has occurred. Approximately 70 percent of the new housing in metropolitan areas has been built outside the central cities of those areas in recent years.

The Seamy Side. In the wake of this development, blighted areas and slums in the central cities have occasioned increasing concern. The role of public housing in remedying such conditions has already been discussed. In addition, a variety of actions have been taken by municipal and State governments and private groups to prevent the deterioration of blighted areas into slums. The condition of the houses in these areas is illustrated by a description of a home in a Baltimore area where a pilot program was launched in 1952 to bring the houses into compliance with the minimum standards of the city housing code:

> The only plumbing on the entire property was an outside toilet which did not function properly and which was enclosed by a small outhouse almost ready to fall over. In the kitchen there was an old iron sink whose drain was so rusted away that waste water ran out onto the ground through a hole in the wall, rather than into a sewer. The structural condition of the house was very bad: Leaking roof; deteriorated and missing rainspouting; broken, worn, and loose doors and windows; floors weak and rickety, paper and plaster falling from walls and ceilings throughout the house, stair treads deeply worn and hazardous, outside and cellar steps dangerously rickety, and electrical wiring defective and dangerous. The house was riddled by rats and infested with bedbugs and roaches. The only heat had been furnished by a little kerosene stove in one room. The cellar was damp and filled with trash. The yard, covered with trash, junk, garbage, and raw sewage, did not drain properly and was surrounded by an extremely dilapidated 6½-foot board fence.[6]

The owners of such houses, which were regarded as blighted but fundamentally sound, were helped to overcome financial barriers to compliance with the housing code by the Fight-Blight Fund—an organization of Baltimore businessmen. The owners were handicapped in some cases by age, inability to work, or low-paying jobs. "Perhaps the most striking characteristic of the cases referred to the Fund," a report on the Fund's activities pointed out, "is the incredible array of misfortunes which beset this entire group of families—often temporarily reducing income or increasing expenses. . . . the single most common factor contributing to financial hardship was the heavy load of short-term debts which the owners had taken on in trying to meet the housing requirements. The total monthly obligations resulting . . . frequently were . . . completely out of line with monthly income."[7]

New Suburbs. Seemingly remote from the blighted area, although actually only a few miles away, is the suburban residential community containing single-family detached homes together with shops, schools, churches, recreation centers, and service establishments. Hundreds of such communities have sprung up around large cities, all connected to the central core by the daily ebb and flow of commuter traffic. As these communities grow, they frequently have difficulty in obtaining sufficient government revenue to meet the cost of schools and community facilities. This leads to efforts to attract industries and business establishments as a means of broadening the property tax base, with the result that the suburbs begin to take on the characteristics of integrated satellite cities. In some instances, such satellite towns have been planned and developed with most of the attributes of self-contained

PLANNED COMMUNITIES—Deliberately planned, entirely new townships of relatively inexpensive homes have sprung up. Wide surfaced roads connect with the main highway. Public buses provide transportation. In a few years, trees and flowers will add to the pleasure of living here. In the distance, see the community shopping center and the community lake.

communities, including local industry. Conspicuous examples are Park Forest, a new postwar city of 25,000 population located 30 miles south of Chicago, and Levittown, Pa., built on a mass-production basis to house employees of a new steel mill and other newly established industries in what was until recently a farming area.

The typical occupants of these new communities are young, growing families, seeking light, air, and play space for their children. A report on Developing Patterns of Urban Decentralization finds that they include "people with a wide range of social and economic characteristics." [8] Factory workers, retail clerks, building craftsmen, and other wage and salary earners can afford to buy houses in the new suburbs. The second and succeeding generations of the immigrants who flooded the Nation's cities early in this century move out and merge with descendants of the immigrants of the 18th and 19th centuries. Sharing common but diversified experiences in military service, in schools and colleges and trade schools, in churches, in labor organizations and other associations, and in their jobs, they take their places in the remarkable social experiments of the new suburbias.

Footnotes

[1] The Housing of the Poor in American Cities (in *Publications of the American Economic Association*, Vol. VIII, Nos. 2 and 3, March and May, 1893, p. 239).

[2] E. R. L. Gould, *The Housing of the Working People, Eighth Special Report of the Commissioner of Labor* (Washington, Government Printing Office, 1895), p. 442.

[3] *Ibid.*, p. 179.

[4] Faith M. Williams and Alice C. Hanson, *Money Disbursements of Wage Earners and Clerical Workers, 1934–36, Summary Volume*, U.S. Bureau of Labor Statistics Bulletin 638 (Washington, Government Printing Office, 1941), p. 4.

[5] *Architectural Forum*, cited in *Nineteenth Annual Report of New York City Housing Authority* (New York, 1952), p. 15.

[6] *The Evening Sun*, Baltimore, January 4, 1954.

[7] M. Mead Smith, Financial Hardship Cases Handled by the Fight-Blight Fund (in *Monthly Labor Review*, August 1955, p. 886).

[8] Noel P. Gist (in *Social Forces*, March 1952, p. 265).

CHAPTER IV

The Homemaker's Job and the Home Scene

> *A comfortable house . . . ranks immediately after health and a good conscience.*
> —Sydney Smith.

Attitudes of workers and their wives toward housekeeping have changed very greatly in the United States since the early 1900's. Many of the changes that have occurred become quickly apparent from a brief review of the homemaker's chores at the turn of the century.

In 1900, a job description for the average worker's wife would have read something like this:

- Shopping for the family's food (daily in families without refrigerators); toting it upstairs if the family lived in a tenement.
- Cooking three meals a day for the family, including the baking of bread, cakes, and pies (helped occasionally by purchases from the local bakery), and washing the dishes and the cooking pots and pans.
- Bringing in water from the public tap in the court.
- Filling oil lamps and trimming wicks daily; washing lamp chimneys and shades every other day.
- Making up beds and keeping them and the house at large free from vermin.
- Cleaning out a privy or a flush toilet shared with other families.
- Keeping the cookstove and, when she had one, the stove in the living room supplied with fuel; emptying the ashes.
- Disposing of garbage and trash.
- Emptying the pan under the icebox.
- Washing all the family clothes and household linens by hand, hanging them out to dry, and ironing them.
- Mopping uncarpeted floors at least once a week and sweeping those carpeted; cleaning carpeted floors with a carpet sweeper once a day.
- Making dresses and underwear for herself and the girl children of the family, as well as "running up" curtains for windows as necessary.
- Mending clothes for the entire family (this ranged from sewing patches on overalls and workshirts with the sewing machine to delicate darns of ceremonial baby clothes which served successive babies in a number of generations).
- Spring and fall housecleaning; that is, washing windows, cleaning cupboards and closets, washing and ironing curtains and drapes, taking up and beating rugs and carpets and putting them down again.
- Nursing the sick in her own family or among her boarders and neighbors.

Interspersed with these aspects of the housewife's job were the responsibilities of looking after the children too young to be in

83

school and the older ones before and after school. Many household chores were of course assigned to older children.

By 1950, the housewife's job description had radically changed, largely because higher real incomes and technological progress had given her a vastly different dwelling in which to live and work, and different tools with which to keep it. But the change was also due in part to the transfer of important duties of the 1900 job from home to factory or to service establishment. In addition, higher standards of municipal housekeeping had resulted in improved and extended city water and sewage systems and garbage and trash collection. Moreover, improvements in disease control and health had cut down on her duties as a home nurse. And, finally, her higher level of education and the wider availability of information on housekeeping methods made her more efficient.

Even so, the housewife's workload has not declined as much as might have been expected from the change in her working conditions in the home. Because income is higher and it is now possible to keep the dwelling and its furnishings and the family clothing cleaner and smarter than in 1900, the worker and his wife and their children expect a higher standard to be maintained. The dwelling is larger and there are more appliances to get out of order.

In addition, the American worker and his wife have gradually acquired a different attitude toward the housekeeping job. With the greater availability and attractiveness of factory and office work for women, particularly since 1940, the worker's family has often applied the earnings of the wife and mother toward the purchase of laborsaving devices or a house of its own. In some families where the wife is working outside the home, much of her housekeeping job is taken over by the husband and the older children.

HOUSEKEEPING IN 1900

Obviously, conditions of housekeeping in workers' families at the turn of the century varied greatly from one group to another and in different parts of the country. Doing the job in a city tenement was a very different matter from keeping house in the best of the small factory towns, where single-family houses predominated.

For many housewives, industrial homework complicated the housekeeping task, both in large cities and some smaller towns, particularly in the Northeast. Most industrial homework was connected with the garment industries and related trades, and thread, ravelings, snips of cloth, and bundles of goods in process often cluttered the homes where it was carried on.

Condition of Houses

No comprehensive data are available on workers' housekeeping in the early 1900's. In the 1901 expenditure survey made by the United States Bureau of Labor, however, "an effort was made to ascertain the condition of the homes as to sanitation, furnishings, and cleanliness." But since the Bureau's field agents often did not have the opportunity to inspect the premises thoroughly, having no authority as sanitary officers, "in many families it was quite impossible to secure a knowledge of these conditions." [1] However, the observations that were made gave a basis for the following impressions:

Item	Percent of dwellings rated—		
	Good	Fair	Bad
Sanitation	61	33	6
Furnishings	61	27	12
Cleanliness	79	15	6

The report on the survey commented on the relatively high proportion of the workers' homes which were described as "cleanly" as follows:

> The fact that nearly 80 percent of the families were found in a good condition as to cleanliness, while only 61 percent lived under good sanitary conditions and had homes well furnished, indicates that there was a disposition to live under as good conditions as possible. Many families that could not afford to live under good sanitary conditions or have their homes well furnished could be, and were, cleanly.[2]

At that time, refuse collection and disposal were coming to be recognized as municipal responsibilities, but less widely so than the water supply. In 1902 and 1903, of the 175 cities of over 25,000 population, 80 reported that ashes were disposed of by the householder, and in 45, garbage disposal was also a household chore.

Bituminous coal was the dominant fuel used for both cooking and heating in wage earners' and clerical workers' homes in most parts of the country, but anthracite was used extensively in New England and the Middle Atlantic States and wood was the main fuel in the smaller mill towns of the South. In many neighborhoods where workers lived, children were regularly sent to pick up coal along the railroad tracks, to collect wood from discarded crates, packing boxes, and scaffolding at wharves, warehouse districts, and construction projects. Manufactured gas was available in many cities, but it was expensive. Workers did use it for lighting but they seldom used it for heating. An observer in Homestead, a suburb of Pittsburgh, pointed out that in 1908 "housework may be materially lightened by the use of gas instead of coal, and in Homestead with its supply of natural gas, the relative cost is not great . . . . But even with care its use for baking, washing and ironing as well as heating makes the bills grow and an income of $12 a week does not permit a gas bill of $2.50 a month, that of one careful housekeeper, nor the purchase of gas ranges."[3] Reliance on gas even in Homestead was, therefore, apparently a solution to housekeeping problems only for workers with above-average incomes.

A study of living conditions among cotton mill workers in 1908 indicated that although some had electric lights, most of them were using oil lamps for light. For the housewife, this meant keeping the lamps filled with oil and trimming wicks in addition to cleaning the chimneys. Frequently, however, the lamp chimneys used in the early 1900's protected gas mantles, and the chimneys were further covered by a decorative china lamp shade. A gas mantle thus shaded provided a well-diffused soft light which made quite a pleasant illumination. They were in contrast to the ugly, unprotected gas flares found in less prosperous and less well-tended homes.

Furniture and Equipment

No actual inventories of furniture and homefurnishings exist for workers' homes early in the century. The 1901 expenditure survey showed only that about 15 percent of the families reported no expenditure for "furniture and utensils."

Pictures, however, show that those of the more prosperous had living rooms with curtains at the windows, drapes, an organ or piano, large upholstered chairs or sofa, and a carpet on the floor. The carpet was usually an Axminster, woven in 27-inch strips, sewn together and then stretched and tacked down to the floor over layers of newspaper and straw. Antimacassars ("tidies"), which had to be washed periodically, protected the backs of chairs and sofas. The presence of a "baseburner" stove, which was essential if the living room was to be used in the winter, was an almost infallible index of a family's economic status.

Families with only a cookstove spent much time in the kitchen in the colder months of the year, in much the same fashion recalled by the present musical director of the National Broadcasting Co., whose family lived in a "3-room railroad flat" in New York City about 1900:

Perhaps because of the accessibility of the light refreshment that it was customary to offer guests, the kitchen rather than the parlor became the living room until bedtime, and all social life centered in it. Made comparatively presentable after a long day of cooking, eating, and the washing of dishes and laundry, it was the scene of formal calls at our house and of the visits of friends and prospective suitors.[4]

The bedrooms of the more prosperous workers were furnished with heavy matching wood furniture—bedsteads, chiffoniers, dressers, washstands, and wardrobes, or with metal beds (iron painted white, with brass trimmings) and hand-painted furniture. Families with grandmothers or maiden aunts adept at needlework had finely quilted bedspreads in bright patchwork or more formal flower patterns. The floor was covered with straw matting, or "floor oilcloth," as the type of linoleum produced in 1900 was then known.

Homes of some of the workers with above-average earnings had dining rooms with matching dining room sets of oak or walnut, usually made in a nearby factory. Kitchens in such homes had (in addition to the stove on which the family meals were cooked and which also provided heat in winter) a table used not only for food preparation but frequently also for family meals, several plain wooden chairs, and wooden cupboards for dishes, pots, and pans.

If the 1900 family had an ice chest, it was often placed on the "back stoop" just outside the kitchen door. This protected it from the heat of the cookstove in summer and took advantage of the refrigeration provided by nature in winter, but also increased the number of steps taken by the housewife in getting and clearing away meals. If the family did not have an ice chest, food on hand might be stored in a "safe" or "cooler"—a cupboard with hooked, tightly fitted screened doors to keep out flies and provide ventilation—which had many shortcomings as a way of storing perishable foods. If the house had a cellar, the safe might be placed there, even though it increased the housewife's workload. There was generally no problem about where to put the telephone, because, in 1900, most families could not afford private telephone service.

The furniture and furnishings in the homes of workers with smaller earnings varied widely from this typical end-of-the-century design, depending on location, history of the family and its wanderings, and family income in relation to the size and composition of the family.

Washing and ironing the family clothes and the bed and table linen was one of the heavier jobs of housewives in workers' families. Except in cases of sickness, they rarely sent the laundry out. The equipment to be used for getting the laundry done in American homes was described in one of the national women's magazines in 1901:

> The things absolutely necessary in doing a family washing are tubs, washboard, boiler, clothes-stick, pail, long-handled dipper, clothes lines and pins, irons, and ironing board. In addition to these, when possible one should have a good wringer, mangle, hot or cold, separate boards for shirts, shirtwaists, and sleeves, shirt bosoms, and trousers.[5]

Many workers' wives at the beginning of the century did not have all the "absolutely necessary" things. They were more likely to have only one tub (wooden or galvanized iron), a washboard, a clothes line, and an iron and an ironing board. Some of them, however, had washing machines based on the principle of removal of dirt by friction, which had been used in washing clothes throughout recorded time. Handcranked wooden washers retained the rubbing principle through grooved sides and bottoms and paddles, and one had a device resembling a three-legged stool attached to its cover. If the kitchen had the requisite water supply, washers powered by water could be used by attaching a hose to the faucet. The 1908 report on the Homestead study reported that one of the steelworkers had such a machine. However, use of such a washing machine would not have been possible in a large proportion (if not in most) of the workers' homes in 1900, because their homes did not have running water.

At the beginning of the century, relatively few of the workers' families still had to make soft soap for laundering and other cleaning. Bars of heavy yellow soap were the rule in the kitchen and although some soap powders were on the market, soap flakes were a rarity.

Methods of cleaning house for most families centered upon the broom and a brush. When the broom was the chief cleaning instrument available, preparations for cleaning a room were more extensive than the actual cleaning. This was particularly true during the annual spring cleaning. Bric-a-brac was dusted, draperies were taken down, and rugs were carried outdoors to be aired and hung on a line and beaten with a stick or heavy carpet beater. Cleaning the intricate carvings and designs on woodwork and furniture was also a time-consuming task. All furniture was covered or carried out of the room before the vigorous sweeping with the broom began. The object was to sweep just as hard as possible; the more dust raised, the cleaner the rug would be—so it was believed. Actually, all that this effort accomplished was to spread the dust over a broader area. Quite often, tea leaves or coarse meal and water were scattered over the rug and swept off to remove dust and to brighten colors. Following these operations, the room was aired and perhaps a carpet sweeper was used. Finally the rug was wiped with a cloth dipped in ammonia and water.

BEGINNINGS OF MECHANIZED HOUSEKEEPING

The first extensive information on housekeeping accessories was provided by the Bureau of Labor Statistics as part of its 1917-19 study of expenditures by families of wage earners and lower salaried workers. Even that survey is largely an indirect source of information; the report tells what families bought in one year, not what they owned. The figures on purchases imply, however, that a larger proportion of the workers' wives had the help of automatic devices than was the case in 1900.

Unfortunately, this survey did not call for separate figures on purchases of carpet sweepers and vacuum cleaners, although the latter represent one of the most important instances of the mechanization of housekeeping. The percent of all families purchasing one or the other of those household helps rose sharply with income, and the average expenditure for families buying one or the other seems to indicate that quite a large proportion of those whose incomes exceeded the average of about $1,500 (equivalent to at least $2,400 in 1950) were then buying vacuum cleaners. (Although there had been an estimated 150 makes of vacuum cleaners on the market in 1911, electric cleaners did not become common in the homes of wage earners until at least 20 years later.)

Sewing machines were much more generally bought than washing machines—8.1 percent compared with 3 percent of all families surveyed. Significantly, the percent of families buying washing machines increased progressively from the lowest to the highest level of family income; in the case of sewing machines, it increased from the lowest to the next level of income, then became fairly stable, but actually declined in the highest income level. The small proportion of families at the highest income level buying sewing machines may indicate that such families bought more of their clothing readymade, particularly in view of the fact that 7 in 10 of them reported income from the earnings of older children. Moreover, it is somewhat more probable that these families had purchased machines in earlier years.

The proportion of families buying washtubs was nearly 4 times as large as the proportion buying washing machines, and over 3 times as many bought wash boilers. A new washtub or a wash boiler was still something many women wanted; the percent buying them rose steadily with income. Still more rapid was the rise in the percentage of families buying window and door screens.

KITCHEN STILL IS KING—In the old-fashioned boardinghouse type of kitchen, the cook labored mightily to produce turkey as a special treat. Scientific breeding has improved the quality and availability of turkey, and the modern kitchen, with its gas stove or electric stove and laborsaving devices, gives the housewife more time to herself.

Expenditure figures from the 1917–19 survey indicate rather widespread use of laundry service outside the home. The proportion of white workers whose expenditures included laundry services was largest in the South Atlantic States, as shown in the following tabulation:

Region	Percent of families reporting expenditure	Average amount spent per year per family purchasing
North Atlantic States	69.2	$13.20
South Atlantic States	78.8	31.97
North Central States	63.8	13.60
South Central States	72.2	26.47
Western States	73.4	17.12
United States	69.6	17.91

Even in the North Central States, where the overall percentage of families reporting such expenditures was lowest, 31 percent of the families in the lowest income range bought some laundry services. Nevertheless, the sums thus used were so small as to indicate resort by most families to outside laundry service only in emergencies or as an occasional luxury.

The proportion of families making expenditures for domestic service at the end of World War I also varied from region to region, obviously in relation to the wages for domestic workers. The extremes occurred in the North Atlantic and South Central States: 11 and 34 percent of the workers' families recorded expenditures which averaged $22 and $30 a year in the respective regions. Data on regional differences in wage rates imply that the families in the South Central States received more hours of work per dollar than those in the North Atlantic States.

The survey also affords evidence of other important changes. The proportion of families buying carpets rose sharply with income, the buying of linoleum and floor oilcloth rose very slightly as income increased, and the buying of matting rose hardly at all. The percent of families buying carpets (24 percent) was, on the average, not quite double that for linoleum and floor oilcloth, but it was almost 8 times the percent buying matting.

Data collected for 1917–19 include the first comprehensive information about a highly significant trend among workers' families, namely, the use of installment credit. Installment buying had been introduced to wage and clerical workers in this country as early as 1870, primarily in the purchase of sewing machines, furniture, and pianos, but the 1917–19 survey provides the first record of the extent of its use countrywide by these occupational groups.

The 1901 survey had shown that about one-tenth of the families surveyed had obtained credit during the year, but since these were families who had incurred a deficit, it is unlikely that they had so reported installment debt. More probably, installment payments were recorded simply as current expenditures.

A recent tabulation from the original 1917-19 family spending schedules shows that 23 percent of the families surveyed reported some installment buying of furniture and furnishings. The largest proportion for any region was in the South—28 percent. Among Negro families surveyed at the time, 34 percent used installment credit.*

The kinds of goods bought on credit by workers' families, white and Negro, ranged widely. By way of example, 40 percent of the sewing machines bought were purchased on the installment plan; 37 percent of bureaus, chiffoniers, dressing tables; 33 percent of couches, davenports, sofas; 30 percent of tables; 28 percent of bedsprings; 20 percent of carpets. A few families even reported installment purchases of such items as mops and brooms.

The information is indicative of the rise of living standards, or ambitions for living, above the actual levels of living. These serve to emphasize the extent to which workers' living standards were higher than their actual levels of living and the eagerness with which they grasped the opportunity presented by the development of installment credit to buy time, quite literally, in improving their homes.

THE MID-THIRTIES

In the middle 1930's, when figures on family expenditures were gathered from employed workers in large cities, some information was obtained on the kind of household equipment being used. Those families were better off than the average worker's family in 1934-36, because the survey was restricted to families in which at least one earner had a specified amount of employment and excluded families who had received relief during the year.

The economic climate of the middle 1930's, as well as the distinctive characteristics of the wage earners and clerical workers whose expenditures were studied at that time, profoundly affected their current outlays for housefurnishings and equipment. Total consumer expenditures for durable goods dropped in the years 1930-33. The reduction was naturally accompanied by a considerable decline in consumer installment credit outstanding, and, until 1933, in consumer credit extended. By 1934-36, the gradual

---

*Possibly there is an element of historical continuity with the transitional period after the Civil War. During the period, "going in debt" was ingrained by the almost complete dependence of Negroes as sharecroppers, between harvests, on supplies extended by the planters and later by crossroads and village stores. For a time, in many areas, virtually no money was exchanged.

improvement of the economic situation had brought a return of optimism. Overall expenditures for consumer durable goods and the volume of installment credit extended to consumers rose more during these 3 years than disposable personal income. But average spending for furniture and furnishings by the families of employed workers studied in 1934-36 was not significantly different (in dollars of equivalent purchasing power) from that shown in the 1917-19 survey.

The proportion of the families buying all kinds of furniture except that for the living room was smaller in 1934-36 than in 1917-19. The same thing was true of most types of housefurnishings and equipment, insofar as the lists of commodities used in the two studies permit comparison. There were, however, some interesting exceptions to this rule. The proportion buying linoleum (inlaid or felt base) was very close to that at the end of World War I, but only 15 percent bought carpets, compared with 24 percent in the earlier period. The proportions of the 1934-36 group buying vacuum cleaners and carpet sweepers and refrigerators and iceboxes were larger than for the 1917-19 group. Families buying washing machines were 6 percent of the 1934-36 group, as compared with 3 percent in 1917-19. And, although about the same proportion of families bought irons, they had switched from flatirons to electric irons.

On the other hand, in the relatively favored group surveyed in the mid-1930's, the proportion of families sending their laundry out at any time during the year was about 32 percent—somewhat less than half the proportion reported at the end of World War I. The proportion buying washboards and washtubs was also much lower. This latter change may have been affected by the increasing number of dwellings with built-in laundry tubs, and it was undoubtedly influenced by the appearance of the automatic washing machines on the market for those who could afford them.

WARTIME AND POSTWAR PURCHASES

Presumably, workers' families were able to increase their purchases of furniture and equipment in the later years of the 1930's as the proportion of the unemployed declined. During World War II, however, prices of durable consumer goods rose sharply, and output of many types of consumer durable goods was halted.

By the end of World War II, the pent-up demand for furniture and equipment was very large. Wartime savings available for such purchases were larger than had been expected, but considerable use was also made of installment credit. Consumer optimism persisted even throughout the "inventory recession" of 1949-50,

Chart 5.

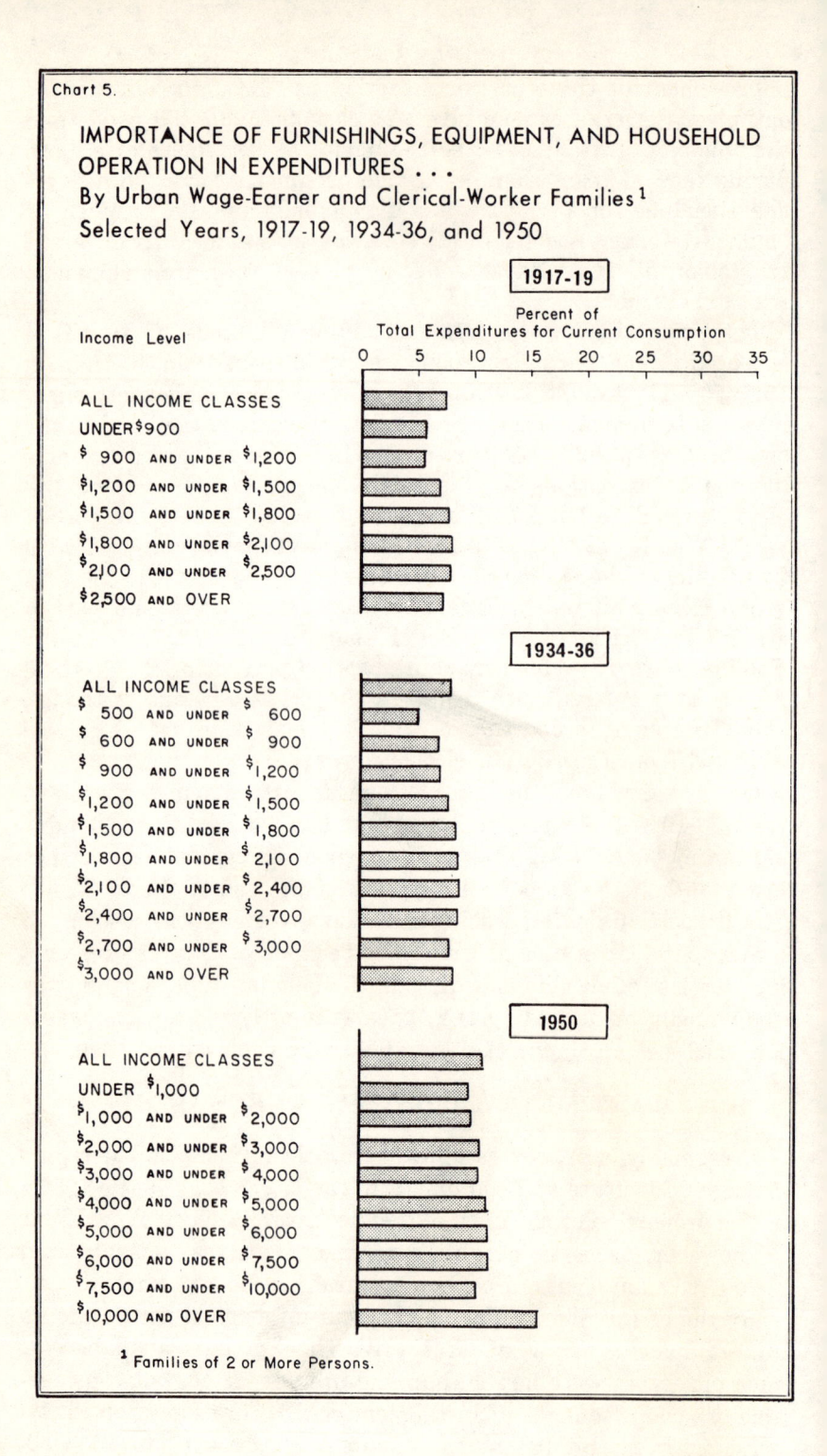

IMPORTANCE OF FURNISHINGS, EQUIPMENT, AND HOUSEHOLD OPERATION IN EXPENDITURES ...
By Urban Wage-Earner and Clerical-Worker Families[1]
Selected Years, 1917-19, 1934-36, and 1950

1917-19

Income Level — Percent of Total Expenditures for Current Consumption

ALL INCOME CLASSES
UNDER $900
$900 AND UNDER $1,200
$1,200 AND UNDER $1,500
$1,500 AND UNDER $1,800
$1,800 AND UNDER $2,100
$2,100 AND UNDER $2,500
$2,500 AND OVER

1934-36

ALL INCOME CLASSES
$500 AND UNDER $600
$600 AND UNDER $900
$900 AND UNDER $1,200
$1,200 AND UNDER $1,500
$1,500 AND UNDER $1,800
$1,800 AND UNDER $2,100
$2,100 AND UNDER $2,400
$2,400 AND UNDER $2,700
$2,700 AND UNDER $3,000
$3,000 AND OVER

1950

ALL INCOME CLASSES
UNDER $1,000
$1,000 AND UNDER $2,000
$2,000 AND UNDER $3,000
$3,000 AND UNDER $4,000
$4,000 AND UNDER $5,000
$5,000 AND UNDER $6,000
$6,000 AND UNDER $7,500
$7,500 AND UNDER $10,000
$10,000 AND OVER

[1] Families of 2 or More Persons.

when unemployment at one time rose to as much as 7.6 percent of the labor force. The confidence of most workers was supported not only by the general economic outlook but also by the knowledge that unemployment insurance would cushion the impact on their family finances if they should lose their jobs. Moreover, unemployment began to decline in March 1950, and after the outbreak of fighting in Korea many consumers feared that the shortages of consumer goods which occurred during World War II would be repeated.

Workers' expenditures for furniture, housefurnishings, and equipment in 1950 were slightly above the postwar trend, despite some enforced economies among workers who were unemployed early in the year. Average expenditures for housefurnishings and equipment were, in dollars of equivalent purchasing power, more than $2\frac{1}{2}$ times higher than those of the 1917–19 group and about $2\frac{1}{3}$ times the amounts spent by the 1934–36 group. Such expenditures had risen far more than average incomes and thus constituted a substantially larger percentage of total expenditures. In combination with the costs of household operation (cleaning supplies, water, telephone, laundry, etc.), they accounted for 11 percent of family spending in 1950, compared with about 7 and 8 percent, respectively, in 1917–19 and 1934–36. But even in 1950, expenditures for furniture, housefurnishings, and household operation rose with family income, although not as rapidly as in the earlier years, indicating that workers had not fully achieved their standards for such items. (See chart 5, p. 94.)

With respect to purchases, the most important differences between 1950 and the earlier periods were concentrated in specific types of goods rather than spread evenly among all types. Mechanical refrigerators, mechanical washing machines (automatic and nonautomatic), vacuum cleaners, and electric toasters and irons were bought in strikingly larger proportions. Purchases of linoleum were also much higher. In addition, sizable numbers of the 1950 families purchased such mechanical equipment as deep-freeze units, automatic ironers and mangles, and mechanical clothes dryers—equipment that had been bought by workers' families in the middle 1930's rarely if at all.

The 1950 purchase rates for furniture are not strictly comparable with those shown by the earlier surveys, because of changes in furniture styles and in the type of information obtained in the surveys. Where they can be compared, however, they are almost universally higher than in 1934–36.

In contrast to these changes in spending for household equipment and furnishings, family spending patterns for household service had not changed dramatically by 1950. As during World

War I, the largest number of families reporting expenditures for maids' wages and tips in 1950 lived in the South, and their average expenditures were, generally speaking, significantly higher than in other parts of the country. Somewhat more than one-fifth of southern families in the $3,000–$5,000 income bracket reported expenditures for maids' wages and tips. Only about one-tenth of the families in this income bracket in the North had such expenditures, and the proportion was slightly lower in the West. Similarly, about one-third of the workers' families in 1950 used commercial laundry or diaper service, compared with 32 percent sending laundry out in the mid-thirties.

Telephone expenses were reported in 1950 by nearly 3 out of 4 urban families, compared with 28 percent of the families in the 1917–19 survey who had telephones and 36 percent of the 1934–36 families reporting telephone expenditures.

THE WORKER'S HOME IN 1950

Perhaps the most revealing 1950 data relate to the ownership of certain kinds of furniture and household equipment, shown in table 10. Data on ownership of pieces of furniture other than those listed in the table were not obtained in 1950. Therefore, the figures understate furniture ownership to the extent that workers bought other kinds, primarily couches and davenports.

The table shows data for skilled wage earners, because they are the largest occupational group among city wage and clerical workers. They are not, however, completely typical of all such workers in the ownership of durable goods. In the case of living room and bedroom suites, for example, ownership was reported by nearly four-fifths of the skilled workers, compared with about three-fifths of the unskilled workers and approximately seven-tenths of the clerical, sales, and semiskilled workers. And, although the highest proportion of each occupational group owning such furniture was generally found in the North, regional differences were larger among unskilled wage earners.

Differences among occupational groups in the ownership of laborsaving devices may be illustrated by data on washing machines for skilled and unskilled workers. The highest proportion of ownership among skilled workers was found in suburbs in the West (87 percent) and among unskilled workers in small cities in the North (73 percent). For both skilled and unskilled, ownership was lowest in small cities in the South, but the proportion of skilled workers in such cities owning a washing machine was double that of unskilled—62 percent compared with 30.

TABLE 10.—*Percent of skilled wage earners owning homes and selected items of furniture and household equipment, by region and type of city, 1950*

Region and type of city	Home	Mechanical refrigerator	Home freezers	Cooking stoves	Vacuum cleaners Upright	Vacuum cleaners Tank	Sewing machines	Washing machines Automatic	Washing machines Nonautomatic
North:									
Large cities	45	80	2	70	43	24	41	27	42
Suburbs	66	90	2	82	44	34	52	29	54
Small cities	54	89		87	40	38	50	22	64
South:									
Large cities	47	80	1	79	20	25	44	28	41
Suburbs	68	81	6	78	30	26	40	41	38
Small cities	49	81	4	75	26	18	46	23	39
West:									
Large cities	58	79	5	74	38	30	53	23	52
Suburbs	70	87	8	83	31	39	53	29	58
Small cities	58	79	2	71	36	26	60	23	57

	Ironing machines	Living room suites	Dining room suites	Dinette sets	Bedroom suites	Upholstered chairs	Wool rugs and carpets
North:							
Large cities	5	80	43	67	83	44	66
Suburbs	10	89	52	70	88	43	75
Small cities	7	81	45	72	82	38	72
South:							
Large cities	4	75	37	57	83	36	41
Suburbs	6	81	47	61	80	32	55
Small cities	7	77	37	58	75	35	40
West:							
Large cities	10	77	42	60	72	46	62
Suburbs	7	78	32	64	72	55	69
Small cities	9	72	38	51	67	37	49

SOURCE: Study of Consumer Expenditures, Incomes and Savings: Statistical Tables, Urban U. S.—1950, Volume XVII, Ownership of Consumer Durables (University of Pennsylvania, 1957), pp. 42, 74, 106, 138, 170.

The ownership figures shown in the table are therefore somewhat higher than they would be if they covered the wage and clerical worker group as a whole. On the other hand, they understate the extent to which certain kinds of equipment are part of the skilled worker's home, because they do not indicate the substantial proportion of rental dwellings which are equipped with such facilities as mechanical refrigerators and cooking stoves. Surveys of tenant-occupied dwelling units in 75 cities by the Bureau of Labor Statistics in 1950 and 1952 showed the following ranges in the percent of units having various facilities included in the rent:

Refrigerator: 3.0 in Scranton, Pa., to 72.0 in Miami, Fla.
Cookstove: 6.2 in Ravenna, Ohio, to 93.1 in Providence, R. I.
Furniture: 2.7 in the northeastern New Jersey metropolitan area to 67.4 in Miami, Fla.

Therefore, it is difficult to judge the overall extent to which rented dwellings had such equipment, so as to derive an accurate measure of the number of workers' homes having certain kinds of equipment and furniture.

TECHNOLOGICAL CHANGES IN THE HOME

The ownership data for skilled workers nevertheless indicate that workers' homes today are better furnished and have household equipment which makes it easier to keep them neat and clean and comfortable than they were at the turn of the century. It is evident that mechanical and electrical energy has replaced a good part of the human energy used in keeping house. It has increased the output per hour of the homemaker to such an extent that houses are better kept in a much shorter time than at the beginning of the century. Over two-thirds of the skilled workers in most areas had vacuum cleaners in 1950, for example, whereas in 1900 the broom and the brush were virtually the only implements used for comparable cleaning jobs. And, although the furniture and furnishings in the homes of workers in the lowest income classes undoubtedly are only a little better now than then, and a small proportion of city workers' homes have neither electricity nor gas to power mechanical housekeeping equipment, the proportion of families living in poverty has dramatically declined.

Since the start of the present century, improvements in the design of the average worker's dwelling and its furnishings have also facilitated housekeeping. Larger windows reflect, at least in part, the increased emphasis on the importance of sunlight for health and for pleasanter living conditions. Lighter window curtain materials may be due in part to the same influences, reinforced by the availability of easy-to-wash synthetic fabrics. The virtual disappearance of heavy draperies in doorways was a natural reaction to changes in house design. Simpler patterns for furniture and furnishings are also related to these basic changes and to the general trend toward more informality in daily life; they also grow out of changes in the technology of furniture production.

Many articles added lately even to the simpler households are the result of revolutionary technological changes of recent decades. Some of those items, notably automatic devices and electrical appliances, were not so long ago unknown to rich and poor alike. Furniture and the simpler furnishings, in contrast, were from time out of mind among the elementary requirements of homes; the transformation of techniques in making them and the nature of the resulting modifications are thus basic changes that warrant comment.

During the first two decades of this century, the furniture industry widely adopted high-speed, special-purpose machinery for operations ranging from the sawing of rough lumber to the finishing of furniture pieces. As a result, small shops expanded into large-scale units, and the quality of furniture available to low- and moderate-income families improved.

The increased demand for furniture in turn induced a further expansion of the industry and the introduction of additional improvements up to the depression of the thirties. During World War II, when nearly all furniture factories were converted to war production, the specialized military needs stimulated the devising of new techniques. Some of the distinctive changes were the use of laminated and core woods, beautiful as well as strong; sprayed-on plastic finishes in place of costly hand finishes; use of manmade fibers in upholstery; resinous glues for permanent joints in the structural frames; and lightweight metal components which made the assembly of furniture a more efficient operation.

Other improvements—of a different kind—have stemmed from the adoption of legislation, in 40 States and the District of Columbia, regulating the manufacture and sale of bedding, and in 24, legislation concerning upholstered furniture. These laws generally were designed to assure proper labeling of the contents. In addition, health departments have taken measures to prevent the sale of bedding and furniture infested with vermin. Because of such laws, dealing with insect pests is a much less frequent chore now than in 1900. Moreover, there are more efficient chemicals to use in eliminating any insects which do penetrate a dwelling.

Chemistry has also eased cleaning chores through the development of new types of cleaning agents. Those available nowadays, in comparison with their 1900 counterparts, make it possible to do necessary jobs in less time and they do not wear out the things to be cleaned, or the homemaker's hands, as fast.

THE HOUSEWIFE'S JOB TODAY

It is even more difficult to generalize about "the job of the average worker's wife" in 1950 than it was in 1900, because there is now a wider range of housekeeping situations within the group and a much greater variety in the available housekeeping tools. No matter how prosperous the worker in 1900, he could not have purchased for his wife completely automatic washing and drying machines, because there were none being produced for sale at that time. Many of the tasks which were most onerous in 1900 are a thing of the past for the majority of the wives of city workers. Yet some of these tasks persist in workers' families because their environments are not very different from those which were typical in 1900.

Summarizing what we know of the jobs which were typical in 1900 which have either disappeared or changed materially will perhaps clarify what has happened to the homemaking job in the city worker's family.

- It is no longer the rule to shop daily for the family food because the majority of workers' homes have mechanical refrigerators, making it possible for the average worker and his wife to buy food in relatively large quantities once or twice a week and bring it home in the car.
- The transfer of much food preparation to factories which turn out millions of cans of ready-to-eat foods, cake and cooky mixes, frozen chicken pies, pizzas, and so on ad infinitum, and of most clothing sewing to factories which make all kinds of clothes for all age groups, has greatly shortened the city homemaker's workday. Mending and some sewing must, of course, still be done, but a majority of the wives have sewing machines.
- The city homemaker's tasks have been greatly simplified by the great increase in the number of gas and electric stoves for cooking, and she no longer need give daily attention to oil lamps.
- The number of city workers' homes without running water and electricity has dropped to a very small proportion of the total in most communities, although carrying in pails of water and cleaning a shared toilet are still burdensome housekeeping tasks in some large city slums.
- Garbage and trash still have to be gotten out of the dwelling, but municipal collection has greatly improved.
- Among workers' families, very few wives have to empty a pan from under the icebox these days. Almost all families not owning mechanical refrigerators appear to have rented houses or apartments with such equipment. Among the unskilled workers' families, particularly in the South, however, a significant proportion still use iceboxes or do not have refrigerators of any kind.
- The problem of getting the family laundry done has changed greatly, not only because of the use of mechanical washing machines and the wider availability of laundry service, but also because modern fabrics are easier to wash.
- Most of the heavy drapes which are seen in pictures of the more prosperous workers' homes in the early 1900's have been replaced with curtains which can be put into the washing machine and which, in some cases, can be left to drip dry and be hung without ironing. The electric iron eliminates many steps and much of the weight carrying required by what were so appropriately called "sad irons" in 1900.
- Cleaning the rugs or carpets is now done with vacuum cleaners in the majority of city workers' homes in the North and West, although in the South, where the proportion having woolen rugs and carpets is lower, considerably less than half the workers' families have vacuum cleaners.
- Spring and fall housecleaning has been much simplified by the new types of household equipment and of cleaning agents and detergents and the change to cleaner fuels for heating and cooking.
- Child care has been simplified by the availability of diaper laundry service, prepared baby foods, cooperative nurseries, improved health and medical care.

These and countless other tasks were easier for the housewife because she had almost certainly received some training for them in a home economics class at a public school. In addition, most city newspapers, as well as many magazines, now carry homemaking columns or sections.

The homemaker shares with her husband a shorter workday than she had at the beginning of the century and the whole family is able to enjoy a cleaner and more attractive dwelling than that available to most workers' families in the 1900's. The extent to which women over 35 have returned to the labor force is a result not only of timesaving equipment and more efficiently designed homes, which free them for work outside the home, but also of the homemaker's desire to acquire these conveniences. Because so many married women have paid employment, it is almost impossible to present a typical job description for the city worker's wife in the 1950's, but one can say without hesitation that the majority of the workers' wives have lighter workloads and less monotonous heavy labor than their predecessors in the 1900's.

Many of the women who are returning to the labor force after their children have reached school age are taking part-time jobs voluntarily. It must be recognized, however, that even when their outside jobs do not take a full 8 hours a day, these women lead complicated lives. Their housekeeping tasks may require less physical effort than in the 1900's, but their lives have taken on new aspects. Because of the numerous demands made on the housewife's time—either holding an outside job or participating in Community Chest drives, raising money for community organizations, taking part in the Parent-Teachers Association, political, and other activities—the homemaker of the 1950's must schedule her own housekeeping tasks more systematically than she did in the early part of the century, and she must also obtain help from other members of the family. In addition, she must learn what to do when her new mechanical equipment gets out of order and how to judge the value for her particular household of the new types of consumer goods which are constantly coming onto the market. On the other hand, she does not have as many calls on her time for assistance in home nursing for her family, relatives, or neighbors because of the increased hospital facilities and their use by workers' families, and because of the decreased incidence of childhood and other contagious diseases. (See chapter VII.) The jobs of most workers' wives in the 1950's are thus very different from the average wife's job in 1900, but they are not necessarily simpler or easier.

Footnotes

[1] *Cost of Living and Retail Prices of Food,* Eighteenth Annual Report of the Commissioner of Labor, 1903 (Washington, Government Printing Office, 1904), p. 21.

[2] *Ibid.,* p. 22.

[3] Margaret F. Byington, *Homestead, the Households of a Mill Town* (New York, Russell Sage Foundation, Charities Publication Committee, 1910), p. 87.

[4] Samuel Chotzinoff, *A Lost Paradise* (New York, Alfred Knopf, 1955), p. 81.

[5] *Ladies' Home Journal,* February 1901, p. 26.

CHAPTER V

Meals, Menus, and Market Baskets

> *To satisfy one's hunger is not so expensive as it is to gratify one's appetite.*
> —Massachusetts Bureau of Statistics of Labor.

Abundant food has always been a symbol of prosperity, and food the first objective of economic activity. The prospect of more and better food was one of the attractions of the United States for the early settlers. In the improvement of diets—in quantity, quality, and variety—we can see evidence of benefits to the descendants of those early immigrants from the opportunities of the new land. It is commonly observed that the children of each generation seem a little taller, heavier, and generally healthier than their parents. This is attributed in large part to the continuous improvement in the diet.

In the raising of food standards, the families of urban wage earners have probably gained more since the turn of the century than have other groups in the population. Their increasing command of purchasing power has served a dual function in providing for improvement in their diet. They have gained the means of buying more and better foods. But their mass purchasing power has also supported the development of low-cost mass production and marketing of new and better foods, many of them fully processed.

EVOLUTION IN DIETS AND FOOD MARKETING

Variety in the Diet

For the workingman near the turn of the century, diets were usually monotonous. Meats, fruits and vegetables, and milk had to be produced locally. The customary winter diet in one midwestern city during the 1890's was described in the following terms:

> Steak, roasts, macaroni, Irish potatoes, sweet potatoes, turnips, cole slaw, fried apples, and stewed tomatoes, with Indian pudding, rice, cake, or pie for dessert. This was the winter repertoire of the average family that was not wealthy, and we swapped about from

one combination to another, using pickles and chow-chow to make the familiar starchy food relishing. We never thought of having fresh fruit or green vegetables and could not have got them if we had.[1]

Food eaten by the average worker in the United States today is more varied and more healthful, and for lower income workers it is also more bountiful, than it was at the beginning of the century. Today's family market basket* has a little less food in terms of calories and considerably fewer carbohydrates than the 1900 basket, but it contains more proteins, minerals, and vitamins. This comes from the use of fewer potatoes, breads, and heavy desserts, and more meat and poultry, eggs, fruits, vegetables, and milk.

In the merging of many ethnic groups, this country has achieved a widely varied diet. Nearly every nation of the world has contributed its unique dishes, and in many instances those once exotic foods have become part of our daily diet, widely available on the shelves of stores. Such items as spaghetti, pizza, chow mein, enchiladas, kippers, and shishkebab remind us of our dietary debt to other countries.

The availability of these foods, as well as the indigenous staples of the American diet, to families in all income ranges, in all seasons of the year, has been achieved largely by technological developments. The fresh meats, formerly very difficult to obtain during the summer months, are now readily available at any time through the use of modern refrigeration. Cities are no longer dependent on produce from nearby truck farms. Lettuce from the Imperial Valley of California, tomatoes from Florida, peas and beans from Ohio, oranges from California, Florida, and Texas, and numerous other perishable foods flow—and in some cases literally are flown—to Boston, New York, Chicago, Seattle, New Orleans, and other cities during much of the year. These are the benefits of refrigerated high-speed transportation, supported in turn by mass buying power and public recognition of the importance of those foods in a balanced diet.

Stores and Packages

Another aspect of the technological story of food is the revolution in retailing. That remarkable institution of recent origin,

---

*The term "market basket" nowadays is mainly a figure of speech that suggests the transformation in marketing as well as dietary habits. Earlier, the market basket was actually a common mode of carrying food supplies, especially perishables, bought each day in small quantities. Today, the less frequent marketing calls for larger quantities and more kinds of food, often carried by automobile, and much of it stored in refrigerators or deep freezes. Some items, notably milk and bakery products, are widely delivered to individual households. Nevertheless, the term "market basket" survives as a reminder of "the good old days."

the supermarket, has combined in one establishment the once numerous food specialty stores. Both chains and supermarkets purchase directly from the food producer, reducing the cost of distribution through large-scale operations. The chains and supermarkets have in large measure eliminated one social barrier which once separated the rich from the workers' families. Americans in all income groups and occupations now shop in the same stores; they are influenced in their selection by the same advertising; and, although they have tended to develop similar food habits, the wide variety of items continuously available on the shelves allows each customer to satisfy his individual dietary needs and desires.

Many more foods than formerly are purchased either partially or completely prepared. Fruits and vegetables are canned or frozen. Mixes, particularly those for baking, make cooking far simpler. Even fresh vegetables are more nearly ready to serve; spinach, for example, is washed, stemmed, and neatly packaged. Poultry is cleaned and dressed. More and more frequently hams are being sold ready-cooked. Coffee is already ground and packaged (with the customer's option, however, in many stores, of grinding it on the premises). In addition, foods ready-prepared by a variety of establishments, notably frozen-food manufacturers, delicatessen stores, bakeries, and dairies, make it possible to dine at home with virtually no cooking.

A recent time and cost study by the U.S. Department of Agriculture of one day's meals for a family of four illustrates the saving of time in the kitchen through purchase of partially or completely prepared foods to make up the same menu.

Type of meal	Approximate cost at 1953 prices	Hours required for home preparation
Home-prepared meals	$4.90	5.5
Partially prepared meals	5.80	3.1
Ready-to-serve meals	6.70	1.6

To realize many of the fundamental changes which have taken place in workers' food habits, one has only to contrast the modern supermarkets with the small and relatively primitive grocery stores of 1900. At the beginning of the 20th century, food retailing was carried on largely by the store owner himself in a small neighborhood store. Staple articles were sold in bulk or in large quantities. Many articles were sold without weighing—5, 10, or 25 cents' worth judged by eye—and the sizes of boxes, packages, and cans were not standardized. Coffee was roasted or ground on the premises. Milk, delivered to the store in large cans, was

PACKAGING AND FROZEN FOODS—The old-fashioned grocery store has yielded to supermarket efficiency. Today's shoppers choose personally what they want from a tremendously varied stock of packaged and frozen foods. To collect their purchases, they are allowed the use of wire baskets, which they wheel out to the family car on the shop's parking lot.

ladled out to the customer in his own container. Crackers and cookies were sold from large boxes or barrels. Indeed, many older people—those who grew up on farms or in small towns particularly—have nostalgic memories of the cracker barrel; as a gathering place, it was one of the social symbols of the era. Customer purchases were made to a great extent on credit. Many store owners felt that extension of credit assured a steady clientele.

A group of small stores, such as a dry-grocery store, vegetable store, butcher shop, and bakery, would serve the needs of the immediate neighborhood. There might also be a dairy. In the large cities, the majority of the stores were located in tenement buildings whose street-floor levels were constructed especially for store purposes. Perhaps the nearest resemblance to a modern supermarket was found in the large market in which a collection of small specialty food sellers were housed under a single roof (a form of retail outlet which still exists today).

A typical grocery store would measure about 18 feet in width and 31 feet in depth. It was poorly lighted and poorly ventilated, perhaps with a rear room used either for storage or living quarters. Store fronts seemed to be used as added storage space rather than for display purposes. The proprietor had to carry a wastefully large stock in order to meet the varied demands of his relatively few customers; with poor storage and refrigeration facilities, unsold perishables would deteriorate rapidly.

Unsanitary handling of food was common. Even the best stores had food exposed to dust and flies as well as to indiscriminate handling by customers. In addition to the lack of screening and covering of food inside the stores, some products like fruits and vegetables were displayed on the sidewalk outside the store. In butcher shops, meats were similarly exposed, even side by side with live poultry. Although there were a few ordinances for inspection of food establishments and food, principally meats and milk, enforcement was lax.

Chain grocery stores began to appear early in the century. Concerning the development of chain stores, it was said in November 1916 that "the chain grocery store is, in fact, almost the first attempt that has been made to apply the methods of scientific commerce to the retail business in dry groceries."[2] The early chains were not more than a series of small neighborhood shops under common ownership. Through central purchasing, they were able to buy at lower prices than those paid by the independent stores. In other ways, also, the chains were able to lower prices. They introduced self-service, no delivery, cash sales, and large volume at low margins. The independents were forced to follow suit to survive and prosper. In many cities, the independents joined together in cooperative arrangements to pool their advertising and their purchases from producers and wholesalers and to facilitate the use of improved accounting and sales procedures.

The growth of chain grocery stores continued until the 1930's, when the trend toward one-stop shopping and bigness became pronounced. Between 1930 and 1950, chains decreased in number but increased greatly in size of individual outlets and volume of business, and that fairly recent innovation in the field of food retailing, the supermarket, experienced its phenomenal development.

IMPROVEMENTS IN NUTRITION

Food in America has generally been more varied and abundant than in other parts of the world. Meat and vegetables in particular were more plentiful. By 1909, food for an average American workingman's family included approximately 13½ pounds of meat a week, roughly 50 percent more than for an average workingman's family in England or Wales.

This situation still exists today. In 1955, for example, urban families in the United Kingdom used only about half as much meat, poultry, and game as urban families in this country, and very much less of fruits and green vegetables, but twice the quantity of potatoes and bread.

At the beginning of the century in the United States, food was consumed primarily for its fuel value, and bread and meat and potatoes constituted the basic foods. Much less was known about nutritional elements than today. Lower income families had to live on the less expensive energy foods. Higher income groups could afford variety in their diet and therefore achieved a more balanced diet, but with little of rational design.

Since then, diets for workers as well as other groups in the population have been greatly improved and differences between the diets of the "rich" and "poor" noticeably reduced. In 1918, when the study of nutrition was still in its infancy, it was estimated that 15 to 25 percent of children in the United States were actually undernourished. A large-scale survey of food consumption of city wage-earner families in 1934–36 indicated that less than one-fourth of the families had nutritionally good diets while one-third had "poor" diets. The greatest improvement in the nutrition of urban families took place after this period. By the spring of 1955, according to a nationwide food consumption study, only about 10 percent of families had nutritionally "poor" diets by standards used in the earlier period. This study showed that the average amount of food purchased was more than sufficient to provide nutritionally adequate diets.

Research in Nutrition

At the turn of the century, the beginnings of scientific investigations into the nutritive value of various foods were being made. W. O. Atwater, who was in charge of the human nutrition investigations for the Federal Government in 1894, established American dietary standards using the food consumption data of the families studied. Further work on nutritional standards was carried forward in the first decade of the 20th century by Russell Henry Chittenden, Henry C. Sherman, and others. Besides the properties of protein, fats, and carbohydrates on which the standards were based, the importance of mineral elements in human nutrition was recognized at the time, and early Government bulletins included reviews of experimental research in this field and computations of amounts of these elements in typical American diets. It was also in this first decade, in 1906, that Frederick Gowland Hopkins of Cambridge University announced the existence of some substance or substances not previously known but essential to nutrition—later to be known as vitamins.

During this early period, little knowledge of nutrition was made available to the general public and much of the popular literature stressed the digestibility of various foods rather than their nutritive value. Often based on untested theory—if not personal notions—statements such as that meat was difficult to digest and could be harmful, for example, were taken at face value by many. The importance of proper mastication and limiting the intake of food was propounded at great length in a book entitled "Humaniculture," published in 1906. Opinions concerning the ill effects resulting from eating certain fruits and vegetables were not uncommon in the literature of the day.

During World War I, the country became aware of the practical value of scientific knowledge of food and nutrition. Basal metabolism tests were developed partly to settle disputed questions concerning overeating and undereating. Investigations by the Office of Home Economics, which had been established in the Department of Agriculture in 1915, brought drastic changes in dietary thinking and in cooking methods. The subject of nutrition was introduced into the curriculum of some public schools as early as 1918.

The war not only gave impetus to the study of nutrition, but it impelled some conservation expedients which had lasting effects. Greater consumption of fruits and vegetables resulted from the wartime campaigns for saving meat, wheat, sugar, and fat, as well as from the teachings of dietitians.

The economic depression of the 1930's brought a substantial decline in amount of food eaten, but the more widespread knowledge of nutrition probably prevented a proportionate decrease in nutrient values. Government pamphlets presented plans for achieving maximum nutrition at minimum cost, for example, and home economics courses for girls were becoming common.

With the coming of World War II, interest in nutrition was stimulated again and much was done to educate the consumer in the advantages of healthful eating and the dangers of obesity. Many women enrolled in the Red Cross nutrition courses so they could serve as volunteer dietitians' aides in civilian hospitals. Food rationing challenged the ingenuity of many housekeepers and much material was published on ways to maintain good nutrition despite food shortages. Much of the recent emphasis on nutrition education in the schools stems from the discovery that dietary patterns of adolescents are worse than for any other age group.

FOOD IN THE FAMILY BUDGET

According to family living surveys of the Bureau of Labor Statistics in 1941 and 1950, about 31 percent of city family expenditures were for food and beverages—just about the same as for the entire population, urban and rural. The proportion of food expenditures to the total has declined from 43 percent at the beginning of the century—an indication of the improvement in wage earners' levels of living over the last 50 years. (See chart 6, p. 111.)

Food is essential, but there is a physical limit to a family's capacity. As the worker's income rises, so do his expenditures for food. But after he has satisfied his family's food wants, he begins to buy other things which he could not previously afford. Therefore, the *proportion* of both his income and his expenditures devoted to the purchase of food tends to fall as income rises.

Not only does the decline in the share allocated to food apply to the average expenditure but also to spending by families all along the income scale. In 1901, more than half of total outlays by workers' families in the lowest income group were for food and beverages, while those with the highest incomes devoted only slightly more than 35 percent to food. (See table 3, p. 40.) In 1950, city workers' families in the two lowest income classes spent about 35 percent for food; those in the top income group, about 26 percent (table 6, p. 46). This is particularly remarkable in view of the fact that food prices by 1950 had risen more since 1901 than prices for all other items commonly bought by city families. The special significance of these changes is that, in the lower ranges of income, they indicate a widening of the margin of earnings for additional spending beyond food.

Chart 6.

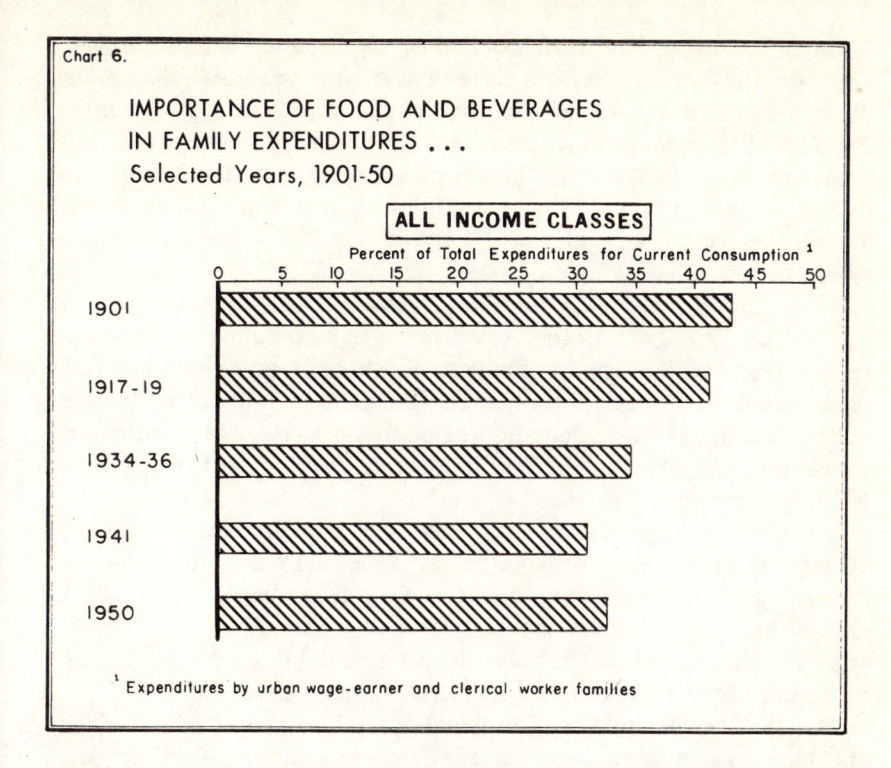

IMPORTANCE OF FOOD AND BEVERAGES
IN FAMILY EXPENDITURES...
Selected Years, 1901-50

ALL INCOME CLASSES

Percent of Total Expenditures for Current Consumption [1]

1901	~42
1917-19	~43
1934-36	~35
1941	~33
1950	~33

[1] Expenditures by urban wage-earner and clerical worker families

One aspect of family food habits since 1900, reflected only indirectly in costs of food purchased, i.e., the decline in home production of food, deserves some mention. At the beginning of the century, some workers' families who lived in large cities owned livestock and chickens, enabling them to reduce purchases of milk and eggs and, to some extent, meat and poultry. By 1950, this practice had virtually disappeared among city workers. Gardens also were much less common in 1950 than in 1900 and were generally more of a recreational hobby than an economic necessity with workers living in suburban areas. In 1950 and subsequent years, therefore, virtually all food eaten by city wage-earner families came from retail stores or restaurants.

Eating Out

In 1909 (the earliest date for which such information is available), only 3 percent of the food costs of city workers' families included in a study made in the United States by the British Board of Trade were for food and beverages purchased and consumed away from home. A relatively small part of this was for meals at work, since workers usually carried their lunches from home.

111

Carrying meals to work continued to be a common practice through the 1930's. At the time of the BLS 1917-19 study, only about one-third of the families reported the purchase of lunches. By 1934-36, considerably more of an urban worker's food bill was for food away from home and nearly two-thirds of the average amount spent for eating out was for meals at work. The majority of workers still carried lunch to work in paper bags, dinner pails, or lunch boxes.

Since the thirties, the number of eating and drinking places has grown rapidly. Motor travel brought the "drive-in" restaurant. Decentralization of business to suburbs and the repeal of prohibition also were factors in the increase in number of eating and drinking places. Demand for such facilities was reenforced by rising personal incomes and increasing employment of married women.

By 1955, nearly one-fifth of the food and beverage expense of city families was for food away from home. This expense includes meals in restaurants, cafeterias, drugstores, and in-plant cafeterias, and between-meal snacks in coffeeshops and candy stores. By this time, in-plant feeding had become a $3 billion business, serving about 23 million meals each working day.

The higher the income, the greater is the percent of the food and beverage budget spent for meals of one sort or another outside the home. This is true today to a less marked degree than in 1909 or 1917-19. Whereas in 1909 expenditures for meals away from home were negligible for the lowest income families, in 1950 even that group reported 15 to 20 percent of total food expenditures for food away from home. Only the small percentage of families in the highest income brackets spent a much larger share than this.

Food in the Family Kitchen

Despite the growth of the custom of eating out, about four-fifths of the outlay for food by city families continues to be for food that is prepared in the family kitchen.

The foods commonly grouped under the title "meat, poultry, and fish" have always constituted the largest major component in the food budget of the American household. (See table 11, p. 113.) Early in the century, this component accounted for 34 percent of food expenditures. Changes in dietary thinking, income, and other factors then brought about a decline in its importance. Since the mid-thirties, however, consumption of meat has increased considerably. In 1955, amounts expended for meat, poultry, and fish by city families again represented more than a third of the total expense for food to be eaten at home.

TABLE 11.—*Percent distribution of expenditures for food consumed at home [1] by urban wage-earner and clerical-worker families, selected periods, 1901–55*

Group	1901	February 1909 [2]	1934–36	Spring 1942 [3]	Spring 1951 [3]	Spring 1955 [4]
All food at home	100.0	100.0	100.0	100.0	100.0	100.0
Meat, poultry, and fish	33.8	29.0	26.2	27.3	32.1	34.5
Cereals and bakery products	[5] 15.8	18.5	15.8	11.4	12.2	10.1
Eggs	5.1	6.3	5.7	6.4	4.7	4.0
Dairy products	16.1	15.5	18.7	19.0	16.7	16.6
Butter	8.8	7.7	5.3	4.2	2.4	1.7
Other	7.1	7.8	13.4	14.8	14.3	14.9
Fats and oils	2.9	2.7	3.2	3.1	3.4	2.4
Fruits and vegetables	14.8	17.5	20.8	22.8	18.1	19.9
Fresh	14.8	14.8	15.6	15.9	9.4	12.2
Processed		2.7	5.2	6.9	8.7	7.7
Sugar and sweets	5.3	4.1	3.4	2.8	3.4	2.9
Beverages, nonalcoholic	4.9	5.3	[6] 4.0	4.5	6.1	5.5
Miscellaneous	1.3	1.1	2.2	2.7	3.3	4.1

[1] Excludes alcoholic beverages.
[2] Families of British descent living in northern cities.
[3] All urban housekeeping families and single persons.
[4] All urban housekeeping families.
[5] Includes "not specified" food, judged to be chiefly unlisted items of cereals and bakery products.
[6] Excludes "other drinks," considered to be alcoholic beverages.

SOURCE: *1901*—Cost of Living and Retail Prices of Food, Eighteenth Annual Report of the Commissioner of Labor, 1903. *1909*—Cost of Living in American Towns, Report of the British Board of Trade on the Cost of Living in the Principal Industrial Cities of the United States. *1934-36*—Money Disbursements of Wage Earners and Clerical Workers, 1934–36, U. S. Bureau of Labor Statistics Bulletin 638, and Diets of Families of Employed Wage Earners and Clerical Workers in Cities, U. S. Department of Agriculture Circular 507. *1942*—Family Spending and Saving in Wartime, U. S. Bureau of Labor Statistics Bulletin 822, and Family Food Consumption in the United States, Spring 1942, U. S. Department of Agriculture Miscellaneous Publication 550. *1951*—Family Income, Expenditures, and Savings in 1950, U. S. Bureau of Labor Statistics Bulletin 1097 (Revised) and unpublished BLS data. *1955*—Food Consumption of Households in the United States, Report No. 1 of Household Food Consumption Survey, U. S. Department of Agriculture.

The changes in meat consumption were at least partly caused by changes in family spending for dairy products (except butter), eggs, and fruits and vegetables. These foods became increasingly important in the family food budget from the turn of the century through the World War II period but since then have taken a smaller share of the food dollar. There have also been particularly striking declines in expenditures allocated to butter and to cereal and bakery products. For sugar and sweets, the proportion of the food dollar spent (though not total quantities consumed) has decreased noticeably. The reduction for cereals is partly a result of lower consumption by today's weight-conscious American consumer. Reduced purchases of sugar in the grocery store are offset by greater consumption away from home of ice cream, soft drinks, candy bars, and the like, as well as relatively low prices, and by increased purchases of processed foods containing sugar. Much the same story is evident in the physical quantities of food purchased as summarized in table 12, which shows average weekly consumption of the major groups of food by city families of three persons.

TABLE 12. *Average number of pounds of food purchased per week for consumption at home by urban wage-earner and clerical-worker families, estimated for 3 persons, selected periods, 1901–55*

Group	1901	February 1909 [1]	1917–19 [2]	1934–36	Spring 1942 [3]	Spring 1948 [3]	Spring 1955 [4]
Total pounds of food	([5])	([5])	67.3	[6] 71.2	[7] 85.0	92.4	87.6
Meat, poultry, and fish	9.2	9.6	6.6	7.7	9.0	9.6	12.6
Cereal and bakery products	[8] 14.2	17.6	14.8	12.9	11.4	11.7	9.8
Eggs	1.4	1.6	1.4	1.8	2.9	2.4	2.5
Dairy products	9.1	8.2	13.4	14.4	20.2	23.7	22.5
Butter	1.2	1.0	1.0	1.1	1.1	.7	.6
Other	7.9	7.2	12.4	13.3	19.1	23.0	21.9
Fats and oils	.9	1.1	1.3	1.3	1.5	2.0	1.8
Fruits and vegetables	([5])	([5])	25.9	27.7	34.5	33.8	28.7
Fresh			24.1	24.3	27.9	25.5	20.6
Processed			1.8	3.4	6.6	8.3	8.1
Sugar and sweets	3.4	3.3	3.0	3.8	2.6	3.7	3.1
Beverages, nonalcoholic	.6	.8	.8	[6] 1.3	[7] 1.8	4.1	3.8
Miscellaneous	([5])	([5])	.1	.3	1.1	1.4	2.8

[1] Weighted averages of all nationality groups.
[2] Since the 1917–19 survey excluded 2-person families, in which per capita consumption usually exceeds that in larger families, these estimates are based on consumption of 2.6 "equivalent adult males," corresponding to an average 3-person family in 1934–36. Consumption by adult females was estimated at 90 percent of that for an adult male; that by children aged 3 or under, 4–6, 7–10, and 11–14 years, at 15, 40, 75, and 90 percent, respectively.
[3] All urban housekeeping families and single persons.
[4] All urban housekeeping families.
[5] Not available.
[6] Excludes "other drinks," considered to be alcoholic beverages.
[7] Excludes tea and coffee.
[8] Includes "not specified" food, judged to be chiefly unlisted items of cereals and bakery products.

SOURCE: See table 11; 1917–19 data are from Cost of Living in the United States, U. S. Bureau of Labor Statistics Bulletin 357; spring 1948, from Food Consumption of Urban Families in the United States, U. S. Department of Agriculture Information Bulletin 132.

Families at different income levels apportion their household food expenditures to major food categories a little differently. Poorer families concentrate on cheaper foods and energy foods, whereas the more well-to-do usually eat a greater variety, higher quality foods, and more delicacies. Normally, therefore, relative expenditures for meat increase a little with income, while those for cereal products decrease. There are other differences (not large) in the way the food dollar is divided, but proportionally the distributions of expenditures do not differ radically for various income groups.

Absolute quantities consumed vary more with income. In general, wealthier families eat more of everything. Some individual items are notable exceptions—skim milk, margarine, lard, corn meal, salt pork, collards and other similar greens, canned peas, etc. Many of these items are replaced by more expensive ones bought in greater quantity by higher income families. These families similarly buy better cuts of meat, and fresh or frozen fruits and vegetables other than potatoes in preference to canned or dried fruits and vegetables, etc. The higher prices paid by higher income families can be illustrated by the following data for the spring of 1948:

Annual family income	Average price per pound paid for—		
	All meats, poultry, fish	Beef	Pork
Under $1,000	$0.56	$0.61	$0.56
$1,000–$1,999	.61	.68	.60
$2,000–$2,999	.64	.69	.64
$3,000–$3,999	.64	.69	.65
$4,000–$4,999	.67	.70	.68
$5,000–$7,499	.69	.73	.69
$7,500 and over	.74	.82	.72

The average costs per pound for other items, such as fresh vegetables and coffee, are also a little higher for more well-to-do families.

The substantial increase in earnings since 1900, particularly for lower income families, has tended to lessen differences in food habits due to income. In 1909, consumption of eggs ranged from as little as 2 eggs per person per week for the poorest families to over 5 eggs for the highest income families. In 1955, average consumption per person was higher but it varied much less between low- and high-income families. Consumption of meat, poultry, and fish, which in 1909 was around 100 pounds a year per person for families at the lower end of the income scale and slightly over 200 pounds at the upper end, by 1955 varied less—from about 200 to 250 pounds a year across the income scale.

Importance of Meats. Since meat is high priced compared with other foods, the share of the total food bill that must be allocated to this group of items is of first concern to families (chart 7, p. 117).

The apportionment of expenditures of city families among the various kinds of meat, poultry, and fish has changed materially since 1901, as shown below. (The data used here and in subsequent tabulations in this chapter are from the expenditure surveys indicated on tables 11 and 12.)

In 1901, families of wage earners and lower salaried persons bought a little more than 3 pounds of meat, poultry, and fish a week per person, not counting home production. Of this quantity, about 2½ pounds consisted of beef, pork, or other red meats. The British Board of Trade survey indicates amounts used in 1909 to have been a little higher. In these early surveys, fresh beef was the largest item. Only about one-third as much fresh pork was eaten, and slightly less salt pork than fresh.

Subgroup	Percent distribution of city family expenditures					
	1901	February 1909	1934–36	Spring 1942	Spring 1951	Spring 1955
All meats, poultry, and fish	100.0	100.0	100.0	100.0	100.0	100.0
Meat	84.2	87.3	79.7	80.4	78.5	75.4
Beef	50.1	43.0	31.1	33.1	32.2	32.4
Pork	25.3	30.0	25.3	27.4	27.7	25.1
Other meats [1]	8.8	14.3	23.3	19.9	18.6	17.9
Poultry	8.6	5.7	11.9	12.0	13.6	15.5
Fish and other seafood	7.2	7.0	8.4	7.6	7.9	9.1

[1] Includes canned meats.

The pattern of meat consumption varied among the different sections of the country, largely because of soil and climatic conditions, but also because of preferences of particular nationality groups concentrated in certain areas. Pork was the natural product of the South, where hogs could be turned loose to forage for themselves. Cattle, on the other hand, were harder to raise because grasses did not grow as well as in other areas. In New England, feed for hogs was scarce, but grass grew abundantly for cattle feed. As a result, the population of New England ate mainly beef and mutton, whereas in the South fresh or salt pork was more important than beef. Similarly, pork and salt meats were little used in the West, where livestock could be fed on abundant grass. Salt beef was rarely consumed except in the North Atlantic States.

Within these broad geographic regions, there were other differences because of the inherited tastes of inhabitants. Veal, for example, was more important in the diet of German, Scandinavian, South European, and Slavonic groups in 1909 than in that of other nationality groups studied at the time. As late as 1934–36, the persistence of French eating habits showed up in greater consumption of veal and fish in New Orleans than in otherwise similar southern cities.

Consumption of red meats reached a low point about 1935, after which an upward trend began, which has continued to the present time. According to surveys of the U. S. Department of Agriculture, urban families consumed more than 3 pounds of red meats a week per person in the spring of 1955—as much as the 1901 consumption of red meats, poultry, and fish combined.

In addition to red meats, about one-fourth of a pound of poultry per person per week was purchased in 1901. Besides this, a fair amount of home-produced chickens was consumed. In many households, roast chicken was the traditional Sunday dinner.

Chart 7.

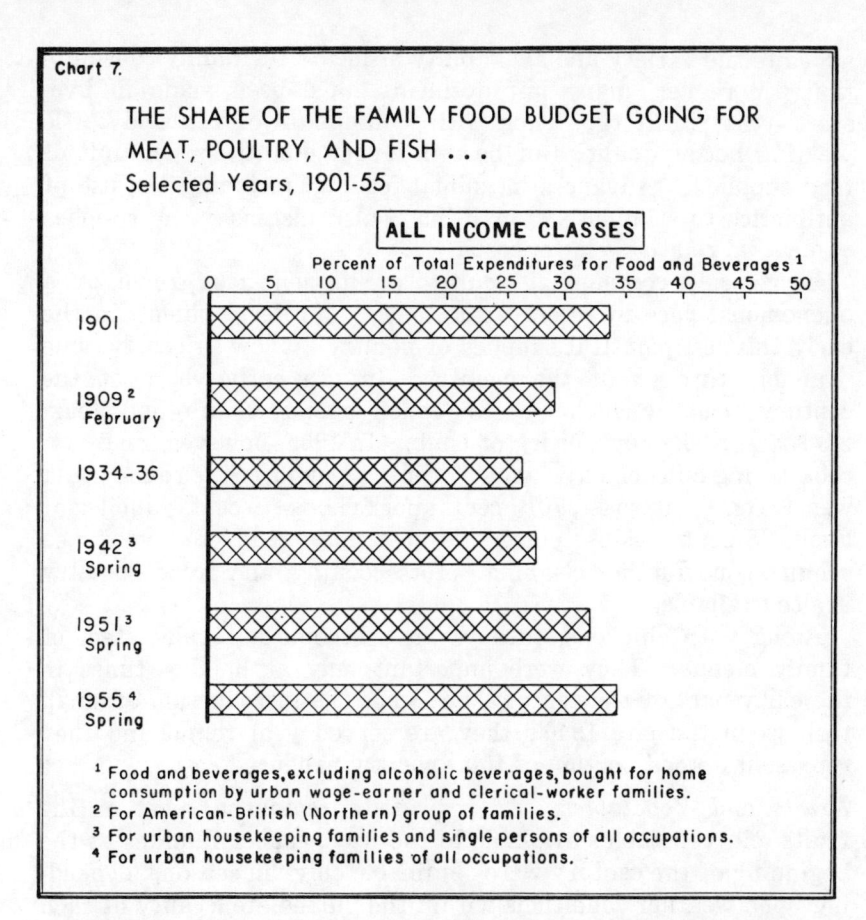

THE SHARE OF THE FAMILY FOOD BUDGET GOING FOR MEAT, POULTRY, AND FISH...
Selected Years, 1901-55

ALL INCOME CLASSES

Percent of Total Expenditures for Food and Beverages [1]

1901

1909 [2]
February

1934-36

1942 [3]
Spring

1951 [3]
Spring

1955 [4]
Spring

[1] Food and beverages, excluding alcoholic beverages, bought for home consumption by urban wage-earner and clerical-worker families.
[2] For American-British (Northern) group of families.
[3] For urban housekeeping families and single persons of all occupations.
[4] For urban housekeeping families of all occupations.

Fresh fish has consistently accounted for 7 or 8 percent of meat, poultry, and fish expenditures since 1901. Lack of adequate shipping and storage facilities in the early years of the century prevented wide distribution of fish. As a result, consumption was confined to coastal areas and to cities adjacent to the Great Lakes and large rivers like the Mississippi. Dry salt fish, smoked or pickled fish, and canned fish were not important items of diet.

Many of these changes in meat consumption patterns stem from technological and marketing developments. Before the introduction of refrigerated railroad cars about 1875–80, all fresh meat was slaughtered locally and, in hot weather, needs had to be supplied from stocks of "packed" or salted meats, particularly pork. Since then, meat inspection and grading have improved the quality of meat supplied the consumer, and canning, freezing, and packaging are bringing meats to him in more convenient form, some ready for serving.

The ubiquitous chain store or supermarket, with long freezer counters for precut and packaged meats, as well as many improvements in curing, canning, and precooking of meat products, has added to the variety and availability of meats for family consumption. Moreover, many improvements have been made in livestock—the "meat type" hog with a minimum of fat, and cattle yielding better qualities of beef in larger quantities per unit of feed supplied. Advances in animal feeding, including the use of antibiotics to stimulate growth, have also increased the supplies of meats at relatively lower costs.

Large-scale commercial poultry production has grown at a phenomenal pace in recent years. With its development, in the early thirties, plentiful supplies of poultry, at low prices, became available throughout the country. In the early years of the century, roasting chicken cost as much or more than round steak, rib roast, pork chops, or leg of lamb. In 1955, however, ready-to-cook frying chickens averaged 57 cents a pound, while round steak was 90 cents; rib roast, 70½ cents; pork chops, 79 cents; and leg of lamb, 68 cents. Most poultry is now sold "ready to cook," i.e., requiring no further cleaning before cooking, and frozen poultry is also available.

Along with chickens, turkeys have become a regular item of family menus. They were important only at holiday times in the early part of the century, but since the introduction of small turkeys in the late 1940's they are served year-round and they represent a good portion of total poultry produced.

Fruits and Vegetables. As indicated previously, most of the fruits and vegetables available to the wage-earner families at the beginning of the century were obtainable only "in season," depending upon weather conditions within the immediate locality of each city. When home gardens or nearby truck farms were not producing, the family depended largely on potatoes, dried beans and peas, canned tomatoes and peas, dried fruit, fruit preserves and jams, and, if it had its own garden, home-canned vegetables to supplement its meat and cereals. The chief item was potatoes, consumption of which was close to 4 pounds per person per week. It was not at all unusual early in the century to serve potatoes regularly for breakfast as well as at lunch and dinner.

The purchases of an Irish trucker's family in New York City for a 2-week period in the summer of 1895, selected as typical of the working group, included the following fruits and vegetables: Potatoes, onions, beets, dried peas and beans, fresh and canned tomatoes, strawberries, turnip greens, string beans, and canned peas—a limited selection by today's standards, which would include leafy vegetables, yellow vegetables, and fruit juices. According to estimates of the U. S. Department of Agriculture, well over half of the vegetables consumed in 1909, excluding potatoes, were homegrown. By contrast, fruits and vegetables of all kinds are available today in fresh, frozen, canned, or dried form throughout the year, although the housewife still shops for seasonal price advantages.

The vitamin contents of fruits and green vegetables were still unknown in 1900. One writer classed lemon and grapefruit as hyperacid fruits, not to be considered eating fruits, and apples as a relish rather than a food. Another claimed that fruits and vegetables were mainly valuable for their salts. Not until about the time of the first world war was much publicity given to the nutritional values of fruits and vegetables. Civilians were urged to develop "victory gardens" and consume more vegetables and less staples such as flour, wheat, butter, and sugar, which were more easily shipped overseas to supply the troops. The search for the causes of poor health of men drafted for the military service intensified study of the importance of vitamins and minerals. Vitamin A (present in large amounts in most leafy green and yellow vegetables) had been reported in 1913. By 1920, the function of Vitamin C—the most important sources of which are the citrus fruits—in the health of human beings was well understood, although this vitamin had not yet been identified chemically.

Advertisers were quick to capitalize on these discoveries. Every housewife heard of the importance of vitamins and minerals. Slogans regarding oranges, raisins, and spinach became part of the consumer vocabulary.

Extensive use of canned goods by the military services gave impetus to the growth of the canning industry. Between 1904 and 1935, the annual volume of canned goods packed rose from 34½ million to nearly 200 million cases.

The increasing use of canned and, later, frozen items and the growing knowledge of nutrition effected a gradual transformation in the distribution of family expenditures for different types of fruits and vegetables, as shown in the following tabulation:

Subgroup	Percent distribution of city family expenditures				
	February 1909	1934–36	Spring 1942	Spring 1951	Spring 1955
All fruits and vegetables	100.0	100.0	100.0	100.0	100.0
Fresh	84.8	74.8	69.8	51.8	61.2
Fruit	22.9	30.6	27.2	22.3	24.3
Vegetables	61.9	44.2	42.6	29.5	36.9
Potatoes, sweet potatoes	30.4	11.1	11.0	8.3	7.8
Other	31.5	33.1	31.6	21.2	29.1
Dried	5.3	5.7	4.2	4.7	3.7
Canned	9.9	19.5	26.0	35.8	26.0
Frozen				7.7	9.1

Frozen fruits and vegetables, a high-priced novelty in the 1930's, were still not of sufficient importance in workers' food bills to be noted as a separate expenditure item in 1942. However, according to the U.S. Department of Agriculture, annual consumption of frozen fruits and vegetables had grown to approximately 2 pounds per capita by the beginning of World War II. By the 1950's, families in all walks of life were using frozen foods as a matter of course.

With the substantial increases in earnings in recent years, the differences in quantities of fruits and vegetables eaten by different income groups have diminished. Between 1942 and 1948, for example, consumption of citrus fruit and tomatoes by lowest income families increased 40 percent, whereas that for highest income families changed little.

As with most foods, fruits and vegetables are packaged very differently today from those purchased around 1900. Prepackaging of fresh fruits and vegetables gained rapidly between 1950 and 1955, and it is estimated that 20 percent of all produce is now bought in that form. Today's packages and cans also tend to be smaller to suit the needs of today's smaller families. Most packages of frozen foods serve at most 3 to 4 persons. Instead of a 25-pound box of prunes, today's market carries 1- or 2-pound packages.

Grain Products. Modern ideas about diet have been influential in reducing the intake of starchy foods, while higher incomes of working people have made possible greater use of higher priced foods like meats and fresh fruits and vegetables. As a result, consumption of cereal products as a whole by city families declined continuously from 5.9 pounds a week per person in 1909 to 3.3 pounds in the spring of 1955. This occurred despite the fact that price increases for flour and bread in this half century have not been as large as for other foods. In 1901, 5 pounds of flour roughly equaled in price 1 pound of round steak, for example, but in 1951, although the price of flour was about 4 times as much, it cost only half as much as round steak.

As regards grain products, a shift from the purchase of flour and unprepared cereals for home cooking to the purchase of bread, prepared cereals, and other baked goods is apparent from the tabulation at the top of p. 121.

Early in this century, many housewives baked the family's bread and prepared all other grain foods from the basic raw materials, chiefly flour, oatmeal, and cornmeal. In the expenditure studies early in this century, almost all city families reported the purchase of flour, but over one-fifth of the families bought no bread. Today, homemade bread has become a rare delicacy.

| | Purchases per person per week, in pounds ||||||
Subgroup	February 1909	1917–19 [1]	1934–36	Spring 1942	Spring 1948	Spring 1955
All cereal and bakery products	5.9	5.7	4.3	3.8	3.9	3.3
Prepared	2.8	2.8	2.8	2.7	2.8	2.4
Bread	2.0	2.5	2.2	1.9	1.9	1.4
Other bakery goods, ready-to-eat cereals, and prepared mixes	.8	.3	.6	.8	.9	1.0
Unprepared	3.1	2.9	1.5	1.1	1.1	.9
Flour	2.1	1.8	.9	.6	.6	.4
Unprepared cereals	1.0	1.1	.6	.5	.5	.5

[1] Per "equivalent adult male"; for explanation, see table 12, footnote 2.

Average quantities of flour bought by city families have decreased from about 2.5 pounds per person a week in 1901 to about 0.4 pound in the spring of 1955.

Accompanying the decline in total consumption of grain products, there has been a fairly steady increase in the use of partially prepared foods—prepared breakfast foods, cake and piecrust mixes, crackers, cakes, cookies, etc. Ready-to-eat cereals, almost unknown in 1909, accounted for 7 percent of total expenditures for cereals and bakery products in 1955, while prepared mixes accounted for almost as much. In 1952–54, about two-thirds of the total per capita supply of flour was purchased in the form of processed products, compared with only 20–25 percent in 1909.

Even flour and bread bought today are not the same as they were in 1900. Bread now is baked to exact specifications, carefully labeled, and wrapped under sanitary conditions. Early methods for refining flour removed much of the vitamin and mineral content. As early as 1923, both vitamins and minerals were being added to both flour and bread, and in 1941, specific standards of enrichment were established. Later, other products, such as farina, cornmeal, grits, macaroni products, dry breakfast foods, and rice were enriched with vitamins. From 1943 to 1946, as part of the wartime conservation of wheat, bread enrichment was mandatory. Thereafter, many bakers voluntarily or by State law continued to enrich bread, and in 1955, an estimated 80 percent of commercially baked white bread was enriched. This development has raised the average iron, thiamin, riboflavin, and niacin content of diets, despite the reduced consumption of cereal products.

Milk and Other Dairy Products. Perhaps the most outstanding feature of the modern American diet, by comparison with 1900, is the high per capita consumption of fluid milk. Milk and milk products, especially cheese and butter, have for centuries been

THE STAFF OF LIFE—To meet the food demands of a rapidly increasing population, bread must be prepared under mass-production conditions. What today's bread might have lost in flavor, it gains in uniformity and sanitary preparation. Wrapping is customary, and pre-slicing helps the housewife.

staples in the diets of many countries, but in no other part of the modern world has fluid milk achieved the dietary role it plays in the average American household. Milk is served in many schools—either free or at nominal cost—and millions of soldiers acquired a taste for milk during their military service in World War II. Whatever the causes, milk has increased in popularity. Army dietitians have had to raise daily rations of milk to satisfy the young men in today's military forces.

In 1901, wage earners' families purchased about $1\frac{1}{4}$ quarts of fluid milk per person per week. The quantity purchased was much higher in all regions outside the South, where some families had a cow. Buttermilk was used to a certain extent in place of milk, especially in the South in the summer, when it was difficult to keep milk sweet for more than a few hours. By about 1935, each member of city workingmen's families was consuming nearly 2 quarts of fresh fluid milk each week, and by the spring of 1955, the amount used had increased to more than 3 quarts.

Today, the housewife has little worry whether the milk she buys is safe to drink. Use of glass bottles did not become general until between 1910 and 1915, and not until the early 1930's was the sale of bulk milk in stores officially banned in New York. Pasteurization of milk, begun in 1886, was practiced mainly by the large dairies in 1909. By the early 1920's, the greater part of milk sold in cities was pasteurized, and currently over 95 percent of all milk sold is so treated. Homogenized milk and milk enriched with Vitamin D were in general use by 1940.

Sweetened condensed milk has decreased in importance in the family food budget while evaporated milk has increased. In the early years of the century, sweetened condensed milk was used by many workingmen's families because it was more economical than fresh milk. In some areas, it was used as a spread in place of butter and jelly and jam. Evaporated milk began to gain in importance before World War I, and has continued to do so, in large part because of its use in the preparation of formulas for babies. An "instant" form of dry skim milk, called "dry nonfat milk," which came on the market about 1955 at prices below those for an equivalent quantity of fluid milk, may soon increase the importance of powdered milk.

Important among processed dairy products is cheese, consumption of which has been on the increase, averaging about 3 pounds a year per person for urban families in 1901 and 1917–19, and 16 pounds in 1955. Since the end of World War I, processed cheeses in which many cheddars are combined to produce a uniform quality and flavor, as well as cheese foods and cheese spreads, have been introduced. Prepackaging of natural and processed American cheese, frequently in slices, in convenient-sized units has contributed to the popularity of this food.

Purchased ice cream was not important in the early part of the century. In 1918, the average reported purchase was 1¼ quarts a year per person. By the spring of 1942, it was up to 5 quarts. Part of this increase reflects the disappearance of homefreezing by handcranking, once a familiar Sunday activity in American family life.

As the following tabulation shows, the family budget for milk and milk products is now allocated very differently than in 1900, with much less going for butter. This does not, of course, necessarily indicate that the consumption of butterfat has declined; while city families are eating only half as much butter, they are eating nearly three times as much milk, cream, ice cream, and cheese.

Subgroup	Percent distribution of city family expenditures					
	1901	February 1909	1934–36	Spring 1942	Spring 1951	Spring 1955
All dairy products	100.0	100.0	100.0	100.0	100.0	100.0
Milk, cream, and ice cream	40.0	42.6	63.7	68.8	73.5	76.3
Cheese	5.0	7.8	8.0	9.0	12.2	13.1
Butter	54.6	49.6	28.3	22.2	14.3	10.6

Butter, now used sparingly, was used liberally in cooking around 1900. Major cause of this change was the introduction of lower priced oleomargarine, based on animal fats, which attained commercial importance as early as the 1890's. Low-income families quickly accepted oleomargarine wherever it was available. With the heavy demands for animal fats in World War I, vegetable oils were substituted for part or all of the animal fats used, and the name was changed to margarine, the product now found in many kitchens. By the spring of 1955, city families were purchasing equal quantities of margarine and butter.

Desserts and Nonalcoholic Drinks. The dessert as a standard part of the meal has declined in importance in recent years. Although the elaborate cakes, pies, preserves, and jams which once invariably accompanied a full meal are no longer typical, the consumption of sugar has not declined. In fact, the per capita use of sugar in all forms by the population as a whole has increased by about a third over the last half century. This is explained by the substantial amount used in processed foods and between-meal snacks.

Nonalcoholic beverages—tea, coffee, and cocoa, and more recently, soft drinks—account for 4 to 6 percent of food expenses. (Fruit juices are included with fruits and vegetables in this chapter.) Most of the group represents coffee, "the national beverage," consumption of which increased substantially—from a little less than 9 pounds per person per year in 1901 to over 16 pounds by 1948—according to family expenditure studies. Per capita coffee consumption dropped to 12 pounds in 1955, following sharp price rises beginning in late 1949. High coffee prices brought about some increase in tea drinking, ordinarily much less popular than coffee in this country.

The price of coffee may also have played a small part in the increasing popularity of soft drinks, just as typically American as the cup of coffee. Not until the 1934–36 survey were bottled soft drinks listed as an item of family food expenditures. In 1950, the average family spent 25 cents a week for soft drinks for home consumption and a great deal more for between-meal snacks away from home. The industry has increased manyfold in this half century.

PROOF OF THE PUDDING

To sum up, perhaps the most significant developments affecting our national diet in the 20th century have been the rise in personal incomes, the improvements in methods of processing and preserving foods, and the increase in scientific knowledge regarding the functions of various food resources in maintaining the human organism. The effects of these developments, along with the gains in medical care described elsewhere in this volume, are seen in the physical condition of the population. As noted, Americans are becoming larger. The span of life is lengthening. Much still remains to be learned about the relationship of foods to physical and mental growth and to various disabilities, but we have achieved general recognition of the importance of the problems, and will continue to find solutions. The gains already made have contributed materially to the productivity of the American wage earner.

Footnotes

[1] Robert S. and Helen M. Lynd, *Middletown* (New York, Harcourt, Brace and Co., 1929), p. 156 (quoted in *An American and His Food* by Richard Osborn Cummings, Chicago, University of Chicago Press, 1940, p. 72).

[2] Theodore H. Price, The Chain Grocery Store, in *Seven Articles by Theo. H. Price* (New York, Theodore H. Price Publishing Corp. [1919?]), p. 45, reprinted from *The Outlook*, November 22, 1916.

CHAPTER VI

Clothing and Personal Care

> *As for clothing . . . perhaps we are led oftener by the love of novelty and a regard for the opinions of men, in procuring it, than by a true utility.*
> —H. D. Thoreau.

In the first half of the 20th century, the dress of American city workers and their families underwent a greater transformation than in any other 50-year period in this Nation's history. Not only did styles change radically, but there were also improvements in the number, design, and quality of garments owned, and in the variety of clothing, fabrics, and colors. Improvements in dress were accompanied by improvements in grooming which went far toward eliminating differences in appearance between the Nation's factory workers and their families and other economic groups. The transformation grew out of interrelated social, industrial, and technological changes.

The increase in real incomes which went along with these developments resulted in greater use of textile materials by low- and moderate-income families than ever before. In 1956, per capita consumption of textiles among the entire population in the United States, as measured by weight, was 50 percent higher than in 1900—about 39 pounds compared with 26. Each person was using about one-sixth more cotton, somewhat less silk and wool, and less than one-sixth as much linen fibers. More importantly, rayon and other synthetics unknown in 1900 constituted over one-fourth of the total per capita consumption in 1956, and cotton accounted for only about two-thirds, compared with over seven-eighths in 1900. The trend is even more striking when we consider that a pound of textile fiber today goes much farther in terms of garments than at the turn of the century.

NATURE OF THE REVOLUTION IN DRESS

Manners and dress have become more and more informal in all economic groups throughout our country. Everywhere there have been shifts in the direction of wearing simpler and more comfortable clothes and adapting behavior to the situation rather than adhering to traditional ways of doing things. Wage and clerical workers were affected by these changes in customs at the same time that a considerable rise in their purchasing power made it possible for them to pay more for clothes and personal care.

New industrial techniques brought about very considerable changes in the production and marketing of textiles and clothing. These in turn affected designing and styling. In the clothing trades, the transition to increased machine operation and from home to factory production raised the supply of clothing available to all classes of consumers and provided better clothing at prices workers and their families could afford. Increases in output per man-hour in the production of textile fibers, notably the synthetics, and in the garment trades made possible higher incomes for workers in those industries. In the first decade of the century, wage earners in the garment trades pioneered in reaching agreements with employers for improved working conditions. They also took the lead in arousing the public to an understanding of the economic and social implications of industrial homework, until it was regulated or abolished by law. The garment workers also contributed substantially to developing more equitable methods of computing pay, regularizing production and therefore employment, and shortening the workweek. Changes in the garment trades set precedents for other industries and played an important part in the upward trends in real incomes and leisure for all workers. Those changes, in turn, affected the kind and the variety of the clothes workers wear.

In 1900, men's and boys' clothing was mostly factory-made, although the wife sometimes made nightshirts and summer underpants for her husband and sons. Shoes were factory-produced, as they are today, sometimes in small plants, sometimes in large ones, with machines rented from the United Shoe Machinery Corp. Stockings for women and girls, their heavy winter underwear, their summer undershirts, the women's corsets, and the girls' underwaists were also mass-produced. Their outer clothes were, for the most part, either made at home or in small dressmaking shops equipped with sewing machines but operating on such a small base that a really low-cost division of labor was impossible.

By 1920, production of clothing for all members of the worker's family had, in large part, been transferred from home and shop to factory. Nevertheless, the demand for yard goods survived. Clothing shortages during World War II and the later upsurge of the "do-it-yourself" vogue may even have brought about a minor revival of designing and sewing in the home.

Textile Fibers

The invention of man-made textile fibers was one of the most important causes of the revolution in dress. These fibers have been developed to the point where, either alone or in combination with natural fibers, they provide a much greater variety of light and less expensive clothing materials within the range of the workers' buying power. Meanwhile, new finishes have been perfected for use with materials made of traditional fibers which keep them in shape longer and make them easier to clean.

"Artificial silk," the first commercialized synthetic fiber, was marketed as early as 1911, but it was disappointing in use. The rapid growth of production began in 1921, following a decade of technological advances, and in the 1920's the industry adopted and began to popularize the word "rayon" instead of "artificial silk." Another synthetic, nylon, came onto the market in small quantities in the late 1930's. During World War II, production was greatly increased, but output was largely channeled into the making of parachutes and other wartime goods. Since 1945, use of clothing made exclusively of nylon, particularly women's hosiery, or of nylon in combination with other fibers, has risen sharply among city workers and their families as well as other parts of the population. Meanwhile, other synthetics developed for special purposes have increased the variety and types of clothing workers can buy.

With the change in textile materials, there also occurred a change in the materials used for making shoes. In 1900, the shoe with a rubber sole was a rarity, and shoes made of textiles were seldom seen.

Garment Production

Technological changes in clothing production had an important influence in changing the apparel of low- and moderate-income families in the United States in this 50-year period. The first big step in the modernization of the garment industry had occurred with the invention of the sewing machine in 1846. An illustration of its revolutionary impact on labor is found in the making of men's overalls, as reported in a study of hand and machine labor by the U.S. Commissioner of Labor in 1895. The manufacture manually of 12 dozen pairs in 1870 required about 720 work hours, mostly in sewing. The women who made the overalls were paid $36 a gross, or 5 cents an hour. (Then, 50 cents a day was no uncommon wage for women.) The making of 12 dozen pairs in 1895 required only 71 hours, or about a tenth of the time in 1870, the main reduction resulting from the use of mechanically powered sewing machines. The labor cost was about $11, an average per hour of 3 times the hourly pay in 1870. Real earnings increased even more, as the cost of living had declined by nearly one-fifth during this period.

The changes in technology which occurred after 1900 had to do notably with the development of automatic devices used to spread out cloth for cutting (a task which was performed in the 19th century by small boys), and the improvements in high-speed, electrically driven cutting devices such as rotary discs or reciprocating knives which cut layers of cloth up to 9 inches thick. The pressing machine, which had been perfected early in the century and introduced into garment factories before 1910, was also important in raising productivity.

> More than 200 specialized forms of the power-driven sewing machine are in use [in garment factories]. These operate at speeds ranging up to 4,600 stitches per minute and perform specialized tasks such as the sewing of buttons, buttonholes, basting, hemstitching, spiral braiding . . . . A pressing machine also has been invented. It consists of a bed plate made to fit a particular garment or part of a garment. This bed is piped for steam, as is also the head which the operator brings down after the garment has been placed on the bed.[1]

Since the 1930's the chief means of raising average output per man-hour and lowering costs have been changes in the organization of production, the specialization of work, and the design of garments. Those changes did not have the dramatic effects of the shifts from hand to machine methods, but continuing reductions have been made in the amount of work required per unit of output.

Styling

In addition to the technological developments affecting all clothing, important changes in the styling of women's garments have tended to put modish apparel within the reach of the worker's wife. One of the first schools of fashion and design was the Needle Trades High School established in New York City in 1925 by the New York City Board of Education. Originally established to help overcome an impending shortage of skilled workmen in the needle trades, this high school soon proved its value, and labor and management representatives became interested in developing its potentials. In addition, a 2-year junior college to train talented youths in design and management, known as the Fashion Institute of Technology, was created in 1944 with the financial backing of the Educational Foundation for the

Apparel Industry (a voluntary organization of labor and management representatives) and the New York City Board of Education. Owners and employers in the apparel industry have praised the graduates of the institute, many of whom have been instrumental in introducing modern production techniques into the plants where they have been employed.

Similar developments occurred in the Midwest in the early 1930's. The School of Fine Arts of Washington University in St. Louis established a program of dress design, and business and professional groups helped to provide scholarships for students majoring in dress design and to employ its graduates in the local garment industry.

The result of these and other efforts in the same direction has been a diffusion of knowledge about style among groups in the population who had earlier never thought of modish clothing as being for them. With increased division of labor and improved technology in the industry, style changes which have become popular in a new season can be transmitted in an incredibly short time from the top of the price structure to the bottom.

Another important reason for the appearance of the latest styles in the lower price ranges is that in recent years some of the large retailers of mass-produced apparel get by airmail from their own agents the designs and specifications of the fashions shown at the Paris openings. In this way, simplified and standardized editions of fashions originated in Paris (and for that matter, New York and Hollywood) to be sold at three-digit dollar figures appear at popular prices in Main Street store windows a few months after they are first seen in the salons of the couturiers.

Environment

The changes in types and styles of clothing, particularly women's and children's garments, have been dramatic. An important reason for the changes has been the increase in the proportion of houses, offices, factories, and schools which have central heat. Most workers now use either private automobiles or well-heated public conveyances, and exposure to outdoor cold is much less than formerly. The tremendous increase in the relative number of girls and women with jobs outside the home has also had much to do with the changes. Women working in offices and factories and going to and from work in public conveyances found that long skirts were not practical or even safe. Skirts were shortened, cautiously at first and then more rapidly, until 1920. Thereafter, skirt lengths varied from time to time, but they never returned to the extreme and cumbersome lengths of the early 1900's. Shorter skirts brought about changes not

MILADY AND HER DAUGHTER'S DAUGHTER—Women's clothing styles have changed dramatically. Today their clothes are of lighter weight, more comfortable, and permit greater freedom of movement. Usually the clothes are made of synthetic fibers, and designed in brighter colors.

only in the garments worn under the dresses but also in shoes and stockings, with high and heavy shoes and heavy dark stockings going out of fashion.

In part, the change in the styling of garments is due to increased informality of living. While new styles for women are more talked about than the new styles for men, actually the latter's contributions to the changes in taste which began after World War I have been quite as decisive as those of women. Men gave up wearing high, starched collars in favor of lower, soft collars, and derby hats in favor of soft felts or no hat at all. Sports clothes have become increasingly popular.

Some observers have attributed the change in clothing habits during the past 3 decades in part to the growth of the new suburbs, where most of the householders are within a relatively narrow age range and relatively young. A study of 6 such communities where skilled workers and salesmen had bought homes alongside small businessmen in the $4,000–$7,000 income bracket showed great informality of dress. Slacks or shorts, we are told—

> . . . are standard wear for both men and women at all times, including trips to the shopping center. Visiting grandparents invariably are shocked and whisper: "Why, nobody dresses around here!" Children, regardless of sex, wear dungarees or shorts and a cotton T-shirt until puberty. One mother expressed the attitude of most: "Kids don't wear anything you bother with. It cuts down the time needed for dressing, washing, and ironing." [2]

Yet workers and their families own a greater variety of clothing. This is due in no small part to their shorter work schedules in factories, offices, and stores, and to their ownership of automobiles, which make possible their participation in a greater number of recreational activities than had been the case in 1900. Most workingmen nowadays have, in addition to work clothing and dress clothing, some sports clothing for outdoor recreation. The same is true, although perhaps to a lesser extent, of their wives. Children's clothing has become simpler and more durable, and even their dress-up clothes allow greater freedom of movement and informality of behavior than dress-up clothing in 1900.

TRENDS IN CLOTHING EXPENDITURES

Since 1900, the average share of the worker's dollar spent for clothing has declined as real income rose, despite the fact that the 1901 study of workers' expenditures by the U. S. Bureau of Labor revealed a definite tendency for clothing expenditures at each successive income level to take a larger proportion of income. Workers' families currently, with relatively high earnings, allocate a smaller share of their total expenditures for clothing than did those of 1901. The 1950 expenditure survey by the Bureau of Labor Statistics showed 11.5 percent of family expenditures on clothing, compared with 13.0 percent in the earlier year.

Workers even in the lower ranges of earnings in 1950 generally had more real buying power above basic necessities, and therefore a wider range of free choices as consumers, than did workers in 1901 in the upper ranges of earnings. The textile and apparel industries, compared with some other industries, had undergone a more thorough mechanization and technological transformation, with noteworthy reductions of cost. There was a much wider range of items in 1950 than in 1901 (automobiles, television sets, summer vacations, by way of examples) to compete for the worker's dollars; and the competition had been intensified by the rise of consumer credit. The choices of wearing apparel were more varied, but the kinds usually worn were simpler and lighter and likely to be made of less elaborate materials. Perhaps of minor significance was the fact that work, whether in the home or on a job outside the home, had become prevailingly less strenuous, with less wear and tear on clothing and shoes.

By the time of the 1950 survey of family expenditures, it was clear that American workers had found that they could be better dressed with a smaller relative outlay than could their grandparents. They were more apt to use increases in earnings for buying new automobiles and new kitchen or laundry equipment.

Clothing Expenses of Different Family Members

In the families of industrial wage earners in 1888-91, clothing outlays for the wife were almost one-third less than those for the husband. The New York City Committee on the Standard of Living showed the same relationship in its estimate of necessary clothing in 1907. By the end of World War I, as rising incomes had made possible a more liberal clothing budget, the relative importance of the wife's clothing outlays had increased; average clothing expenditures for wives were only 11 percent less than those for husbands. Since that time, the women in the family have had the largest share of the clothing budget.

In 1934-36, in families of employed workers, women and girls 18 years of age and over spent, on the average, 13 percent more than men and boys in the same age group (clothing expenditures were classified by age and sex, but not by marital status). Clothing expenditures for girls in school rose somewhat more as they grew older than those for boys and continued to rise at an even sharper pace after age 18 (table 13, p. 135). Expenses of both men and women decreased after they reached their early or middle twenties, whether they stayed at home or worked as wage or clerical workers.

The women, however, consistently spent more than men of the same age and in the same work status—nearly 1½ times as much in some instances. These large differences were probably due in part to the fact that the clothing worn by women in different roles was more sharply differentiated than the clothing worn by men, as it is today. When men work around the house or in the garden, they are apt to wear clothes grown old with factory or office wear, but women do not ordinarily cook, clean house, or care for small children in clothes discarded from an office or factory job. When women take part in social affairs they are usually expected to "dress for the occasion," but the man of the family, as a rule, puts on a clean shirt and makes sure that his suit is well pressed.

Expenditures of women clerks in 1934-36 were relatively high as compared with those of women in other work groups. Women between 54 and 60 years old who did clerical work usually spent 75 percent more for clothing than women of the same ages who were working only as housewives, and slightly more than women between 24 and 30 years old who had no jobs outside their homes. However, the older women clerks spent much less than younger ones.

TABLE 13.—*Annual clothing expenditures for members of families of employed wage and clerical workers,[1] by age, sex, and occupation, 1934-36*

[Expenditures expressed as ratios of annual expenditure ($56.68) of male wage earners and clerical workers aged 21 and under 36]

Age	Male				Female			
	Under 5 or at school	At home	Clerical	Wage earner	Under 5 or at school	At home	Clerical	Wage earner
Under 2	0.19				0.19			
2 and under 6	.34				.38			
6 and under 9	.48				.47			
9 and under 12	.53				.56			
12 and under 15	.63				.77			
15 and under 18	.88	0.74	1.02	1.02	1.01	0.94	1.08	1.08
18 and under 21	1.01	.80	1.14	1.13	1.28	1.05	1.60	1.63
21 and under 24		.57	1.14	1.07		1.04	1.66	1.60
24 and under 27		.48	1.13	1.00		1.02	1.64	1.46
27 and under 30		.46	1.10	.96		1.00	1.62	1.36
30 and under 36		.44	1.04	.92		.96	1.58	1.23
36 and under 42		.43	.94	.87		.88	1.48	1.07
42 and under 48		.41	.87	.81		.78	1.35	.94
48 and under 54		.39	.80	.75		.68	1.18	.84
54 and under 60		.37	.75	.69		.58	1.03	.76
60 and over		.35	.65	.60		.40	.78	.67

[1] Data based on clothing expenditures of families of white employed wage and clerical workers in 42 cities.

SOURCE: Money Disbursements of Wage Earners and Clerical Workers, 1934-36, U. S. Bureau of Labor Statistics Bulletin 638, p. 364.

The relationships shown in table 13, and particularly the relatively low expenditures for both women and men at home without paid jobs, may have been considerably affected by attitudes induced by the depression. The presence in the population of large numbers of persons wanting to work but unable to find jobs frequently made those who were employed very conservative about postponable purchases for themselves or other family members. Persons at home were naturally able more readily to get along with old clothes than were those who had jobs.

Clothing outlays in 1950 for women and girls 16 years old and over in families with incomes from $3,000 to $5,000 were 11 to 41 percent above those of men and boys of the same age. The gap was narrowest in the northern small cities and in the southern suburbs and small cities, and largest in northern suburbs, as shown in the following tabulation:

	Average 1950 clothing expenditure		
Region and class of city	Men and boys	Women and girls	
		Amount	As percent of men's and boys'
Large cities:			
North	$121	$151	125
South	127	149	117
West	127	153	120
Suburbs:			
North	113	159	141
South	114	128	112
West	109	132	121
Small cities:			
North	110	124	113
South	121	134	111
West	121	143	118

SOURCE: Study of Consumer Expenditures, Incomes and Savings: Statistical Tables, Urban U. S.—1950, Volumes XIV and XV (University of Pennsylvania, 1957), pp. 114 and 113, respectively.

In the light of the 1934–36 data on clothing expenditures for women and girls at different ages and in different work status groups, it seems likely that the relatively larger average expenditures for women in 1950 were due primarily to the increase in the proportion of women in the labor force, either employed or looking for jobs, as indicated on page 141.

TYPES OF CLOTHING PURCHASED

More satisfactory than expenditures as a measure of the real change in workers' clothing purchases would be a list of the clothing represented by the expenditures recorded in the various family spending surveys. However, the kinds of clothing bought by families of workers in 1901 were not spelled out in detail in the U. S. Bureau of Labor's report on the expenditures of families of wage and clerical workers across the Nation in that year. Therefore, information presented here on actual clothing purchases for the period before the end of World War I comes from other, less comprehensive surveys. The three major later studies of family outlays by the Bureau of Labor Statistics—1917–19, 1934–36, and 1950—do show detailed data on clothing purchases.

The 1917–19 survey covered the outlays of wage and clerical workers' families in 92 cities in 42 States and the figures are more satisfactory than the earlier data, even though they apply only to white families.* The 1934–36 study covered employed workers in 42 cities who did not receive any relief during the year. Since more than half of the city families headed by wage and clerical workers in the 91 cities surveyed in 1950 were in the $3,000–$5,000 income bracket, data from this group are used for the analysis in this chapter. The figures for this group are probably very close to the average purchases by individuals in the families of wage and clerical workers, because differences in the kinds of garments worn by persons in families of the same economic status (but supported by different kinds of work) have greatly diminished.

Men's Apparel

Expenditure figures for men's clothing a decade before the end of the 19th century are of interest even though they cover only broad categories of clothing. The following tabulation summarizes annual outlays for the husband's clothing in 1888–91 in wage earners' families consisting of husband, wife, and children.

Garment	Percent of families reporting expenditure	Average expenditure Per person buying	Per family
Coats, vests, trousers	79	$18.20	$14.42
Overcoats	22	15.81	3.46
Boots and shoes	95	6.29	5.98
Hats	84	2.61	2.20
Underclothes	75	4.62	3.48
Shirts	69	2.75	1.89
Miscellaneous items	88	3.42	2.38
Total			$33.81

SOURCE: Nelson W. Aldrich, Retail Prices and Wages, Senate Report 986, Part 3 (United States Senate, Committee on Finance, 52d Cong., 1st sess., July 19, 1892).

*The information obtained from Negro families was published only in summary form by major categories of expenditures. (See Monthly Labor Review, May, June, and July 1919.) If the clothing expenditures of Negro families were included in the 1917–19 summary, the averages would be somewhat lower, since the incomes of the Negro families were lower.

The most detailed account of city workers' annual clothing purchases in the first decade of the century appears in a report on a survey of family expenditures of workers in New York City. The study was undertaken at the request of the New York Conference of Charities and Correction in order to arrive at a "reliable representation of the standard of living, first, absolutely, for a given time, place, and class of laborers; second, relatively, in comparison with the standard of different times, places, and classes of men." [3] No dependent families were included. Attention was concentrated on families comprising husband, wife, and 2 to 4 children under 16 years old, with family incomes from $500 to $1,000 (the equivalent of about $1,250 to $2,500 in 1950). An annual clothing budget was estimated for a family of 5 "on the basis of the averages of expenditures and the details given in typical schedules."

The clothing needed by the worker himself in 1907 was estimated on this basis to cost $33, distributed as follows:

2 hats or caps	$2.00	4 ties	$0.50
1 overcoat*	5.00	4 handkerchiefs	.30
1 suit	10.00	Summer underwear	1.00
1 pair pantaloons	2.00	Winter underwear	1.50
2 pair overalls	1.50	6 pair hose	.60
3 working shirts	1.00	2 pair shoes	4.00
2 white shirts	1.00	Repair of shoes	1.50
6 collars	.60	Gloves or mittens	.50

*Costs $10 to $15, lasts 2 or 3 years.

SOURCE: Robert C. Chapin, The Standard of Living Among Workingmen's Families in New York City, 1907 (New York, Russell Sage Foundation, Charities Publication Committee, 1909), p. 166.

The purchase of a new suit with an extra pair of trousers every year for the worker himself seems surprising in view of the restricted list of other garments which he purchased. Apparently, insofar as these workers had nightwear, it was made by their wives; there is no discussion of home sewing in the report, although it is stated that a few of the families did some sewing. The data from the New York City survey can hardly be taken as representative of men workers' clothing expenditures throughout the country. There is, it is true, a similarity between the New York City estimate of the cost of clothing needed by the workingman in 1907, and the average expenditures of husbands in families of wage earners in 1888-91. Certain discrepancies, however, limit the conclusions that can be drawn with assurance.

Table 14 shows the number of garments of different types purchased by men covered in 3 studies made by the Bureau of

TABLE 14.—*Average number of garments[1] purchased annually by men and boys over 16 years of age in families of city wage earners and clerical workers, 1917–19, 1934–36, and 1950*[2]

| Garment | 1917–19[3] | 1934–36[4] | 1950—Large cities |||
			North	South	West
Hats and caps	1.6	1.0	0.8	0.9	0.8
Overcoats and topcoats	.2	.3	.2	.2	.2
Raincoats	.1	(5)	(5)	.1	(5)
Suits	.7	.5	.5	.4	.3
Jackets and sport coats		.2	.3	.3	.3
Trousers and slacks	.6	.8	.9	1.2	.9
Overalls, dungarees, work trousers, etc	1.5	.6	1.7	1.8	2.2
Sweaters and jerseys	.2	.2	.2	.2	.1
Shirts	3.9	3.6	4.5	4.9	4.7
Collars	4.4	.2			
Ties	2.3	2.6	1.7	1.8	1.5
Socks, pairs	11.2	12.0	12.4	11.5	11.0
Shoes	2.3	1.7	1.6	1.6	1.4
Underwear:					
Union suits	1.5	1.1	.3	.1	.3
Undershirts	1.0	1.9	3.1	3.3	2.6
Drawers	.9	.2	.2	.1	.1
Undershorts		1.7	3.4	3.9	3.5
Pajamas and nightshirts	.4	.5	.4	.5	.4
House slippers	.2		.1	.1	.1
Galoshes, etc	.6	.4	.2	(5)	.2
Umbrellas	.1				
Handkerchiefs	5.6	5.1	3.8	4.7	2.8
Gloves	4.1	2.8	2.7	1.5	2.4
Average expenditures:					
In current dollars	$71	$49	$121	$127	$127
In 1950 dollars	$121	$95	$121	$127	$127

[1] Garments for which the average quantity is less than 1.0 were not purchased every year; for example, an average quantity of 0.2 means a purchase once every 5 years.
[2] See text (p. 137) for differences in the groups studied in the different periods.
[3] Relates to husbands only.
[4] Includes persons 18 years and over.
[5] Less than 0.05.
SOURCE: *1917–19*—Cost of Living in the United States, U. S. Bureau of Labor Statistics Bulletin 357; *1934–36*—Money Disbursements of Wage Earners and Clerical Workers, 1934–36, U. S. Bureau of Labor Statistics Bulletin 638; *1950*—Study of Consumer Expenditures, Incomes and Savings: Statistical Tables Urban U. S.—1950, Volume XV.

Labor Statistics: one at the end of World War I, one for the middle 1930's, and one covering 1950.

Although employment was at generally high levels in 1917–19, the advances in the earnings of most workers had hardly more than kept pace with the increases in the cost of living since 1907, the year of the New York survey mentioned above. Therefore, it seems unlikely that the kinds of clothing they were buying were generally very different from those of 11 years earlier. (The supply of clothing in the markets was not materially affected by the war situation in World War I.) The revolution in dress which has occurred during the first half of the 20th century had scarcely started at the time of the 1917–19 survey.

139

A comparison of the average number of garments purchased by the men in the 1934–36 survey group with the averages for 1917–19 shows that important changes in dress had occurred in the 17-year interval. The purchase of separate collars had almost disappeared, but this had not yet led to an increase in the average number of shirts men bought. Buying of hats and caps had been cut by slightly more than one-third. The small drop in purchases of suits was offset at least in part by the buying of jackets and separate trousers and slacks. The effect of central heating was already reflected in the increased popularity of undershirts and undershorts as compared with union suits, or undershirts and long underdrawers.

By 1950, the change to more casual clothing for men was established—the vest, for example, had all but disappeared. Men wage and clerical workers bought fewer hats, suits, and ties in 1950 than had the 1934–36 group, but larger numbers of trousers, slacks, and shirts. They continued to buy as many jackets as the 1934–36 group and bought, in addition, sport coats. The comfort and convenience of cotton undershirts and shorts appealed to the men, who bought almost twice the number purchased in 1934–36, and they bought fewer union suits and fewer drawers. People now were less exposed to cold and wet weather and had little need for heavy underclothing. These changes may also explain declines in purchases of men's galoshes, boots, and gloves, and even house slippers; the lighter and more casual styles of men's shoes in 1950 could provide "slipper comforts." Since 1917–19, men have bought slightly fewer overalls and dungarees but more work trousers. Purchases of these items by the 1934–36 group were very low, partly because under depression conditions even employed men "made do" with old clothes, especially for the type of work for which overalls would be used.

In 1950, the average number of garments of different kinds purchased by men workers was very similar in large and small cities and in suburbs in all parts of the country. However, there were some variations which appear to reflect either the milder climate or the greater informality of living in the South and West: in those regions men bought fewer suits and more separate shirts, trousers, slacks, and overalls than in the North; on the other hand, they bought hats and caps somewhat more often in the South. However, these distinctive area patterns did not add up to consistent area differences in the total amounts spent for clothing at given income levels. Apparently the lower expenditures for heavy clothing in the South and West were more than offset by purchases of a greater variety of lighter clothes.

What the statistics do not show is the change in the weight of suits worn by men. When the Bureau of Labor Statistics first studied the weight of wool yard goods used in making suits in 1935, it was found that the most used type of winter suiting weighed 14–16 ounces per yard of 58-inch fabric, and of summer suiting, 11–13 ounces per yard of 56-inch fabric. At the present time, the material used in the most commonly purchased types of winter suits weighs 12½–13½ ounces per yard of 60-inch fabric and in the summer suits, under 10 ounces. The change in the summer suits reflects the use not only of lighter weight wool, but also of mixtures of wool with dacron, nylon, silk, mohair, or rayon.

Women's Clothing

Changes in clothing for women in the first half of the 20th century have been affected by all the factors which brought about changes in men's clothing—more noticeably in the case of styling—and, in addition, by changes in their work status. In April 1957, nearly 35 percent of the females in the population who were 14 years of age and over were either working at jobs outside their homes or looking for such jobs. Exactly comparable figures for 1900 are not available, but from the census figures gathered at the time, it would appear that the proportion of women in these age groups who were in the labor force was not more than 20 percent. Changes in the labor force participation of women 35 to 64 years of age are very much more striking; almost 42 percent of them were working outside the home in April 1957, compared with about 14 percent in 1900.

The woman with a job outside her home has clothing needs quite different from the woman whose work is child care and keeping house for her family. In addition, the family in which the homemaker has money earnings has a larger money income than it would otherwise have had, and she presumably has more to say about how it is spent. Of course, the family with a working wife must make money outlays not necessary when the wife is a full-time homeworker and cannot make economies which were customary before the wife took an outside job. Nevertheless, the increase in the proportion of earners among married women is no doubt one of the factors which has brought about the use of a higher proportion of the family clothing dollar for women's clothing.

The style of women's and girls' clothing has been altered more than that of men's and boys' over the half century. In 1900, women who spent most of their time in heavy physical work at home or in factories wore clothing which was cumbersome and difficult to clean or repair. To be sure, women at home frequently wore a "wrapper" while working around the house. Its uses were related to those of today's "duster," which, however, is more attractively designed. Most women wore full skirts of floor or ankle length, high collars, and long sleeves, tight below the elbow, when they worked outside the home, as well as on ceremonial occasions, if one may judge from surviving pictures.

The data from the study of wage earners' average expenditures in 1888–91 provide the following condensed picture of annual clothing expenditures by workers' wives at the end of the 19th century.

Garment	Percent of families reporting expenditure	Average expenditure Per person buying	Average expenditure Per family
Cloaks and shawls	21	$7.56	$1.57
Dresses	91	10.04	9.14
Boots and shoes	97	4.78	4.62
Hats	67	3.72	2.49
Underclothes	68	4.89	3.31
Miscellaneous	88	2.94	2.04
Total			$23.17

SOURCE: Nelson W. Aldrich, op. cit.

The table of necessary clothing expenditures for the women of the family in New York City for the 1907 study mentioned in connection with men's clothing again shows a striking similarity to the 1888–91 study in the dollar total, but gives more details.

The clothing needed by the woman in a normal family in New York City in 1907 was estimated to cost $23, detailed as follows:

1 hat	$1.50	Winter underwear	$1.00
1 cloak*	2.50	6 handkerchiefs	.45
2 dresses of wash goods	2.50	Gloves or mittens	.50
1 woolen dress	5.00	3 aprons	.50
3 waists	1.50	6 pairs of stockings	.60
1 petticoat	.50	2 pairs of shoes	3.00
Summer underwear	.50	Repair of shoes	1.25
Sundries, linen, etc.	1.70		

*Costs $5, lasts 2 years.
SOURCE: Chapin, op. cit., p. 166.

There is in the report no clue as to whether the cost for the wife's cloak and dresses was for yard goods she would make up, or for ready-to-wear clothes. The report does state, however, that the clothing budget as a whole "presupposes, on the part of the mother, a high grade of efficiency in mending and remaking." In the light of the styles of the period, it seems likely that the money provided only for a length of dress goods and not for a dress. The $1.70 included in the estimated budget for "sundries, linen, etc." also seems very small in view of the fact that it included such substantial articles as corsets and nightgowns.

The 1917–19 family expenditure survey shows no great change in the kinds of clothing bought by workers' wives, with two exceptions. They were beginning to buy silk stockings (32 percent purchased one or more pairs). And some of them were buying lightweight girdles rather than heavy corsets.

The study of employed workers' expenditures in 1934–36 reflects the types of changes which occurred in women's clothing outlays between the end of World War I and the mid-1930's. The decade of the 1920's had been a period of rapid changes in the clothing habits of women, as drastic changes in styles occurred and technological developments caused a substantial drop in clothing prices.

The 1934–36 record shows women spending very much more for silk stockings; on the average, 13 percent of their total clothing outlays in 1934–36, as compared with 1.5 percent in 1917–19. They were spending very much less for hats in the 1930's, and a much larger proportion of the clothing dollar than earlier went for silk and/or rayon dresses. Rayon and cotton gloves were then competing with leather and wool gloves. Underwear had changed radically; corset covers had almost entirely disappeared, and only about one-third as many union suits were purchased. In the mid-1930's, the most commonly worn underclothing for women consisted of a girdle, underpants, a brassiere, and a slip, the last two taking the place of the undershirt, corset cover, and petticoat worn earlier. To a large extent, rayon had replaced cotton as the material for women's underwear.

Changes in women's clothing from the mid-1930's to 1950 were not primarily in the types of garments worn. Women in workers' families bought more clothes in 1950 because they had higher incomes, but they followed earlier trends in the choice of wearing apparel. They bought more suits and sweaters and blouses, more slips and brassieres, many more anklets and socks, and a few more stockings and shoes, than women had bought in the families of workers in 1934–36, as shown in table 15. Hats assumed less importance as younger women continued the wartime habit of wearing head-scarves or going bareheaded. The number of gloves purchased dropped slightly, and the number of handkerchiefs bought was cut by more than one-half, presumably because of the increasing use of paper tissues.

The greatest changes from the mid-1930's were in clothing materials. New fibers (nylon, dacron, orlon, and other synthetic fibers) had been developed, and new finishes made clothing of both the traditional and the new synthetic fibers much easier to care for.

The proportion of the woman's clothing dollar spent for hosiery has varied widely since the early years of the century. In 1907 it was about 2½ percent and in 1917–19 it was 4.7 percent for purchases averaging 5½ pairs of cotton stockings and slightly less than 1 pair of silk. For women and girls 18 and over in employed workers' families in 1934–36, it was 13.7 percent, with average purchases of 10 pairs of silk stockings and 1½ pairs of

TABLE 15.—*Average number of garments[1] purchased annually by women and girls over 16 years of age in families of city wage earners and clerical workers, 1917–19, 1934–36, and 1950* [2]

Garment	1917–19 [3]	1934–36 [4]	1950—large cities		
			North	South	West
Hats	1.2	1.6	0.9	0.9	0.8
Coats	.4	.3	.5	.3	.3
Suits	.2	.1	.3	.4	.3
Jackets		.1	([5])	([5])	.1
Skirts	.6	.1	.6	.6	.5
Sweaters and jerseys	.1	.2	.5	.4	.5
Blouses	1.8	.3	1.2	1.2	1.3
Dresses, street	1.0	2.0	2.3	2.1	1.8
Dresses, house	1.7	1.5	1.1	.9	.9
Aprons	.9	.5	.3	.2	.2
Stockings, pairs	6.3	11.8	13.3	12.4	9.8
Anklets and socks			1.3	.9	1.6
Shoes	1.9	2.2	2.4	2.6	2.3
Slippers	.3	.4	.3	.3	.4
Play clothes, all sports and seasons		.1	.2	.2	.3
Underwear:					
Slips	[6] 1.0	1.7	1.9	2.0	1.5
Pants	1.0	2.2	3.1	4.0	3.3
Girdles and corsets	.9	.5	.5	.3	.5
Brassieres	.3	.8	1.7	1.8	1.7
Union suits and combinations	1.6	.6			
Undershirts and corset covers	2.8	.4			
Nightgowns and pajamas	1.1	.9	.9	1.3	1.0
Wrappers and robes	.1	.1	.2	.2	.2
Rainwear:					
Rain coats	([5])	([5])	([5])	.1	.1
Boots and galoshes	.4	.3	.2	([5])	.1
Umbrellas	.1	.1	.1	.1	.1
Handbags	.3	.6	.7	.7	.6
Gloves	.8	.8	.6	.6	.7
Handkerchiefs	4.3	3.6	1.4	1.2	.7
Average expenditure:					
In current dollars	$64	$55	$151	$149	$153
In 1950 dollars	$107	$108	$151	$149	$153

[1] Garments for which the average quantity is less than 1.0 were not purchased every year; for example, an average quantity of 0.2 means a purchase once every 5 years.
[2] See text (p. 137) for differences in the groups studied in the different periods.
[3] Relates to wives only.
[4] Includes women and girls 18 years and over.
[5] Less than 0.05.
[6] Petticoats.

SOURCE: See table 14.

144

cotton, wool, or rayon hose. For women and girls 16 and over in 1950 in families with incomes from $3,000 to $5,000, the proportion of their clothing dollar spent on nylon stockings ranged from 7.8 percent in suburbs in the West to 11 percent in large cities in the North. Their average purchases ranged between 7 and 13 pairs of nylon stockings, and 1 to 2 pairs of cotton anklets and socks.

Clothing for Children

Since 1900, the availability of new textile fibers and new finishes, as well as increases in productivity in garment manufacturing, have affected clothing expenditures for children as well as for their parents. In addition, the trend toward standardization and greater simplicity of dress is even more apparent in their clothing than in that of their parents. Little girls, as well as little boys, now wear T-shirts and blue jeans, and the overall and the sunsuit have become almost a uniform for the toddler and his slightly older brother or sister.

For the high school boy, school clothes usually include sport shirts, sweaters, leather coats, corduroy and cotton twill slacks or jeans, and "loafer" shoes. For the high school girl, simple blouses, sweaters and jackets, woolen and cotton skirts, socks, and loafers are the rule. These clothes, in standardized designs, can be factory-made in large quantities; this reduces costs and yet provides garments which are comfortable, attractive, and long-wearing.

These more efficient designs for young people's clothing have not, however, reduced the clothing expenditures for the young in relation to those of their parents. The New York City budget for "necessary clothing" compiled on the basis of the 1907 consumption study showed that clothes for a girl aged 10 cost 45 percent as much as her father's and those for a 4- to 6-year-old boy, 36 percent as much. In 1917-19, clothing expenditures for elementary school boys and girls were 55 percent of their father's. In 1934-36, relative expenditures for such children in families of employed workers had dropped to 50 percent, presumably because of the prevailing sense of economic insecurity.

By 1950, however, the younger members of the family were getting a larger share of family clothing outlays. In northern cities, in the income brackets from $3,000 to $5,000, clothing expenditures for boys 6-15 years old ranged from 69 to 77 percent of their father's outlays, and for girls, from 79 to 87 percent. In the South and West, relative expenditures were lower; for boys, they ranged from 54 to 65 percent, and for girls, from 65 to 79 percent of their father's outlays.

All the available evidence on the clothing of children of city wage and clerical workers is that it has improved markedly over the half century. Lower costs resulting from technological improvements in the production of textiles and of clothing, simpler and more functional designs, and the higher average incomes of these families have enabled them to dress their children far more neatly and attractively in the 1950's than in the first decade of the century.

TRENDS IN EXPENDITURES FOR PERSONAL CARE

In the early 1900's, money expenditures by wage and clerical workers for personal care were almost entirely limited to payments to the barber and to the grocery or apothecary shop for soap, hair tonic, and occasionally cologne or perfume.

Minimum budgets set up in the first decade of the century included with "necessary clothing" the annual cost of "barbering" for father and the boys and, under sundries, toilet and laundry soap. The most usual allowance for each man and boy for barbering was $5.20, which, it would seem, covered haircuts only.

Separate expenses for personal care were first recorded in the family expenditure survey of 1917–19. The proportion used for personal care varied little by income level, being 1.1 percent for families with incomes under $1,500 per year, and 1.0 percent for all other families. By 1934–36, families were allotting from 2.0 to 2.3 percent of their expenditures for personal care, depending on income. In 1950, the percentages were substantially the same. (See tables 4, 5, and 6, pp. 42, 44, and 46.)

Technological and price changes have altered the amount and direction of expenditures for personal care items, as for other types of consumer goods. Such items as electric razors and devices for "hairdos" have greatly changed personal care customs. Women's expenditures for beauty parlor services have usually come to exceed men's at the barber shop. Women's expenditures for materials to use in personal care at home have also increased greatly. The woman who polished her nails at the turn of the century did so with a buffer and a little rice powder, but not many women in the families of wage earners and clerical workers appear to have fitted nail polishing into their weekly schedules. Today, with more free time and more money, they customarily give themselves a weekly manicure. In addition, there are materials for skin care and home hairdressing which supplement, or in some cases replace, services at beauty parlors.

The better grooming of workers and their families in the 1950's than early in the century is in no small part a result of the improvement in the plumbing facilities in their homes. It is possible to be well-groomed without a basin with running water and a bathtub or a shower, but difficult; it takes much more time, planning ahead, and the cooperation of all family members, and it is hard to fit in after a long workday.

The following description of grooming problems in the early 1900's among some recent immigrants in New York City highlights the difficulties caused by overcrowding and inadequate plumbing facilities in the large city. Such families were in the minority, but it comes from a man who experienced those conditions and wrote his reminiscences.

> Old people had, in general, an acrid smell . . . . Young people and children merely smelled unwashed . . . . It was natural, though not desirable, for children to have lice in their hair and for grownups to harbor them in the seams of their clothing and underwear . . . . In the visible world, half of which we knew firsthand, and the other half of which we could only imagine, there were, for us, certain unchangeable phenomena: children were dirty and were obliged to scratch their heads; mothers were unkempt and slatternly . . . . my mother periodically subjected my head and my little sister's to whole kettles of water heated to a temperature we were barely able to endure [and] adopted the preventive measure of doing the family wash (in scalding water) as often as twice a week! [4]

As the century has progressed, scientific developments in the control of insect life have reduced the incidence of these problems. But in spite of all the improvements in income, in plumbing, in soaps and detergents, and in hair lotions, personal care and cleanliness problems persist.* Some families still live in dwellings with only a cold water faucet in the kitchen sink or no water at all, and others share a bath with other occupants. The proportion has greatly declined, but the actual number remains large. A 1950 survey by the Bureau of Labor Statistics in 22 cities showed that from 5 to 10 percent of the dwellings had no running water in 6 cities, only cold water in 5 cities, and a shared bath in 8. Yet the recent migrants, as those of earlier decades, expect that they will acquire new skills, earn larger incomes, and have the means to be as well-groomed and as well-dressed as the workers with whom they have deliberately chosen to associate themselves.

---

*The very plethora of cleaning agents, lotions, beauty aids, and cosmetics, with a superabundance of advertising claims and counterclaims, creates a problem not simplified by the marketing of some useless and even harmful preparations and devices, in spite of the efforts of Federal and local pure food and drug agencies.

Footnotes

[1] E.B. Alderfer and H.E. Michl, *Economics of American Industry* (New York, McGraw-Hill Book Co., Inc., 1942), p. 367.

[2] Harry Henderson, The Mass-Produced Suburbs: How People Live in America's Newest Towns (in *Harper's Magazine*, November 1953, p. 29).

[3] Robert C. Chapin, *The Standard of Living Among Workingmen's Families in New York City, 1907* (New York, Russell Sage Foundation, Charities Publication Committee, 1909), p. 3.

[4] Samuel Chotzinoff, *A Lost Paradise* (New York, Alfred Knopf, 1955), pp. 59 and 190.

CHAPTER VII

Health Care: Past Gains, New Goals

> *Health is a state of complete physical, mental, and social well-being and not merely the absence of disease or infirmity.*
>
> *The enjoyment of the highest attainable standard of health is one of the fundamental rights of every human being without distinction of race, religion, political belief, economic or social condition.*
> —Constitution of the World Health Organization.

In the United States, the worker and his family have benefited immeasurably from the triumphs of medical science over disease and the success of public and private agencies in mastering or limiting many of the health hazards which existed at the beginning of the century. At the same time, workers have contributed substantially to this medical progress through their determination to improve living conditions and their interest in health education.

HEALTH PROBLEMS OF URBAN WORKERS IN 1900

The health outlook of the worker and his family in the United States in 1900, compared with today, was much less promising. Many factors contributed to the comparatively poor health prospects of the industrial worker of that day. Knowledge of health hazards was generally inadequate and the worker was unable, in many instances, to pay for adequate medical care even if it was available. Moreover, employers and government were only beginning to recognize their responsibilities in the fields of safety and health.

Lack of Knowledge

All groups in the population suffered from lack of knowledge of the cause and control of many contagious diseases. The importance of good nutrition had not yet been established and few families—even those with greater educational opportunities than those available to the worker—recognized the possibilities of preventive medicine. Municipal control of sanitation was ineffective, and in some cases nonexistent. The public in general was only beginning to recognize the need for basic legislation in matters affecting public health.

Working Conditions

In addition to these general health problems, the industrial worker was faced by others arising from hazardous working conditions over which he had little control, and for which employers and government had as yet accepted little responsibility. Throughout most of the 19th century, little consideration had been given to the health hazards that city life and factory work presented to the worker and his family. Cities were founded or grew from smaller towns with little knowledge or consideration of the complex health problems of urban living. Few factories or other workplaces were built with scientifically planned heating, lighting, ventilation, sanitation, and there was little protection from dangerous machinery, noxious chemicals, and other hazards. This, coupled with the lack of knowledge of how to control conditions even when recognized, resulted in a high industrial accident rate, crippling diseases, and a low life expectancy for workers in many industries. Moreover, in some industries, such as steel in western Pennsylvania, substantial numbers of employees worked 12 hours a day, 7 days a week. Such an exhausting work schedule naturally left these workers an easy prey to disease and to accidents.

The effect of such conditions on working children was particularly severe. The health of children at work was described in a survey of child labor made by the U.S. Bureau of Labor early in the century:

> Many of the children seen in the establishments visited appeared to be undersized, the pinched worn faces, the thin arms and puny bodies of many of them giving evidence that they were underweight. Among the children reported many were physically unfit for the labor required of them. A few who began work before they were 10 years old, though not actually broken down, were at 15 so worn, their energies so far exhausted, that advancement in productive power much beyond the point already reached seemed quite improbable unless a period of complete rest should intervene.[1]

Homework was common in some industries, particularly the garment trades. In the tenements where thousands of immigrants both lived and worked, conditions were primitive, with hazards of tuberculosis, diphtheria, scarlet fever, and other communicable diseases. In 1893, one writer, after describing vividly the sweatshops located in the slums of New York City, stated: "Clothing made in these sweatshops is scattered over the country, carrying germs of diseases to wearers who never dream of the awful conditions under which the goods are made." [2]

In pointing up the advantages to the public of the first label sponsored by a consumers' group to identify goods "made under clean and healthful conditions," the National Consumers' League in 1899 stated that the purchasing public derives from the use of the label the assurance that goods so endorsed have been found to be made in clean and wholesome factories free from contagion and vermin and under the best conditions known in the trade at that time. Certainly the public needed such assurance.

Housing Conditions

Housing conditions as affecting health in a mill town (as distinguished from the frequently described city slums) were described in a study made in Homestead, Pa., in 1908, as follows:

> The green of the parks modifies the first impression of dreariness by one of prosperity such as is not infrequent in American industrial towns. Turn up a side street, however, and you pass uniform frame houses, closely built and dulled by the smoke; and below, on the flats behind the mill, are cluttered alleys, unsightly and unsanitary, the dwelling place of the Slavic laborers. The trees are dwarfed and the foliage withered by the fumes, the air is gray and only from the top of the hill above the smoke is the sky clear blue.
>
> * * * * *
>
> The glaring evils and startling injustices found on every hand in the congested sections of large cities supplied the first and strongest impetus toward social reform in this country. But many of the unwholesome living conditions which we associate with the poorer city neighborhoods are repeated in the average mill town with less excuse and with as bitter effects.[3]

Provisions for sanitary water supplies and sewage disposal were often inadequate. Although nearly all incorporated places of 2,000 or more had public water systems, the water was frequently not filtered or treated to eliminate contamination. A U. S. Bureau of Labor survey in 1898 indicated that 45 percent of the systems used underground sources of supply and 55 percent used surface sources. About 2 percent of those using underground sources filtered the water (in areas using wells, filtration was not always necessary), while about 19 percent of the surface water sources were filtered. Chlorination was not introduced until 1908. Even though the literature of the day emphasized the worst conditions, the following description of the water supply of the mill town mentioned above is interesting:

> The water supply of the borough is drawn from the Monongahela River. This stream is contaminated by the sewage of many small towns, as well as of two cities, McKeesport and Connellsville, the former with a population of about 40,000 and the latter of 10,000.

In addition, the water, some of which drains from the mines, has been used over and over for the processes of steel and coke manufacture, and is impregnated with chemicals, especially sulphuric acid. One Homestead resident said, "No respectable microbe would live in it." . . . While these chemicals may destroy the bacteria to a considerable extent, they are not in themselves ingredients of good drinking water.[4]

Illness and Medical Care

At the beginning of the 20th century, several of the most severe contagious diseases had been brought under some measure of control, e.g., smallpox, yellow fever, typhus, and cholera. Most of these had taken high death tolls in repeated epidemics in earlier years.

Contaminated water, unpasteurized milk, lack of screens, and other unhygienic conditions made typhoid still prevalent, however. Inadequate sanitation, heating, ventilation, and sunlight in many of the homes, with onerous work conditions and poor nutrition, made workers' families particularly susceptible to tuberculosis, influenza, pneumonia, and intestinal disorders, which were among the leading killers of 1900. These conditions also contributed to the high maternal and infant mortality rates, although many of these deaths resulted from ignorance of proper care during pregnancy and childbirth.

When the worker or one of his family got sick, the medical services available were few and comparatively simple. Illnesses viewed as minor were treated with home remedies and patent medicines. For severe illnesses the family doctor was called in. Among families with moderate and lower incomes, even this was not done without serious consideration of the cost involved and whether the family resources could be stretched to cover the bill, or the doctor could be asked to wait for his fee. Often, calling the doctor was delayed until it was too late, especially in cases of childhood diseases. The wife handled the nursing duties with what help she could obtain from relatives and neighbors. When she was ill, the rest of the family and friends did as much as they could, or a practical nurse was called in. In childbirth, midwives often took the place of both doctor and nurse. The dangers were recognized and frequently publicized but the practice continued, particularly among families of recent immigrants and of unskilled native-born workers.

Hospitalization was quite exceptional among all groups. Aside from the cost, many hospitals had served as places for isolating victims of the various plagues of earlier years, and the stigma of their having been "pest houses" still lingered. To many people, a hospital was a place you went to die.

Efforts Toward Improvement

The concern of the Federal Government for workers' health was expressed as early as 1897 by the Commissioner of Labor when he said that if economic efficiency were to be preserved, there must be provision against sickness and unemployment. In the 1901 study of workers' family expenditures, loss of work from illness was reported by over 11 percent of the family heads, with an average of 7.7 weeks of idleness for this reason. An additional 1 percent of the family heads were idle from accidents and another 4 percent from sickness combined with other causes. The social welfare literature of those years records fully the tragedy caused by illness and work injuries.

The public was also beginning to be concerned about statements such as one which appeared in the January 1903 Bulletin of the Department of Labor:

> Every epidemic, be it typhoid, smallpox, scarlet fever, dysentery, cholera, etc., draws its greatest army of victims from [factory workers]. For every death that occurs among the richer and higher classes, there are many in the working class. It is the workmen engaged in unhealthy factories first of all who fill the hospitals and their death chambers. . . . To understand the evils which threaten the industrial classes and to search for their remedy is one of the pressing needs of the day.[5]

Employers in the lumber, mining, oil, and railroad industries had pioneered in the provision of medical care for employees as they expanded into new and frequently isolated areas after the Civil War. Some employers in these industries organized extensive medical staffs and facilities and a few built hospitals which are still in operation. At the turn of the century, progressive employers in other industries were beginning to recognize the importance of improving the health and living conditions of their employees.

In an exhibit prepared for the Louisiana Purchase Exposition in 1903 and designed to "demonstrate the nature of our institutions and their adaptation to the wants of the people," the U. S. Bureau of Labor cited the provision by some employers of such facilities as recreational clubs, free medical and health centers, general educational classes, and instructions in domestic science. The report on the exhibit also commented that "in many factories excellent bathing facilities are now found where formerly no adequate provision was made and quite generally it is found that greatly improved sanitary appliances of various kinds have replaced the conditions of a decade ago." In addition, "the furnishing of hot lunches and even dinners to employees at a nominal price is a feature of very many establishments." Moreover, "free sick and accident insurance are sometimes given . . . while the actual contribution by the employer of the whole or a part of the wages of the disabled employee is the practice in some establishments." [6] However, the major part of the exhibit described the work done by 16 companies to provide modern sanitary dwellings for their employees. While this work was thought to be representative of efforts to help workers in the improvement of home conditions, the report noted that a thorough canvass at that time failed to disclose any other companies that were engaged in similar work.

The workers themselves sought to overcome the obstacles encountered in paying for adequate medical care. Low wages, irregular employment, lack of unemployment insurance and old-age annuities and even workmen's compensation were some of the obstacles.

Among immigrants, in particular, as one author observed, "few households had the resources to take care of their own when illness struck, or accident; fewer still to extend aid to relatives or neighbors. . . . In illness as in death, the mutual benefit society came increasingly to be the main reliance of all immigrants." [7]

Mutual benefit associations had first appeared in the 1860's and 1870's and spread rapidly to a wide variety of industries and businesses. Some were initiated, administered, and financed by the workers, some by employers, and some jointly. Benefit programs were also important in the early days of labor unions, but in only a few cases did labor unions expand their benefit activities to provide medical services.

GROWTH IN HEALTH SERVICES

Hospitals

No area of health services has had a more striking development than the hospital. Not only are there more hospital facilities available today, but the hospital itself is radically different from its counterpart of 1900.

The number of hospitals increased 60 percent between 1909 and 1955, from 4,359 to 6,956, but the number of hospital beds increased 280 percent, showing the trend toward larger hospitals. Even with the growth in the population, the number of hospital beds available for all purposes rose from 4.6 to 9.8 per thousand population during this period. Furthermore, the average hospital stay is shorter today, so more patients can use each bed in the course of a year.

The hospital of the early 1900's would today hardly be recognizable. It was small and often organized for handling a specific disease. Its facilities were very limited and its sanitary conditions were often poor. Prejudice existing against hospitals at that time was not unwarranted.

In contrast, today's hospital provides skilled medical and surgical attention and nursing care. Larger hospitals have organized separate departments for special activities such as diagnosis, dietetics, physical and occupational therapy, medical records, and even social service. Hospitals have tended to become major centers of health activities not only for the direct care of patients but also for medical training and research and for public health education. The hospital clinic and dispensary is important as a free or minimum-cost source of medical care on an "ambulatory" or "outpatient" basis.

Health Service Personnel

Evidence of the improvement in medical care since 1900 is also found in the increases in the numbers of health service personnel and in the improved quality and scope of their services. Because of the growing complexity of medical diagnosis and treatment and the ever-broadening base of health services, many health service occupations exist today that were unknown at the beginning of the century.

The total number of physicians in the United States was about 120,000 in 1900, about 1 physician for every 633 persons. In 1955, there was a total of 218,000 physicians, 1 for every 752 persons. Although the relative number of physicians has become smaller, the amount and quality of their service have increased. With the advent of the automobile, the physician has been able to take care of many more cases than could his predecessor of the horse and buggy days. Moreover, the physician today is better trained for his work, as medical educational requirements have moved upward with the tide of medical advances. In 1910, not only were both premedical and medical educational requirements in general very low by today's standards, but many medical schools were lax in enforcing minimum requirements. On the other hand, today's medical student, after a minimum of 3 years of premedical college study, must successfully complete an intensive 4-year medical course plus 1 year's internship in an accredited hospital. Many also complete postgraduate study. Much of the work formerly done by physicians is now handled by assistants, technicians, and nurses.

The 30,000 dentists in 1900 represented 1 dentist to every 2,564 persons; the 75,000 in 1950, 1 to every 1,695 persons, and approximately this same ratio held in 1955. The high incidence of dental defects among men considered for recruitment in World War I was a stimulus for improving dental services and techniques. The

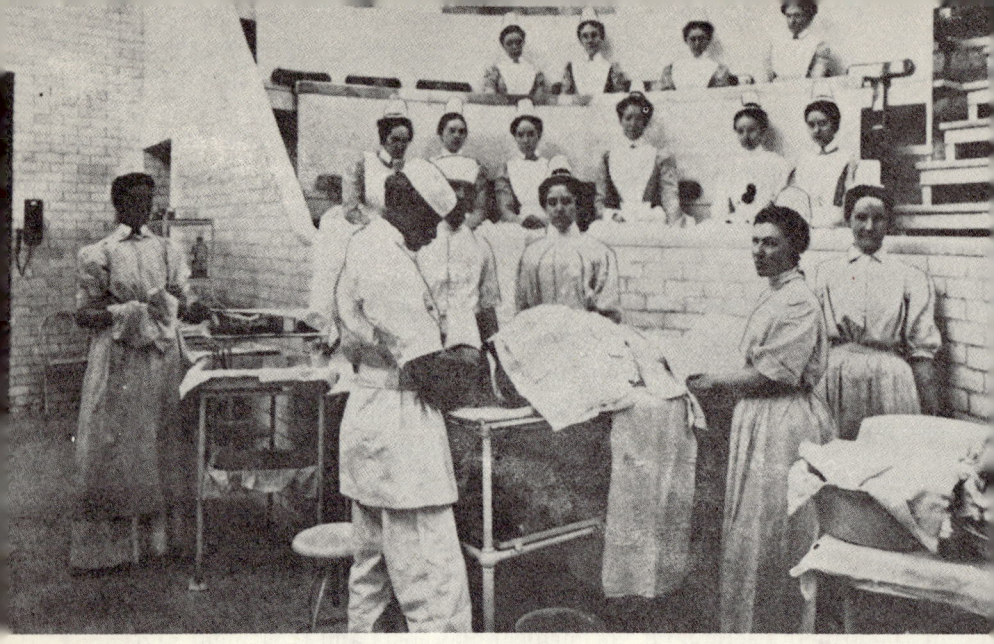

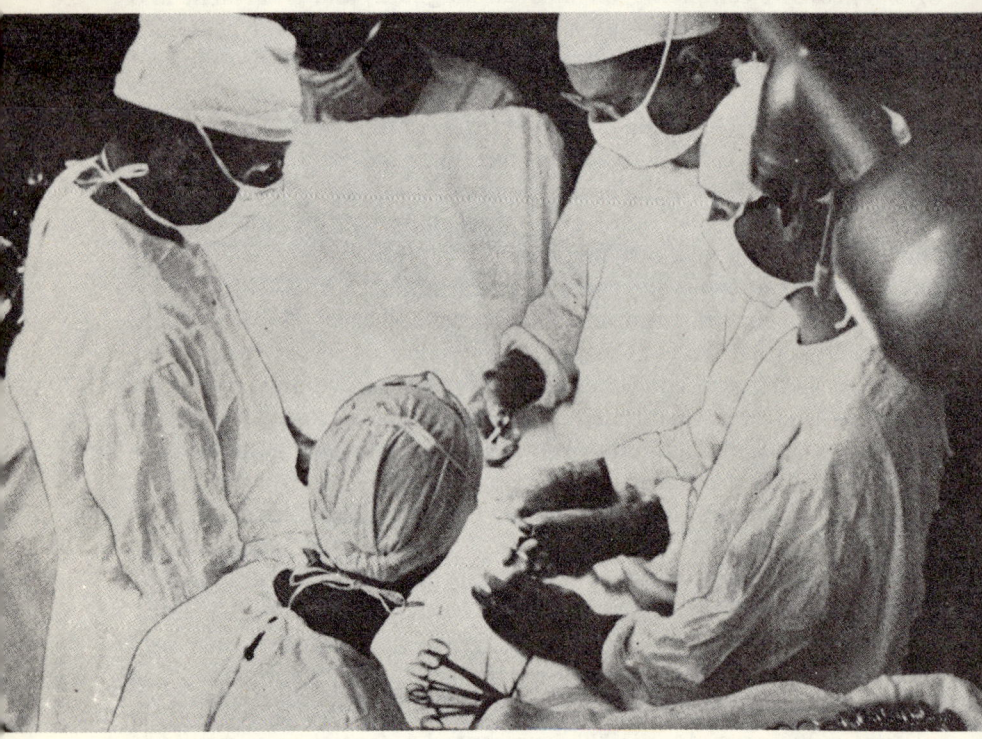

THE CRISIS—Workers of today are longer lived and healthier than their grandparents. Much of this improvement is due to scientific advances in such fields as antibiotics, radiotherapy, and epidemiology. But it is at the point of the surgeon's knife that the question of survival becomes of the most immediate concern to the patient. These are photographs of operating rooms of 1900 and 1950.

dentist's service has also been enhanced through the utilization of dental hygienists and dental laboratories.

The steady and marked increases that took place in the relative numbers of professional nurses reflect the tremendous growth in hospital services. In 1900, there were 12,000 nurses in the United States, or only 1 nurse to 6,250 persons. The nurse-population ratio increased manyfold in the next 30 years; in 1930, there were 214,000 nurses, 1 to every 571 persons. Further increases brought the total to 430,000 in 1955, 1 nurse to every 387 persons. The greatly increased demand for nursing during the first world war focused attention on the need for better nursing education and training. Nursing schools today—in contrast to 1900, when only a few required a high school education for entry, and curriculums and clinical training were generally poor—have high scholastic entry requirements and offer well-rounded programs in basic medical subjects and in actual care of all kinds of diseases.

The changed pattern of the Nation's health force is indicated by the fact that physicians, dentists, and nurses (including student nurses) no longer constitute the bulk of health service personnel. In 1955, they accounted for only about 45 percent of all persons employed in health service occupations. The greatest increases in auxiliary health personnel occurred in the years following World War II. Auxiliary nursing personnel—practical nurses, nurses' aids, attendants, ward maids, and orderlies—increased in number from about 182,000 in 1940 to almost 340,000 in 1950. During this same period, the number of medical laboratory and X-ray technicians, physical and occupational therapists, medical and psychiatric social workers, psychologists, dietitians, and nutritionists rose from 57,000 to 93,000. There also were significant increases in the numbers of such other auxiliary medical workers as pharmacists, optometrists, medical record librarians, and public health educators.

Government Health Assistance

In the effort to improve health conditions, the U. S. Public Health Service has played an important part. By 1900, this agency, established in 1798 to provide hospital care for merchant seamen,* had enlarged its activities, but according to C. E. A. Winslow, a noted sanitarian, sanitation and control of communicable disease still comprised the whole of public health activities. The Service extended its activities in these areas and took on many more, including the control of venereal disease during and following World War I. Its current program covers many phases of

---

*This service was financed by a 20-cent-a-month fee deducted from seamen's wages, probably the first prepaid medical care in this country.

health—efforts to control tuberculosis, pneumonia, cancer, and heart disease, mental and general health services, dental and industrial hygiene, training professional personnel in public health and medical sciences, and others.

Much of the governmental activity in the field of health has been on a cooperative basis. As early as 1917, the Public Health Service cooperated with the States, furnishing them technical, administrative, and financial assistance in carrying out local health programs. (Up to that time, larger communities usually had designated some person or a board as responsible for health, but the extent of the financial resources, authority, abilities, and effectiveness varied widely.) With the passage of the Sheppard-Towner Act, in 1921, a cooperative program had been launched for attacking the maternal and infant mortality problems. Between July 1924 and June 1929, 1,594 permanent local child health and prenatal health consultation centers were established. Several years after the expiration of the Sheppard-Towner Act, Federal grants-in-aid to the States for maternal and child health programs were again made available under a provision of the Social Security Act of 1935. The first large appropriations authorized by this statute for continuation and extension of these grants-in-aid programs stimulated communities to increase the resources available for this purpose. Since World War II, under the Hill-Burton Act of 1946, one of the major cooperative programs has involved the construction of public and nonprofit hospitals, diagnostic and treatment centers, rehabilitation centers, and nursing homes.

Other Federal or State government programs which make provision for personal health services include hospital and medical care for veterans, aid to crippled children, vocational rehabilitation, public assistance for needy persons, workmen's compensation, and temporary disability (or sickness) insurance.

Total health expenditures under government programs which provide either directly or indirectly for personal health services are estimated to have risen from $275 million in the year ended June 30, 1929, to $3.2 billion in 1956. These expenditures represented about 9 percent of the total cost of such services in the earlier year and more than 21 percent in 1956.

Voluntary Health Agencies

Invaluable health services have been provided through a wide variety of nonprofit organizations, most of them supported in whole or in part by contributions for religious and philanthropic purposes. In 1955, 13 percent of an estimated $5,900 million of such contributions was donated for health purposes. Additional contributions to welfare agencies, many of which provide some health services, brought the total for health and welfare purposes to $1,925 million. The share of total contributions allocated to health agencies had more than doubled since 1940, and the amount was nearly 11 times as much, representing nearly 7 percent of the $11.6 billion spent in 1955 by consumers for medical care (including expenditures for hospital construction).

Part of these funds went to nearly 70 health agencies that solicit funds nationally, including such organizations as the National Tuberculosis Association, which was founded more than 50 years ago, and the American Red Cross. These agencies not only provide individuals with care and services but also support educational and research programs dealing with many diseases, e.g., cancer, poliomyelitis, arthritis, muscular dystrophy, multiple sclerosis, and cerebral palsy.

Churches and private social service agencies, through private hospitals and community centers, have also long been active in health work. Important sources of funds for these agencies are the united funds and community chests in various communities—1,873 such fund-raising campaigns were carried on in 1955.

A most impressive expansion in the activities of local health agencies has occurred in the case of clinics. In 1900, there were probably less than 150 clinics in the country, including those attached to hospitals (out-patient clinics) and those conducted independently. By 1931, there were over 50 times as many (7,727), with an estimated 36 to 45 million visits by patients. Since patients made an average of 3 to 5 visits per year, the total number of patients treated may be estimated at 7 to 11 million.

Out-patient clinics attached to hospitals were set up in sections of the country with the greatest industrial development and generally in the largest cities. The large influx of immigrants between 1900 and 1914 and the consequent increase of low-income wage earners in large cities prompted doctors to take the lead in developing out-patient clinics.

Independent clinics, primarily the work of voluntary and governmental health agencies, were generally established to develop preventive measures for health education purposes. In addition to the United States Public Health Service, voluntary agencies such as the nationwide health associations have been active in the establishment of these clinics.

Industrial Medical Services

Numerous industrial concerns provide in-plant medical services of one kind or another for their employees. The Public Health Service estimated that in 1947 about 40 percent of the country's industrial workers were employed in concerns offering some health protection, with the majority of these employed in manufacturing. A 1948 survey of 333 companies of all sizes in over 30 manufacturing and nonmanufacturing industries (with total employment of 1.6 million) by the National Industrial Conference Board showed that medical services provided employees included emergency care for sickness and injury on the job, physical examination, diagnostic and other special services such as health education, counseling, and industrial and mental hygiene programs. Naturally the scope of such programs varied from company to company; a few illustrations suggest the prevalence of the various services. Periodic physical checkups were either required or provided at the employee's request in over half of the companies and about one-fourth provided X-rays, urinalyses, and blood studies. More than one-fourth of the companies made available anti-influenza and cold vaccines and vitamin tablets.

A number of unions have established health centers which provide medical, and in some cases dental, service for members and their families. Currently, there are about 50 such centers in the United States.

More widespread protection has, of course, been achieved through the health and welfare provisions of collective bargaining agreements, which currently cover upwards of 12 million workers. As only a minority of these plans are the service type—as distinguished from insurance or indemnity plans—they are discussed in the section on Paying for Medical Care (p. 171).

HEALTH ADVANCES

Pure Food and Drugs

Most of the patent medicines which were so widely used in 1900 appear to have been ineffectual but harmless except when substituted for needed professional care. Some were found to be dangerous, but their sale was not effectively controlled. Moreover, adulteration of food, sometimes in an effort to preserve it, led to health hazards. An important step toward remedying such conditions was the passage by the United States Congress of the 1906 Pure Food and Drug Act. The Food, Drug, and Cosmetic Act of 1938, which superseded the 1906 law, materially strengthened the power of the U. S. Food and Drug Administration to protect the public against contaminated and harmfully adulterated foods. In the case of drugs, the new law required that adequate directions for use and warnings against misuse and possible deterioration be placed on drug labels. It also required label declaration of drugs likely to be habit forming and, with qualifications, listing of ingredients and amounts thereof contained in drugs.

These requirements are enforced through inspection activities, and violators are subject to criminal prosecution or injunction actions.

Control of Disease

Early in the 20th century, disease prevention centered on a group of communicable diseases eventually controlled through sanitation measures. Typhoid, for example, was handled by treating water supplies, controlling sewage disposal, and pasteurizing milk, with a consequent reduction in the death rate per 100,000 population from 31.3 in 1900 to 7.6 in 1920. Typhoid caused only 50 deaths in the United States in 1955. Helpful, too, was the war on insect carriers of disease, even the simple and direct expedient of screening doors and windows. Complementing these environmental controls, advances in the vaccines have contributed greatly to the prevention of infectious diseases.

Reductions in infant and maternal death rates were achieved by a combination of increased birth attendance by physicians, better hospitals and drugs, and widespread educational programs on proper care. Maternal deaths per 10,000 live births dropped from 60.8 in 1915, when a system of birth-registration areas was established, to 4.7 in 1955. Mortality rates for infants under 1 year declined from 99.9 per 1,000 live births in 1915 to 26.4 in 1955. Death rates per 100,000 population from diphtheria, measles, and whooping cough were 40.3, 13.3, and 12.2, respectively, in 1900 and 0.1, 0.2, and 0.3, respectively, in 1955.

In recent years, special emphasis has been directed to the chronic diseases, including such major problems of the past as diabetes, pernicious anemia, syphilis, and malaria. Tuberculosis, congenital heart disease, and rheumatic fever are among 30 other chronic diseases that are now being brought under control.

Improved vaccines have been effective in curbing many of the virus diseases. The fact that several of these diseases, influenza and poliomyelitis among them, are now in a measure preventable represents substantial progress in this area.

Among the new therapeutic aids that have greatly increased the cure rate of a number of diseases are the antibiotic drugs. The discovery of the sulfa drugs, beginning in 1935, was followed by the development of penicillin in the early years of World War II. Experiments with a new source, the actinomycetes, in the ensuing years have added other drugs to the growing list of antibiotics. These drugs have proved highly efficacious in the treatment of a great variety of infections—meningitis, pneumonia, whooping cough, and osteomyelitis, for example.

Heart diseases comprise the leading cause of death in the Nation today. Concentrated research has been carried on in recent years on the heart diseases of middle and old age—hypertension and arteriosclerosis (hardening of the arteries). A great deal of progress has also been made in the heart diseases of childhood, largely as a result of research regarding rheumatic fever and congenital heart disease, where new surgical techniques have been developed.

Extensive research has been carried on for the past 30 years in the Nation's second cause of death—cancer. The cause is still unknown, but the researchers have found clues as to where the solution lies in the study of genetics and of viruses and hormones. In cancer, surgery and irradiation are still the only recognized treatment. The cure rate for operable cancer is now more than 30 percent.

The contributions of medical research in the control of disease have been accompanied by marked gains in surgical techniques in many fields of medicine. Much has been done, for example, through surgery to restore to useful lives persons who would otherwise have been permanently disabled.

Lengthening the Life Span

What effect have these medical advances had on workers' families and their way of life? Progress in medical knowledge has contributed to an increase in the average life expectancy for white boy babies from 48.2 years in 1900 to 67.3 years in 1955; for white girl babies, 51.1 to 73.6 years. For nonwhite infants, the rise in life expectancy has been even more striking: for boys, it increased from 32.5 to 61.2 years, and for girls, from 35.0 to 65.9 years. Longer life expectancy and improved health have increased the earning power of the worker, and given him assurance that normally he will live to raise and educate his children, that his wife will not die in childbirth, and that his children will survive childhood without dangerous illnesses. This knowledge has contributed to his willingness to change his spending and saving habits. The emphasis placed on sanitation, nutrition, and recreation in health education programs has undoubtedly stimulated demand for a wide range of consumer goods and services from vitamin capsules to a modern house in the suburbs.

COSTS OF MEDICAL CARE FOR WORKERS' FAMILIES

The costs of medical care, unlike most other family expenses, are largely uncertain and subject to extreme variations among families and from time to time for the same family. In the early part of the century, workers' families experienced great difficulty in meeting medical expenses. Many workers' families were unable to pay for adequate medical care and did not receive it. (The very poorest families often received free medical care, mainly from charitable sources.) Family incomes in the early 1900's provided only a small margin beyond requirements for food, housing, and clothing. Since the late 1930's, higher real incomes of workers and new methods of payment for medical care, coupled with greater availability and higher quality of many health services, have made it possible for workers to obtain more and better medical care. However, this greatly improved medical care has increased in cost, particularly with respect to hospital charges.

The net effect of these changes is revealed by the changing pattern of expenditures for medical care reported by workers' families in surveys in 1901, 1917-19, 1934-36, and 1950. Some idea of the adequacy of the medical care received can be gained by comparing these expenditures with estimated costs of adequate care as specified in various family budget and medical studies.

Medical Care Expenditures

Over the first half of this century, city workers' families generally more than doubled the proportion of their total expenditures used for medical care. The 1901 survey of family expenditures indicated that they then used, on account of "sickness and death" (not merely medical care but funeral expenses as well), an average of only 2.7 percent of their total expenditures. Workers' families in 1950 devoted to medical care (not including such items as funeral expenses) an average of 5.1 percent. The change has added meaning because the 1901 families averaged 4 members, the 1950 group, 3.4. Even more significant, families were spending roughly 4 times as much for medical care in 1950 as in 1900, in dollars of equivalent purchasing power, and each dollar bought better care.

Types of Medical Services Obtained. Little is known of how the 1901 expenditures were distributed among the various types of services. It is reasonable to assume that most of the expense was for services of doctors, dentists, and midwives and for medicines, medical supplies, and appliances with relatively little for hospital care. The reports also included burial expenses.

Table 16 shows how urban workers' families allocated their medical care expenditures to various goods and services in 1917–19, 1934–36, and 1950. Although the categories are not strictly comparable, it is evident that proportionately less is being spent in direct payments for doctors' and hospital services and more in indirect payments for these services through various insurance plans. Nevertheless, it becomes apparent that the importance of hospital care has increased when allowance is made for the fact that it accounted for an estimated two-thirds of prepaid medical care expenses in 1950. (See discussion of health insurance, p. 173.)

TABLE 16.—*Percent distribution of medical care expenditures by wage and clerical workers' families, 1917–19, 1934–36, and 1950*

Type of expenditure	1917–19	1934–36	1950
Total medical care:			
Amount	$64	$59	$200
Percent	100	100	100
Direct expenditures:			
Physicians	[1] 53	39	34
Hospital	[1] 8	10	5
Nursing care	5	1	1
Dentist	14	18	15
Eyeglasses	3	5	4
Medicines, drugs, and appliances	17	17	17
Other medical care	[2]	3	5
Prepaid medical care	[3]	7	19

[1] Hospital expenses in 1917–19 include physicians' fees while patient was hospitalized.
[2] Less than 0.5 percent.
[3] Some of the reported expenditure of $3.47 for "lodges, clubs, societies" can be assumed to have been for sickness and death benefits.

SOURCE: *1917–19*—Cost of Living in the United States, U.S. Bureau of Labor Statistics Bulletin 357; *1934–36*—Money Disbursements of Wage Earners and Clerical Workers, 1934–36, U.S. Bureau of Labor Statistics Bulletin 638; *1950*—Unpublished Bureau of Labor Statistics data for wage and clerical worker families in a 17-city subsample from the Survey of Consumer Expenditures in 1950.

Comparison of workers' medical care expenditures with those of the population as a whole provides another measure of the adequacy of the care obtained by the workers. A study of expenditures for all personal health services in 1953 made by the Health Information Foundation (a group sponsored by the drug, pharmaceutical, chemical, and allied industries) indicated that United States families in general spent 37 percent for physicians, 20 percent for hospitals, 15 percent for medicines, 13 percent for other medical goods and services, and 16 percent for dentists. The distribution of expenses by wage and clerical workers' families in 1950 given in table 16, when adjusted by allocating two-thirds of prepaid medical care to hospitals and one-third to physicians, is very similar to the Health Information Foundation distribution.

Differences by Occupational Group and Region. Within the three broad geographic regions, medical expenditures in 1901 were about equal for families of clerical and sales workers and skilled wage earners. In the North, families of semiskilled workers tended to spend less than the clerical and skilled, and unskilled workers the least. Medical expenditures of semiskilled and unskilled workers in the West and South, however, exceeded those of clerical and skilled workers, which may be due in part to their greater expenditures for "burial insurance," which were included in the medical care category.

For all classes of workers combined, the level of "sickness and death" expenditures in 1901 was the same in the North and West and somewhat higher in the South. Fewer families in the West than in the North or the South reported medical care expenditures, which suggests a lower incidence of illness in that less populated area as well as a more limited availability of services. Medical care expenditures (averaging $9.23) by only 39 percent of workers' families in the Far West (Colorado, California, and Washington) are further evidence of the existence of these conditions.

In 1950, the relative positions of the regions with respect to the average medical care expenditure of workers' families (including 1-person families) had changed. There was practically no difference in the proportion of families reporting medical expenses, but the average expenditure in the South was lowest, and in the West was highest. Within each region, the average expenditures of the clerical and the skilled workers' families were about the same. Semiskilled workers' families spent less than clerical and skilled workers in all three regions, but used about the same percent of their incomes for medical care. Expenditures of the unskilled workers, especially in the South, were substantially lower than those of the other groups.

Item	Medical care spending by urban wage and clerical workers' families [1] in the—		
	North	South	West
	1901		
Average expenditure:			
All families	$20	$24	$20
Families reporting such expenditure	27	27	30
Percent of families reporting such expenditure	76	86	68
	1950		
Average expenditure:			
All families	$189	$152	$200
Families reporting such expenditure	193	160	206
Percent of families reporting such expenditure	98	95	97

[1] The 1950 data include 1-person "families"; the 1901 survey covered families of 2 or more.

The preceding tabulation compares expenditures, in dollars, by region, in 1901 and 1950. Comparative prices of the various items of medical care for the 2 years are not available, but consumer prices in general were roughly 3 times as high in 1950 as in 1901.

Influence of Family Size and Income. Studies at the beginning of this century do not tell us exactly how medical care expenditures differed for families of different size and income. That many of the very lowest income families received free medical care, if they had any at all, is suggested by the following comment from one local first-hand study in 1908:

> ... expenses incurred for health count as a luxury to be indulged in only with increasing income. When, for instance, a child is ill, the state of the pocketbook, no less than the seriousness of the disease, determine whether the doctor shall be called. Tonics for the rundown in springtime are dispensed with in a laborer's home. Perhaps the tendency in this direction that is most serious in its results is the custom of relying upon midwives in confinement. While this is more frequent among the foreigners, many English-speaking women call in midwives because their fees are much smaller and because they help in housework. There are no visiting nurses ... whose assistance can be secured for an hour or so.[8]

In 1917–19 and again in 1934–36, surveys showed that workers' families increased their medical care expenditures as incomes increased, and at about the same rate, so that medical expenses represented about the same percentage of total spending at each income level. With the much higher real incomes of 1950, relative spending for medical care decreased as income increased. In that year, families of wage earners and clerical workers used an average of 6.7 percent of their total expenditures for medical care in the lowest reported income range (under $1,000) and 4.0 percent in the highest range ($10,000 and over).

The 1950 pattern is that usually associated with items considered as "necessities" in the family budget. The fact that it has begun to appear for medical care in the spending patterns of workers' families indicates the high order of importance they place on such expense. It also suggests that some measure of satisfaction of this need has been attained, because as workers go up the income scale they do not devote *all* of their increased income to medical care or even increase their expenditures for this purpose proportionately.

Although the proportion of total workers' family expenditures allocated to medical care in 1950 decreased with increases in income, the number of dollars spent per person rose with income except in the 3 lowest income classes, as shown below:

Income class	Family size	Average expenditure— Per family	Average expenditure— Per person	Expenditure per family as percent of total expenditures
All incomes	3.4	$200	$59	5.1
Under $1,000	2.3	112	49	6.7
$1,000 and under $2,000	2.9	102	35	5.3
$2,000 and under $3,000	3.1	150	48	5.4
$3,000 and under $4,000	3.4	194	57	5.4
$4,000 and under $5,000	3.5	221	63	5.0
$5,000 and under $6,000	3.7	246	66	4.7
$6,000 and under $7,500	3.9	294	75	4.8
$7,500 and under $10,000	4.2	333	79	4.7
$10,000 and over	4.5	411	91	4.0

Similar declines in proportionate expenditures for medical care with rises in incomes were found for all United States families in the 1953 survey of the Health Information Foundation. The share of income going for medical care was 11.8 percent for families with incomes under $2,000, 6.1 percent for incomes of $2,000–$3,499, and 3.0 percent for incomes over $7,500.

Adequacy of Expenditures

One important question is left unanswered by the records of family expenditures for medical care: How adequate were these expenditures to buy the medical care needed by these families? From time to time in the past 50 years, there have been attempts to establish the cost of various standards of living. For this purpose, budgets which described the quantities of goods and services needed to achieve a specified level of living for a workingman's family were developed and their costs estimated.

In the earliest of these budgets, little special attention was given to medical care; the average expenditure usually was assigned to this item without any attempt to determine its adequacy. As techniques for developing budgets advanced and improved standards of adequacy were developed, more valid estimates of the cost of adequate medical care were made.

Thus, meaningful comparisons can be made between expenditures and budget estimates beginning with the middle 1930's. The Works Progress Administration's maintenance and emergency budgets for March 1935 represent the first major attempt to arrive at costs for a large population. (See item 18, table 28, p. 237.) These budgets were prepared for 59 cities throughout the country and the costs for all cities combined were also calculated. The maintenance budget's estimated cost of medical care of $52 for a 4-person family compares with an expenditure of $59 in 1934–36 by families of employed wage earners and clerical workers, with average family size 3.6 persons, or a budget cost of $13 and an expenditure of $16 per person. Thus, the average amount spent by employed workingmen's families on medical care during this depression period was slightly above "an adequate standard of living at the lowest economic level."

In 1947, the Bureau of Labor Statistics developed the City Worker's Family Budget—a "modest but adequate" level of living for a wageworker's family of 4 persons—husband, wife, a boy 13 years old, and a girl 8 years old. (See items 19 and 20, table 28, p. 237.) The items included in the budget were determined from information on the pre-World War II spending patterns of families who had attained this level of living. The report for this study describes the allowances for medical and dental care as follows:

> The amount of medical care received . . . can best be measured in the number of home and office calls on physicians. These ranged from a low of about 2.3 calls per person in the lower brackets to about 6.0 calls per person in the higher income brackets. The budget level is determined at about 4.4 calls per person.
>
> The dental care budget was worked out in the same fashion and is slightly over 1 case every 2 years per person.
>
> The needs for medical and dental care, as services directly related to physical health, probably will eventually be formulated in a set of actuarial standards approved by the medical and dental profession and other informed authorities. At present, the detailed and authentic statistical data necessary to the formulation of such a set of standard requirements do not exist. It is, therefore, not possible to adapt the budget determination of the medical care requirements to any set of standards corresponding to those used for food and housing.
>
> The medical and dental standards established in this budget are characteristic of an income level above that of the other groups of goods and services. This corresponds to the generally accepted observation that the majority of United States families have not been receiving a satisfactory volume of these essential services. There is considerable evidence that the medical care sought by families at all income levels is gradually increasing. This increase reflects both more widespread use of insurance plans, credit arrangements, and medical prepayment plans and also increased public education in the necessity of more adequate medical and dental care.[9]

When this budget was priced in 10 cities in October 1949, the costs of medical care for this 4-person family ranged from $176 to $248, with a median cost of $182. On a per-person basis, this would be a range of $44 to $62, with a median of about $46. Wage-earner and clerical-worker families in 1950, averaging 3.4 persons, spent an average of $200 per family, or about $59 per person. (Average prices of medical care rose less than 2 percent between 1949 and 1950.) Since the budget included medical goods and services characteristic of those received by relatively high-income families in prewar years, the fact that the 1950 average expenditures exceeded the 1949 median budget cost is additional evidence that workers' families have gone a long way toward meeting their medical care needs.

Variability in Medical Costs. "The principal problem in the costs of medical care devolves not from the average cost but from the variation in cost." [10] This statement from a 1928–31 study echoed the theme of reports on conditions of workers' families in 1900 and is still true today. If all families could expect to have only the average expenditure for medical care, currently about 4 or 5 percent of their income, this could be budgeted and probably met without undue hardship. In the 1928–31 study, however, it was found that the average medical expenditure for families with incomes of less than $1,200 was $49, but that 11 percent of these families incurred over 50 percent of the total medical expenses reported by that income group.

Similar findings were reported from the 1950 BLS expenditure survey: 11 percent of all the families had 40 percent of the total medical expenditures and 8 percent of the families with incomes of less than $1,000 incurred about 50 percent of the medical care costs of that group. A relatively small proportion of families paid for a large proportion of the total bills for each income class. (See chart 8.) Of the families whose medical expenses exceeded $400, the proportion who had health insurance decreased as the level of expenditures rose. This suggests that the extent of participation in prepaid or insured health plans may be a factor in the variability of expenditures for medical care.

Free Medical Care. One further difficulty in assessing the adequacy of medical care received by examining average family expenditures is that frequently families receive some medical care free. Often this is of a preventive nature—periodic physical examinations under an in-plant medical service program, for example—and is overlooked by families reporting in the surveys. They may also neglect to report free medical care for work-connected injuries and for military-service disabilities. In addition to such legally required compensation, workers increasingly have obtained from employers contractual rights under health and welfare or insurance plans which reduce their direct costs for medical care, and the benefits received under these rights may or may not be reported in expenditure surveys. Moreover, it is impossible to assign a monetary value to the benefits which accrue to the individual worker through the very large public expenditures and philanthropic con-

Chart 8.

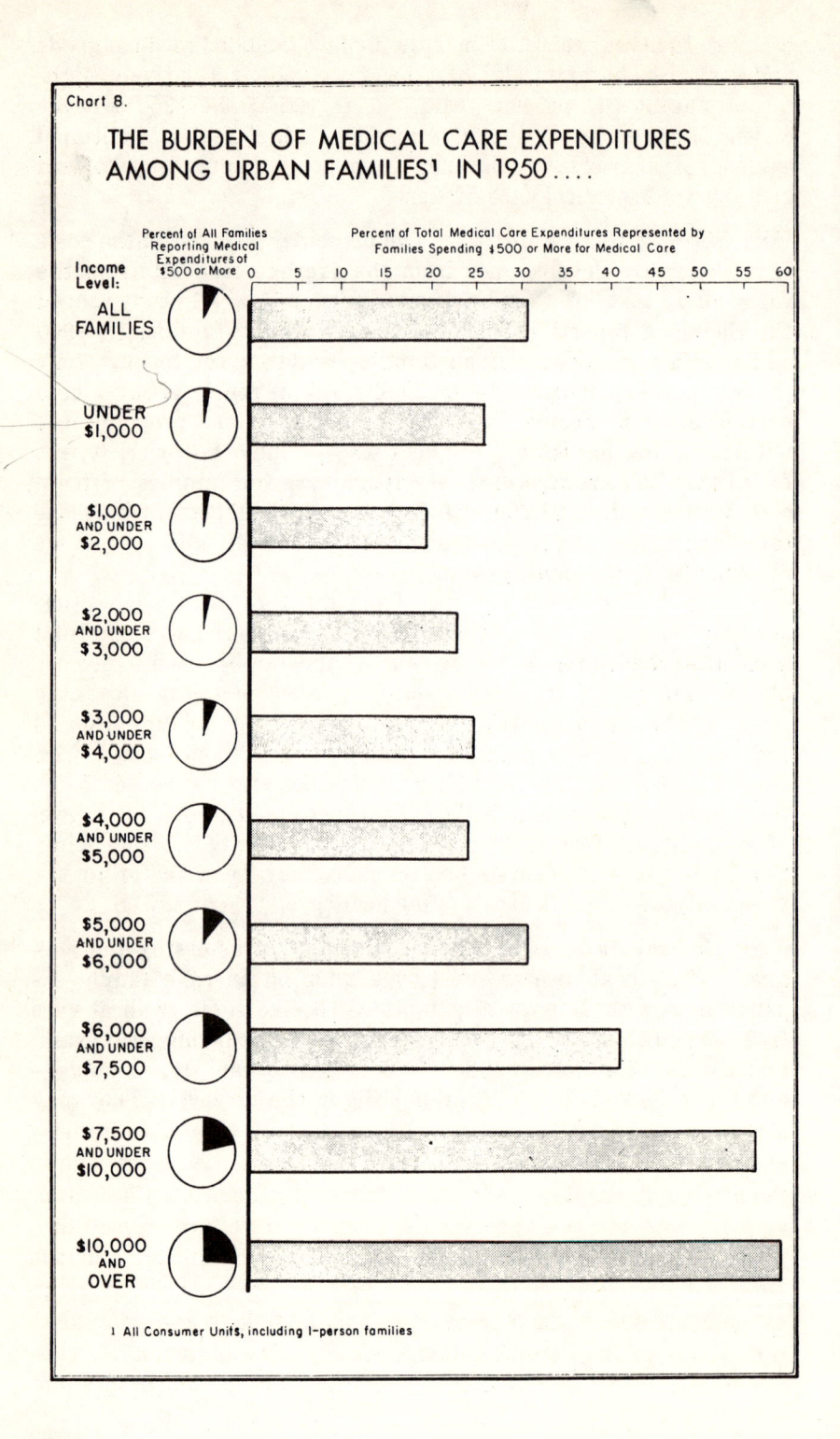

THE BURDEN OF MEDICAL CARE EXPENDITURES AMONG URBAN FAMILIES[1] IN 1950....

[1] All Consumer Units, including 1-person families

tributions for medical and related scientific research, invention, experimentation, and education of personnel. Finally, prepaid systems, in basic conception and mode of operation, also mean that many persons obtain services whose value is far beyond the actual cost, to them, of their particular prepayment fees.

Historically viewed, medical care furnished by clinics and as part of public assistance programs has been important to workers' families, and the educational work of these organizations has had widespread effect on the health of the whole Nation. Medical services provided by employers have undoubtedly expanded—with some such services being available to substantial numbers of workers. There are also a few union health centers which provide services for members either gratis or at nominal fees. From whatever source, about 15 percent of the families of wage and clerical workers reported receiving some free medical care in 1950. This averaged about $18 for all families, or about $120 for those receiving the care.

PAYING FOR MEDICAL CARE

The difficulties which wage earners and salaried employees face in paying for adequate medical care, although still too serious for many of them to overcome, have lessened over the years. Improvements in the workers' economic status and in the health services available have already been detailed. The difficulties have also been alleviated by such developments as workmen's compensation laws, provisions for health benefits in collective bargaining agreements, and group insurance programs.

In 1911, agitation for workmen's compensation legislation began to have effect and within the next decade 42 States passed laws which placed upon the employer the responsibility or "liability" for injuries resulting from the working conditions of his employees. None of the early workmen's compensation laws specifically covered occupational diseases, but the trend toward explicit coverage had been established by 1930, when all or specified types of diseases were covered in 15 of the laws.

Not only did the workmen's compensation laws provide some protection against wage loss, but, being based upon employers' liability, they also tended to moderate opposition to laws for maintenance of minimum standards of safety and sanitation in factories and other workplaces. And, beginning in 1918, States began to incorporate rehabilitation programs into their compensation systems.

Today, all States have workmen's compensation laws which have been vastly improved in recent years. However, these laws vary widely in their coverage and the adequacy of their provisions for medical, disability, and survivor benefits. Some laws restrict coverage to so-called "hazardous" employments (12 States); many exempt employers having fewer than a specified number of employees (29 States); and most of the laws exclude farmwork, domestic service, and casual employment. A majority of the States provide unlimited medical care for injuries "arising out of and in the course of employment," but in 13 States, length-of-time or cost limitations or both are set by law. In addition, 2 States provide no coverage of occupational diseases and 18 States cover only listed or "schedule" diseases.

The increasing public demand for more adequate medical care stimulated widespread discussion of public and private health insurance for the general population, about which there was much debate. The interest thus aroused resulted in the creation of voluntary plans, some of them the results of labor-management agreements.

Some unions were already administering a type of health insurance program. They commonly made some provision—usually a cash benefit similar to that of the mutual-benefit association—for aiding members in illness, accidental disability, or bereavement, either on an informal basis or by means of regularly constituted and administered benefit funds. In 1931, the unions then comprising the American Federation of Labor paid to their members more than $9.7 million in sickness, death, and disability benefits. Some unaffiliated unions, notably in railroading, also provided benefits. The importance of union benefit programs began to lessen during the 1930's.

The really significant union and management activities in the health care field began to develop on a large scale during World War II, when wartime wage controls provided the impetus for collective bargaining for "fringe benefits." In the field of health care, these included the direct provision of medical services, medical care insurance, and payment of cash benefits. Recent trends in this area have been toward covering the workers' dependents and retired workers, adding new benefits, and increasing the level of benefits. In addition, growing numbers of workers are covered by plans which are financed solely by the employer, rather than jointly by the employer and the workers. In 1945, an estimated half million workers were covered by collective bargaining agreements providing benefits for accident and sickness and for hospital, surgical, or other medical care, or protection against death or dismemberment. By mid-1948, the figure had passed 3 million and in 1950 it reached about 7 million. At the end of 1956, estimated coverage of such agreements exceeded 12 million workers, and many also covered workers' dependents and retired workers. The majority of these programs provide medical care insurance.

A few programs provide direct medical services in medical centers and hospitals financed by contributions made under the plan. One of the most noteworthy of these is that administered by the International Ladies' Garment Workers' Union, which pioneered in the establishment of health centers. The ILGWU today operates health centers in 13 cities in the United States, and in 7 other cities operates centers jointly with other unions or by such other arrangements as contracts with private clinics. The union started its first health center in New York City in 1913, as part of a drive to eliminate unsanitary workshops and to control tuberculosis. A few years later the center offered medical and diagnostic services at a nominal charge and it continued to expand. In 1945, a collectively bargained health and welfare plan to which employers contributed took over its financing, and fees for most services were abolished. In 1955, the center served 50,000 patients through examinations, physical and X-ray therapy, various kinds of tests and diagnoses, nutrition services, and a pharmacy.

Probably unique among negotiated health and welfare programs are those provided for in the 1946 agreements between the United Mine Workers and bituminous-coal and anthracite mining operators. The programs are financed by tonnage levies on coal paid to the United Mine Workers Welfare and Retirement Fund. The fund's operations have built, equipped, and staffed a chain of hospitals and clinics throughout the mining areas in communities lacking adequate facilities. Special attention has been given to occupational diseases such as silicosis, to major disabling injuries such as paraplegia, and to the rehabilitation of patients.

For the public at large, but especially important for wage earners and low-salaried employees, group prepayment plans for hospital service, largely sponsored by hospital associations, got an effective start in the 1930's. Much less extensive were prepayment plans for medical service. In the 1940's, private insurance entered the field and by the end of World War II, prepayment programs, especially for hospitalization, were well established.

As of July 1953, 61 percent of the entire population and 70 percent of urban families were covered by some type of health insurance. Of families with insurance, 77 percent obtained it in connection with employment. Among industries, the coverage varied from 33 percent in agriculture, forestry, and fisheries to 90 percent in mining; coverage for all industries combined was about 70 percent. At the end of 1956, about 116 million persons in the United States had some (usually not full) protection for hospital expenses; 101 million for at least some surgical expenses; and 65 million for some medical (largely in-hospital) expenses. American workers, with many exceptions to be sure, have made substantial progress in the handling of their medical care costs.

HEALTH OF WORKERS TODAY

Clearly, the American worker and his family are receiving better medical care than ever before. He is better informed of health hazards and knows more about what has been done in the past, what is available today, and what the prospects are for the future. There is general acceptance, also, of the idea that his health problems are not his alone but the responsibility of the whole community working together. He knows that a vast army of scientific, educational, financial, and legislative experts is waging war against preventable maladies and against unnecessary suffering from unavoidable ills. His earnings, supplemented by benefits from insurance plans, health foundations, labor union and management programs, and public health services, are more nearly adequate than ever before to meet the demands of illness and to maintain his family's standard of living during periods of enforced idleness. His increased income has permitted him to buy the more nutritious foods he learns about through all kinds of educational programs and advertising and finds in modern sanitary markets. He has a much better chance to live in a comfortable home in a community which furnishes him many services that were either unavailable or woefully inadequate in 1900.

This is not to say that all his health needs have been met, or that the unsolved problems are inconsequential. Noteworthy is the inadequacy of the various insurance or prepayment plans as to coverage both of persons and of types of medical costs. Thus, the 1953 surveys sponsored by the Health Information Foundation showed, as previously indicated, that substantial groups of the population had no health insurance. On the basis of family income, only 41 percent of those under $3,000 had any form of health insurance, while 80 percent of families with over $5,000 had some health insurance. Moreover, the foundation reported that prepayment plans covered only one-half of hospital charges, 38 percent of surgery charges, 25 percent of obstetrics charges, 13 percent of physicians' charges, and negligible proportions, if any, of other costs. These "other costs" include dentistry, drugs and medicines, and other medical goods and services accounting for more than two-fifths of medical care costs. Prepayment covered only 15 percent of all medical care charges incurred. In addition, uninsured persons had much less medical care, presumably at least in part because of the costs, than insured persons.

Progress in bringing regular preventive as well as curative medical care under insurance arrangements is, however, indicated by recent growth in group practice plans of various kinds. Advance toward a healthier nation has been and will be costly. The increasing administrative and other costs of medical services through direct payments and indirectly through taxation and contributions to health organizations call for constant study and improved financing lest they become oppressive.

Medical progress has eliminated many of the hazards of childhood and has lengthened the life span, but longer life expectancy has been accompanied by new health problems both physical and mental. Diseases associated with age have become more important. The result of this shift has been to place a large proportion of the burden of the cost of medical care on persons in the older age groups who are least able to pay for it. The tensions and rapid tempo of modern living have increased the incidence of mental illness; at the same time, extension of research and treatment of mental illness has lagged behind that of other illnesses. More than one-half of all hospital beds are occupied by the mentally ill, and well over $1 billion a year are spent by Federal and State governments for caring for the mentally ill in public hospitals and in pensions to veterans with neuropsychiatric disabilities. Despite the increase in facilities, there are not enough accommodations for those who need treatment.

Although the worker or a member of his family is more apt to be killed in an automobile accident than he is on his job, job safety is still a serious problem. Disabling work injuries in 1956 reached a total of 1,990,000, with 14,300 deaths and approximately 81,700 workers suffering some permanent physical impairment. The average length of disability for others injured was 18 days. All States now have workmen's compensation laws, but there are still many gaps in the coverage of both employment and occupational disease, as previously indicated. Benefits under these laws, designed as partial compensation for wage loss, have lagged far behind rising wage levels.

Changing conditions and shifts in industry and population to new sites, with the subsequent deterioration of older residential areas, continually reintroduce slum housing problems. Virtually all urban areas have safe water supplies and provision for sewage disposal, but keeping them thus requires constant vigilance and improvement—a costly process. The most recent addition to the problems of the sanitary engineer is how to prevent contamination of water supplies from radioactive materials. As these have found more common industrial use, new methods of industrial waste disposal are being developed.

In many areas, much still needs to be done to make medical services readily accessible to the workers. For example, in 1956, there was still wide variation among the States in the ratio of physicians to population: 1 for every 500 in New York, compared with 1 for every 1,300 in Mississippi and Alabama.

Despite these problems, there can be little doubt that the advice that more attention be paid to "the improvement of the conditions of health of the working class," [11] given in a 1903 report of the Labor Department, has been followed with greater success than its author could have imagined. A major phase of progress since 1903 has been a dimming of the lines of classes, so that continued advances call for attention to the health problems not so much of the "working class" as of the Nation. In the future, however, as in the past, progress would seem to turn upon a judicious mixture of individual and family alertness, mutual self-help, and a diversity of public policies in areas beyond the competence of individuals and groups. Thus may a substantial measure of reality be given to the World Health Organization's ideal of health—"a state of complete, physical, mental, and social well-being and not merely the absence of disease."

Footnotes

[1] Hannah R. Sewall, *Child Labor in the United States*, Bulletin of the U. S. Bureau of Labor, No. 52 (Washington, 1904), p. 528.

[2] Eva MacDonald Valesh, The Tenement House Problem in New York (in *The Arena*, April 1893, pp. 580-584).

[3] Margaret F. Byington, Homestead, The Households of a Mill Town (New York, Russell Sage Foundation, Charities Publication Committee, 1910, pp. 3, 4).

[4] *Ibid.*, p. 23.

[5] C. F. W. Doehring, *Factory Sanitation and Labor Protection*, Bulletin of the Department of Labor, No. 44 (Washington, January 1903), pp. 2, 3.

[6] G. W. W. Hanger, Housing of the Working People in the United States by Employers, in *The Exhibit of the United States Bureau of Labor at the Louisiana Purchase Exposition*, Bulletin of the Bureau of Labor, No. 54 (Washington, September 1904), p. 1192.

[7] Oscar Handlin, *The Uprooted* (Little, Brown and Company, Boston, 1951), p. 174.

[8] Byington, *op. cit.*, p. 87.

[9] *Workers' Budgets in the United States: City Families and Single Persons, 1946 and 1947*, U.S. Bureau of Labor Statistics Bulletin 927 (Washington, 1948), pp. 14–15.

[10] I. S. Falk, Margaret C. Klem, and Nathan Sinai, *The Incidence of Illness and the Receipt and Costs of Medical Care Among Representative Families: Experiences in Twelve Consecutive Months During 1928–31*, An Abstract of a Report Published for the Committee on the Costs of Medical Care by the University of Chicago Press (Washington, January 1933), p. 17.

[11] Doehring. *op. cit.*, p. 3.

CHAPTER VIII

The Revolution in Transportation

> *Probably more Americans go more places more often than the inhabitants of any other nation on earth.*
> —Thomas R. Carskadon and George Soule.

A reckless forecaster concluded in 1909 that it was "nothing less than feeble-mindedness to expect anything to come of the horseless carriage movement" in the United States.[1] A deterrent to more widespread ownership of the automobile "was thought to be the need of every motorist to keep his car in a costly 'automobile house' equipped with complete repair facilities, drainage pits, washing apparatus, and turntable." Three years later, a proposed 50,000-mile national highway system was attacked as benefiting "a few wealthy pleasure seekers." The revolutionary growth of automotive trucking was not anticipated, a critic contending: "It should be understood in the first place that these highways are intended for . . . automobile touring traffic, since for long-distance freight transportation it is impossible for haulage over any road surface to compete with the low cost of hauling on a railway."

These predictions were no more accurate than those made for the steam locomotive, which men would be unable to endure, so some believed, because of its speed. As for the airplane, some thought that in 1905 it "had reached the limits of success." The apparent consensus was that few Americans would go far from home and that virtually all of them would get about within their own community on the local transit line.

The most outstanding proof of the lack of vision on the part of these early forecasters is that transportation developments since 1900 have been dominated by the acquisition of an automobile by the typical American family. The automobile transformed modes of travel; even more significantly, it altered leisure-time and social activities, changed the concepts of residential areas for workers, and influenced apparel habits. Numerous new industries and millions of jobs were created to produce and service motor vehicles and to serve their passengers—industries and jobs far transcending those displaced or made obsolescent, such as wagon and harness

177

MUD AND CONCRETE—Two views of the same place taken 27 years apart show the influence of automobile travel. Improved vehicles, ever-increasing speeds, and part substitution of trucking for rail and water transportation, have led inevitably to our present program of highway development.

making. Not only private cars, but also motor buses, trucks, and airplanes have greatly accelerated movement of people, mail, and freight in this century. As a consequence, workers' horizons broadened far beyond transit lines, trips on bicycles, and railroad or riverboat excursions.

These developments in transportation since the early years of the 20th century are mirrored in changes in family spending. With their higher real earnings and technology giving them a chance, workers' families have chosen to allocate a much greater proportion of their incomes to travel and transportation. There is no simple explanation for this preference, but some of the causes can be delineated. Memories of the population density and housing congestion prevailing in many urban centers early in the century (see chapter III) heightened interest in more comfortable living and encouraged a surge of migration from central cities to suburban areas. This surge was facilitated by the new forms of transport, but its very volume also created a demand for more and better transportation. The progressive reduction in the length of the workday, the adoption of the 5-day week, and the increasing prevalence of paid vacations, especially among production workers, have provided more leisure which could be devoted to travel. (See chapter IX.)

Two other elements also contributed to the growing importance of transportation, especially as represented by the automobile, in the worker's budget. Social security benefits such as unemployment compensation, health insurance, and retirement pensions have provided greater economic security and encourage less dependence on savings for use in emergencies. Antedating these developments, but undoubtedly given impetus by them, were the development and growth of installment credit to finance the purchase of consumer durable goods, of which the automobile is the most costly item.

Merchandising developments paced the rapid expansion in the use of the passenger automobile and the truck. Rising family incomes and expansion of the size of the middle-income groups led automobile manufacturers to concentrate on production of cars for this market. As the market became more competitive, car manufacturers engineered new features which were displayed in annual models. Success in promoting the sales of new models and availability of replacement parts led to the development of the used car market, a secondhand market exceeded in size only by the market for used homes.

WORKERS' TRANSPORTATION, 1900 TO 1920

In 1900, the urban worker relied largely on his own feet or on public transit for his transportation. He lived ordinarily in a congested city or a mill town, in a dwelling close to his place of employment. In a very large community, subway and elevated lines were his principal means of transport if he lived some distance from his employment. The breadwinner who lived in an outlying section of a large city relied on electrified surface transportation to and from work; within the city limits he usually walked or rode a bicycle. Although rentals were often lower in outlying areas, the time required for streetcar journeys to and from work was an important offset to workers who might be employed for 9, 10, or even as long as 12 hours a day. Moreover, the demands on income for the essentials of living—food, shelter, and clothing—left little resources for excursions or travel, even if less time had been spent at work or if paid vacations had been prevalent. And in addition, transportation facilities were limited, with the exception of local transit.

Public Transportation

The dispersion of city population had, however, begun late in the 19th century. The Interstate Commerce Act of 1887, for example, specifically exempted rail commutation tickets from its prohibition on the granting of special fare rates by railroads. Moreover, the electrification of street railways, which was 97 percent complete by 1902, increased the maximum area from which a central city drew its work force to 12½ square miles, or about 6 times that of the horse-drawn vehicle.

Representatives of the British Board of Trade who surveyed living conditions in cities east of the Mississippi River in 1909 observed of Boston that "relief from much of the normal pressure of congestion [was] afforded by an excellent tramway system," a private electric surface system with 474 miles of track.[2] "The area served was largely beyond the city boundaries," including 12 cities and towns. The same report pointed out that electric car service in Lowell provided transportation "not only between different parts of the city, but also between Lowell and many distant places," including Boston, Lawrence, Haverhill, and Worcester in Massachusetts; Nashua, New Hampshire; and Providence, Rhode Island. "The cars," observed another report, "are an undoubted boon to the working classes in affording access to many unspoiled stretches of country; and in summer, special cars are often chartered for picnics to various points."[3]

Transit rides per capita for the urban population grew sharply and steadily from 177 a year in 1902 to a peak of 287 in 1917—a war year. More than 90 percent of these were by surface railway, the remainder represented elevated and subway services. (See

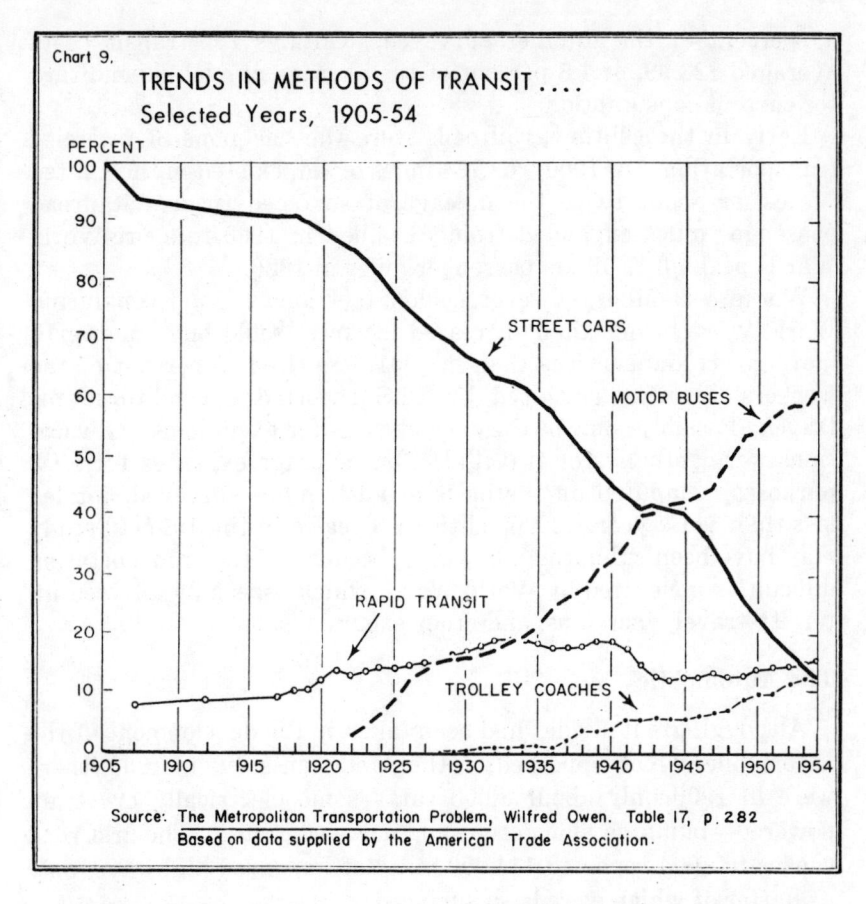

Chart 9.
TRENDS IN METHODS OF TRANSIT....
Selected Years, 1905-54

Source: The Metropolitan Transportation Problem, Wilfred Owen. Table 17, p. 282
Based on data supplied by the American Trade Association.

chart 9.) Motor buses were only being introduced at the time of World War I.

Expenditures for carfare by industrial workers in 1901 were not recorded as a separate item in the BLS consumer expenditure survey of that year. Another source reveals that in 1902 the fare on about two-thirds of the urban street railways in the United States was 5 cents. Over one-third of the transit companies offered fares of approximately 4 cents to patrons under certain conditions, and it was common practice to charge lower fares to school children. And a 1907 study of workingmen's families in New York City indicated an average annual expenditure of $13.91, or 1.7 percent of average income. At that time, only 52 percent of the families in Manhattan and 67 percent in other boroughs reported carfare costs. A similar study in Buffalo in 1908 revealed an annual outlay of $14.83, or 2.5 percent of average income. The differential is partly explainable by the fact that average income was $242 lower in Buffalo. Figures for the United States as revealed in the 1917–19 survey of the U. S. Department of Labor showed expenditures for streetcar fares by

89 percent of the families surveyed. Outlays for transit costs averaged $23.99, or 1.8 percent of the average annual expenditure for current consumption.

Early in the century, railroads were the backbone of intercity transportation. In 1900, 258,784 miles of rail existed in the United States, or about twice the mileage of surfaced roads. Railroad passenger miles expanded from 16 billion in 1900 to a pre-World War II peak of 47 billion passenger miles in 1920.

Workers' families, however, seldom took long trips. Even during World War I, when their increased incomes would buy one-fourth more goods and services than in 1901, less than 10 percent of the workers' families surveyed by BLS reported expenditures for travel. Possibly some of the expenditures for excursions and vacations were actually for travel also, but average expenses for all 3 purposes, computed on the basis of all families surveyed, totaled less than $11 a year. Expenditures revealed in the 1917–19 study may have been subnormal, however, because of the transportation difficulties generated by World War I, which especially affected intercity travel, vacations, and other excursions.

The Automobile

Although great strides had been taken in the development of the automobile, which appeared on the American scene in 1893, there were in 1900 only about 8,000 cars—some electrically or steam powered—bumping along crude and unpaved roads. The first road census in 1904 reported 154,000 miles of improved highways, only a quarter of which were hard surfaced.

Aside from the well-to-do, only a few skilled mechanics were likely to have a car at the turn of the century, when automobile designing was still highly experimental and crude construction placed a premium on the mechanical competence of the owner. More important, the average price of the automobile, then custom built, was about $1,000, well in excess of the means of wage and clerical workers. The average annual family income of such workers was about $650, according to the BLS 1901 income and expenditure survey; indeed, in the South the annual earnings of such workers were under $600. In 1901, Ransom E. Olds began quantity production of a 2-person, 1-cylinder "curved-dash runabout," which sold for $650—still too high for most workers' families. Over one-half of the workers lived on less than this for an entire year and, in any event, the typical family consisted of 4 persons. But most manufacturers—including Mr. Olds' financial backers—preferred to make larger, more expensive cars, and by 1907 the average price ranged between $1,776 and $2,275.

Imperfect materials and unsolved engineering problems added to the cost of owning and maintaining an automobile. In 1905, the manufacturer of the Rambler car published the testimonial of a satisfied owner: "In a thousand miles, we had only 8 punctures and no other repairs or adjustments—except, of course, to the coil, vibrators, and clutch."[4]

By 1910, the automobile was beginning to prove its superiority over horses for personal transportation. Production of cars had advanced from 4,000 in 1900 to 181,000. Doctors, other professional men, and businessmen had begun to shift to the automobile for daily use, and by the end of World War I, carriages had virtually disappeared from city streets.

Most automobile manufacturers recognized during the second decade of the 20th century that technological developments had made mass production possible, and that success in the industry depended on large volume and moderate prices. Ford's nonautomatic assembly line in 1913 reduced the time for attaching the parts to the chassis from 14 hours to 6. A few years later, the use of the first crude automatic device, a mechanically driven conveyor chain, further reduced the assembly time to 1½ hours.

Both wage increases and price reductions accompanied the productivity gains. In 1914, Ford reduced his work schedule to 8 hours per day and instituted the $5 basic daily wage, replacing the minimum prevailing rate of 26 cents per hour. When Ford had begun concentrating on the inimitable Model T in 1908, the initial price of the touring car, $850, was well beyond the reach of wage earners. By 1916, the touring car's price, f.o.b. factory, had declined to $360, or perhaps a third of the average annual income of urban worker families.

These developments, reinforced by widespread advertising and the adaptation of the installment plan to car purchases, led to remarkable expansion in the demand for automobiles, and production rose to almost 2 million in 1920. This represented 1 car for every 13 families. Automobiles led the list of nationally advertised products as early as 1915. Although sales on credit and installment buying appeared much earlier for other durable goods, they first appeared as inducements to the purchase of cars about 1913. By 1919, 32 percent of all sales of General Motors cars involved the use of credit, and in that year the General Motors Acceptance Corporation was organized to expand financing for both dealers and customers.

Despite the automobile's great increase in popularity, only 1 out of every 18 families of urban workers surveyed by the Department of Labor in 1917–19 had an automobile. Undoubtedly, the average income of $1,505 for a 5-person family was too low to permit widespread ownership of a car. However, about 11 percent of the workers whose family income exceeded $1,800 owned cars. Then as now, families in western cities had the highest rate of car ownership—1 in 10 worker families questioned, a rate three times that of families in northern cities where public transportation was comparatively good.

CHANGES DURING THE TWENTIES AND THIRTIES

Family Expenditures for Transportation

Although the next comprehensive study of the extent of workers' ownership of cars was made in the mid-1930's, there are strong indications that the number rose rapidly during the 1920's. Car registrations tripled between 1919 and 1929, and were equivalent in the latter year to 1 car for every 1⅓ families.

In the early twenties, nearly all dealers offered installment credit; and acceptance of customers' old cars as part payment on the purchase of a "newer" one was universal among dealers. By juggling budgets and taking advantage of the extension of credit, many wage earners and lower salaried workers found it possible to buy either a new low-priced car or a serviceable used car.

Even though the buying power of family incomes declined below the 1929 peak during the first half of the thirties,* most families managed to keep their cars or perhaps to acquire used ones. The average car-owning family chose to economize on clothing, housefurnishings, or food rather than relinquish the car—a convenience for driving to work, for job hunting, shopping, and vacations. The Bureau of Labor Statistics observed in connection with the 1935–36 study of consumer purchases that "automobile ownership has been one of the most depression-proof elements in the level of living of families in all parts of the United States."[5] Moreover, data obtained in the 1934–36 survey of expenditures of wage earners and clerical workers indicated that the automobile was regarded as a prestige acquisition as well as a convenient and popular means of transportation. The Bureau reported that "nowadays when the family has had a successful year, it is more apt to think of an automobile as a symbol of success rather than new clothes or furniture for the parlor."[6]

The Bureau's 1934–36 survey of expenditures of wage earners and lower salaried clerical workers in 42 cities revealed car ownership by 44 percent of families surveyed, as shown in table 17, and nearly 1 percent had more than 1 automobile. This represented an eightfold growth in car ownership since World War I. Workers'

---

*Total salaries and wages ebbed 40 percent between 1929 and 1933; consumer prices fell about 25 percent during the same period.

TABLE 17.—*Proportion of wage-earner and clerical-worker families owning and purchasing cars in 42 cities, 1934–36*

Income class	Percent of families—	
	Owning automobile purchased during survey year or earlier	Purchasing automobile during survey year
All incomes	44.4	10.8
$500 and under $600	9.5	1.6
$600 and under $900	21.7	4.3
$900 and under $1,200	32.5	6.2
$1,200 and under $1,500	45.1	9.4
$1,500 and under $1,800	49.8	12.1
$1,800 and under $2,100	56.2	15.1
$2,100 and under $2,400	58.8	18.4
$2,400 and under $2,700	54.6	19.1
$2,700 and under $3,000	61.7	16.7
$3,000 and over	60.1	26.5

SOURCE: Money Disbursements of Wage Earners and Clerical Workers, 1934–36, U. S. Bureau of Labor Statistics Bulletin 638, p. 137.

real family incomes averaged about 10 percent higher in the mid-thirties than in 1917–19, while the average size of families surveyed were smaller.

This fact, coupled with less demand on the family budget for food and clothing and more widespread ownership of cars, resulted in families expending nearly 3 times as much of their income in 1934–36 for travel and transportation as they did in 1917–19—over 8 percent compared with about 3 percent. The sharp rise in the percentage of family expenditures allocated to travel and transportation in the 17-year span extended to all income levels of workers included in the study. (See tables 4 and 5, pp. 42 and 44.)

Expenditures in 1934–36 averaged $87 per year for the purchase, operation, and maintenance of automobiles, compared with $38 for all other forms of transportation. For car-owning families, the average amount which workers' families spent on automobiles was $197. Three-fourths of the cars bought during the survey year were used, and the average cost per car was $300.

Transportation Facilities

These changes in expenditure patterns reflect not only a shift in the value attached to car ownership by the family but also vast technological changes in the field of transportation.

Public Transportation. The volume of passengers riding local transit grew slowly during the 1920's but less rapidly than the population. At the end of World War I, most workers who did not walk relied on streetcars for local transportation. As late as 1922, only 370 public motor buses were in operation by street and electric railway companies or their affiliates, but by 1929, 15 percent of the public transit passengers rode buses.

The use of local public transportation dropped sharply from a total of 17 billion rides by all means of public conveyance in 1929 to a low of 11.3 billion in 1933, and then recovered somewhat to 13.1 billion in 1940. The average number of rides per city dweller fell correspondingly from 252 in 1929 to 160 in 1933 and then rose to 176 in 1940. Much of the decrease during the thirties occurred, of course, because of the large volume of unemployment during the depression, but the losses also reflect the growing use of the automobile. Streetcar losses were heaviest; indeed, buses gained sharply, accounting for nearly a third of all public transit rides in 1940. (See chart 9.)

Meanwhile, railroad passenger service was losing ground; the number of passenger miles operated was little more than half as much in 1936–40 as it had been in 1916–20. Railroad commuter miles declined from almost 7 billion in 1930 to 4 billion 10 years later. At the same time, intercity bus travel was expanding, and in 1930 accounted for one-fifth of the intercity passenger traffic carried by public conveyances. By 1940, this proportion had reached about three-eighths.

Commercial airlines had also gained a measure of public acceptance during the 1930's, and the number of passengers quadrupled between 1935 and 1940. But in the latter year, the airlines still accounted for only 3 percent of the total miles traveled by intercity passengers on public transportation.

Bus travel could not, of course, have become so popular without great improvements in the highway system. In 1921, expenditures for highways by local, State, and national governments totaled $1.3 billion and rose in 1930 to $2.5 billion. During this period, the number of miles of surfaced rural highways also virtually doubled, reaching 694,000 miles in 1930. The expansion quickened during the following decade, pushing the surfaced highway mileage to 1,340,000 in 1940.

Automobile Travel. With the development of this vast highway network, coupled with increasing car ownership, Americans thronged to scenic areas, especially State and national parks. During the 1920's, the number of visitors to national parks tripled. Automobiles, which had superseded railroads as the chief mode of transportation for park visitors by 1925, delivered almost 17 million visitors to national parks in 1940, a fivefold expansion since 1930.

Probably the most significant factor in the growth of car ownership was a drop of 40 percent in factory-delivered prices of cars between 1920 and 1930. Gasoline prices declined a third, averaging

JOURNEY INTO SPACE—In the crowded cities of earlier days, few workers had their own transportation. Most walked, or traveled in publicly owned vehicles. Trips into the countryside were an adventure. The improved highways of today witness daily the commuting of millions of workers in their own cars between home and place of work.

20 cents per gallon in 1930. Tire prices fell even more sharply. Improvement in tire construction and materials, combined with better surfaced streets and highways, tripled tire wear. Automobiles continued in the 1920's to offer more powerful engines, greater comfort and durability, with the development of large-scale competitive automobile selling. Closed cars, which made all-year driving more enjoyable, began to supersede open cars in the mid-twenties.

During the 1930's, manufacturers began to promote style changes and brighter body colors. Cars became easier and safer to drive, as leading manufacturers introduced hydraulic brakes, all-metal bodies, safety glass all around, and lower pressure tires. Mass production by 3 major companies provided millions of new cars retailing for less than $1,000. In the 3 years following 1930, factory-delivered prices of automobiles declined 5 percent but by 1940 had risen slightly above their 1930 level. The average life of passenger tires grew from 15,000 miles in 1930 to 22,000 miles in 1940, as lower pressure "balloon" tires superseded smaller, harder-riding tires. Factory prices of tires declined 18 percent from 1930 to 1934, but turned upward over 40 percent from 1934 to 1939 and then dropped to 1930 levels in 1940. Gasoline prices, including taxes, averaged about 18½ cents per gallon in 1940, compared with 20 cents in 1930. Although refiners greatly improved octane ratings, retail prices of gasoline (without taxes) dropped 3.4 cents per gallon in that decade. However, State and Federal gasoline taxes rose from an average of 3.8 cents in 1930 to 5.7 cents per gallon in 1940.

The average mileage driven per car grew from 25,800 in 1925 to 85,500 miles in 1941, an increase which permitted a substantial reduction in owners' overhead costs. By 1941, the average age of cars scrapped had risen to 10.2 years, as compared with an average life of 6½ years in 1925.

TRANSPORTATION SINCE 1940

Transportation requirements were sharply increased during World War II by the expansion of employment and, for many industries, a return to a 6-day week. At the same time, the production of passenger cars for private use was discontinued between 1942 and 1945, and gasoline and tires were rationed. Thus, although there was widespread formation of worker car pools for trips to and from work, public transportation facilities faced heavy demands. Transit rides expanded by 80 percent over the 1940 level, reaching a peak in 1946 of 23.4 billion a year, or 282 rides per person. Thereafter, local transit use declined rapidly; by 1955, it barely equaled the depression low of 1933, and was no higher than in 1912. Rides per capita of 124 in 1955 set a new low record.

Railroads and intercity buses experienced similar trends. The high level of industrial activity, extensive troop movements, and the virtual banning of intercity and commuter trips by automobile combined to produce an all-time record of 95½ billion revenue passenger miles on railroads in 1944. Similarly, passenger travel by intercity bus more than doubled between 1940 and 1943, when miles traveled reached a peak of nearly 28 billion. By 1955, however, railroad passenger miles had declined to 29 billion, approximately the passenger load in 1941, and the comparable figure for intercity buses was 25 billion.

Revenue passenger miles for scheduled air carriers grew rapidly in the forties from 1.2 billion miles in 1940 to 10.2 billion in 1950. By 1957, when revenue passenger miles approximated 32 billion, it was estimated that the airlines' share of domestic travel was greater than that of the railroads.

The conclusion of World War II released a pent-up demand for consumer durable goods not obtainable during hostilities. Increased buying power enabled a high proportion of urban workers to buy automobiles as well as homes on convenient credit terms. Migration to semirural and suburban areas, which had been checked by restrictions on home construction and by other controls during the war, was resumed at an accelerated rate. (See chapter III.) Production remained high and, although employment declined and prices advanced apace with wages as wartime controls on both were lifted, tax reductions brought increases in spendable earnings. Savings accumulated during the war and allowances granted to World War II veterans provided the remaining essential for a big expansion in the durable goods market. Automobile manufacturers returned to car production, and during 1946–55 they produced almost 51 million passenger automobiles. Scrappage of prewar models tripled and, in that 10-year period, an estimated 26½ million were dumped on the scrap heap.

Consumers bought an unprecedented number—6⅓ million—of new automobiles in 1950, as fear of shortages during the Korean hostilities spurred replacement of pre-World War II cars. In 1950, prices paid for new cars averaged about $2,200, compared with $700 for a used car. Five years later, new car purchases hit their peak; over 7 million new automobiles rolled onto our highways. The average new car buyer paid about $2,940 for his car in 1955. The majority of these cars had 8-cylinder motors, automatic transmissions, radios, and heater-defrosters. The average price paid for a used car in 1955 had risen less sharply—to $780. By this time, the average age of cars being sent to scrap piles had risen to 13 years, twice that of cars taken off the road 25 years earlier. Cars discarded in 1955 had run 3 times as many miles as the average car junked in 1930, so that the cost per mile of car acquisition had declined in spite of substantial increase in their prices.

Growth in Use of Credit

Both rising auto prices and increased use of credit for the purchase of cars are reflected in the rapid growth of installment credit. The pre-World War II peak in auto installment credit outstanding occurred in 1941, when it totaled approximately $2.5 billion, or about two-fifths of the total installment credit outstanding. (See table 18, p. 190.) Installment purchasing rose rapidly after the war* and, in 1956, outstanding automobile installment

---

*Installment credit outstanding increased much less rapidly when viewed as a percentage of income. Disposable personal income rose (without price adjustment) from $83 billion in 1929 to $287 billion in 1956.

TABLE 18.—*Proportion of consumer installment credit represented by automobile paper, selected dates, 1929–56*

At end of—	Number of family units (thousands)	Consumer installment credit outstanding (millions)	Automobile installment credit outstanding Amount (millions)	Percent of all consumer installment credit
1929	(¹)	$3,151	$1,384	43.9
1930	27,980	2,687	986	36.7
1940	32,166	5,514	2,071	37.6
1941	(¹)	6,085	2,458	40.4
1948	37,237	8,996	3,018	33.5
1950	39,303	14,703	6,074	41.3
1951	39,929	15,294	5,972	39.0
1952	40,578	19,403	7,733	39.9
1953	40,832	23,005	9,835	42.8
1954	41,202	23,568	9,809	41.6
1955	41,934	29,020	13,468	46.4
1956	42,843	31,552	14,436	45.8

[1] Not available.

SOURCE: Credit data—Federal Reserve Bulletin, June 1955 (pp. 638 and 690) and October 1956 (p. 1108); Survey of Current Business, February 1957; population data—U. S. Bureau of the Census, Censuses of Population and Current Population Reports, Series P-20, various dates.

credit was about $14½ billion, or almost one-half of all such credit in force. Part of this increase was, of course, due to the growth of the population.

Increased reliance on credit is, however, demonstrated in annual surveys of consumer finances for the Board of Governors of the Federal Reserve System. In 1948, 39 percent of car purchases involved the use of credit, while 59 percent were purchased by full payment in cash. For new cars, the comparable figures were 33 and 66 percent, and for used cars, 42 and 55 percent. By 1955, both new and used car purchases were financed in an approximate ratio of 60 percent with credit and 40 with cash. (See table 19, p. 191.)

The role of installment credit has been especially significant in the buying of cars by wage earners and ordinary salaried employees. In early 1956, about 33 percent of all car-owning "spending units" had automobile indebtedness.* The comparable proportions of workers comprehended within the definition of city workers used in this volume were as follows:

Occupational category	Percent having automobile indebtedness
Clerical and sales	35
Skilled and semiskilled	41
Unskilled and service	42

*A spending unit is defined as all persons living in the same dwelling and belonging to the same family who pool their incomes to meet their major expenses.

TABLE 19.—*Consumers' method of financing automobile purchases, selected years, 1948–55*

Item	Percent				
	1948	1950	1952	1954	1955
All families	100	100	100	100	100
Families owning automobiles	54	60	65	70	71
All passenger car buyers	100	100	100	100	100
Full cash [1]	59	47	35	37	39
Installment credit; other borrowing	39	52	63	62	60
New car buyers	100	100	100	100	100
Full cash [1]	66	54	41	38	39
Installment credit; other borrowing	33	46	57	62	60
Used car buyers	100	100	100	100	100
Full cash [1]	55	41	33	36	38
Installment credit; other borrowing	42	57	65	63	61

[1] Including trade-in allowance.

NOTE: Percentages do not add to 100, because information on method of financing was not obtained in a small number of cases.

SOURCE: Statistical Abstract of the United States: 1957 (U. S. Bureau of the Census, citing Board of Governors of Federal Reserve System, Surveys of Consumer Finances), p. 555.

Family Expenditures

The most recent comprehensive survey of expenditures by wage earners and clerical workers—conducted by BLS in 1950—indicates the degree to which transportation has become a priority item in the family budget. In that year, families allotted to transportation about 1 out of every 7 dollars expended—more than they spent for clothing and less than the outlays only for food and for total shelter costs. Travel expense was reported in 1950 by at least 9 out of 10 families in all but the lowest income class. Even among families at that level (under $1,000), 78 percent reported some travel expense and 16 percent had automobiles. At least two-thirds of the families with annual incomes above $3,000 reported automobile expenses; so did almost one-half of those within the $2,000–$3,000 range, as shown in table 20, p. 192.

The 1950 study indicates clearly that workers in the West devoted a greater proportion of their total expenditures to transportation than those living in northern or southern areas. Expenditures in the North were lower than those in the South, a reflection of greater reliance in northern cities on public transportation facilities and the relatively greater inconvenience of the automobile in densely populated metropolitan areas. The South fell midway in the range, largely because of less adequate public transportation, but also because fewer people lived in densely populated areas. Higher incomes in the West, better access to varied recre-

TABLE 20.—*Percent of wage-earner and clerical-worker families reporting expenditures for automobile and other travel and transportation, by income class, 1950*

Income class	Percent of families reporting expenditure for—			
	Travel and transportation, total	Automobile		Other travel and transportation
		Operation and purchase	Purchase	
Under $1,000	78	16	4	73
$1,000 and under $2,000	92	23	9	85
$2,000 and under $3,000	97	44	18	85
$3,000 and under $4,000	99	66	28	84
$4,000 and under $5,000	100	75	32	87
$5,000 and under $6,000	100	81	38	87
$6,000 and under $7,500	100	83	43	90
$6,500 and under $10,000	100	84	47	92
$10,000 and over	98	84	46	90

SOURCE: Derived from Study of Consumer Expenditures, Incomes and Savings: Statistical Tables, Urban U. S.—1950 (University of Pennsylvania, 1957), Volume XVIII, table 4-10.

ation and vacation spots, greater distances, and the tendency of newer cities in the West to grow horizontally rather than vertically, account for the high proportion of automobile ownership in western urban areas and the largest expenditures for transportation.

The 1950 expenditure data also show clearly that a majority of workers, regardless of region, city size, or occupational class, spent more on the automobile than on public carriers. Expenditures on automobiles and their operation accounted for no less than 73 percent of total transportation expenses for unskilled workers in large northern cities, and ranged as high as 96 percent for skilled workers in small western cities.

The acquisition of an automobile represented 56 percent of all automobile travel costs reported by urban workers in 1950. Greater relative expenditures for acquisition as against the cost of operation were evident in the higher income classes, where the multi-car family is probably more usual and more families may purchase new rather than used cars.

Among white-collar and skilled wage-earner families, the proportions reporting automobile ownership ranged from 97 percent of the skilled workers in the suburbs of western cities to 52 percent of the clerical and sales workers in large southern cities. (See table 21.) Ownership was consistently higher among skilled workers even in classes of cities where their average income was less than white-collar income. Skilled workers' families more often had 2 or more cars and were more apt to have bought a used car than the white-collar families. Except for southern cities, more than half of the semiskilled reported ownership of auto-

TABLE 21.—*Percent of wage-earner and clerical-worker families owning automobiles, by occupation of family head, 1950*

Class of city and geographic region	Percent of clerical and sales workers owning—			Percent of skilled wage earners owning—			Percent of semiskilled wage earners owning—			Percent of unskilled wage earners owning—		
	Any automobiles	2 or more automobiles	Automobiles purchased new	Any automobiles	2 or more automobiles	Automobiles purchased new	Any automobiles	2 or more automobiles	Automobiles purchased new	Any automobiles	2 or more automobiles	Automobiles purchased new
North:												
Large cities	53	3	24	67	5	27	51	4	15	33	2	8
Suburbs	72	6	45	80	8	36	66	5	19	47	3	15
Small cities	56	6	23	83	11	30	59	8	21	53	5	13
South:												
Large cities	52	3	30	63	7	25	44	2	10	22	1	6
Suburbs	72	6	40	83	10	34	71	3	23	41	3	9
Small cities	70	3	35	67	5	32	40	1	6	31	1	8
West:												
Large cities	65	5	32	86	13	29	72	9	18	48	5	10
Suburbs	83	15	49	97	11	28	89	25	27	61	8	13
Small cities	72	5	37	89	16	29	74	10	25	56	7	14

SOURCE: Study of Consumer Expenditures, Incomes and Savings: Statistical Tables, Urban U.S.—1950 (University of Pennsylvania, 1957), Volume XVII, table 7–1.

mobiles. For the unskilled groups, the proportion reporting automobile ownership varied from 22 percent in large southern cities to 61 percent in western suburbs.

How the workers' families used their cars is suggested by a study of the Bureau of Public Roads on motor vehicle use in 17 States in the period 1951-54, which showed that as much as 43.6 percent of automobile travel related to earning a living. Trips to and from work accounted for 25.6 percent and use in related business activities for 18 percent. Social and recreational use approximated one-third. Skilled, semiskilled, and unskilled workers devoted more travel to back-and-forth-to-work and social and recreational purposes, and also to "family business," than did clerical and sales workers. The latter used automotive transportation to a much greater degree in the conduct of their work. (See table 22, below.)

TABLE 22.—*Motor vehicle use in 17 States for selected occupations of principal operator, 1951-54*

Purpose of travel	All occupations	Store and office clerks, salesmen, (excluding traveling salesmen)	Craftsmen, foremen, skilled workers	Operatives, semiskilled workers, unskilled workers, and laborers	Traveling salesmen, agents
All purposes	100.0	100.0	100.0	100.0	100.0
Earning a living	43.6	51.5	46.0	43.8	75.6
To and from work	25.6	29.5	36.9	34.7	24.1
Related business	18.0	22.0	9.1	9.1	51.5
Family business	17.8	12.6	14.4	17.4	5.4
Educational, civic, and religious	3.1	2.2	2.0	2.3	.8
Social and recreational	35.1	33.1	37.5	36.2	18.2
Not reported	.4	.6	.1	.3	

SOURCE: Unpublished data from the Bureau of Public Roads, based on annual studies of motor vehicle use conducted in 17 States (Arkansas, California, Iowa, Kentucky, Louisiana, Mississippi, Missouri, Montana, New Mexico, North Dakota, Oklahoma, Oregon, Pennsylvania, South Dakota, Washington, Wisconsin, Wyoming).

New Problems of Extensive Automobile Ownership

The acquisition of automobiles by most American families has, in conjunction with other developments on the American scene, introduced new problems or aggravated old ones. Increased population densities in metropolitan areas which formerly were quiet suburban communities, extensive decentralization of industry, mass production of housing, insufficient off-street parking coupled with inadequate advance planning for roads and highway systems of sufficient capacity: such circumstances account for traffic congestion which, according to business and automotive groups as reported by The New York Times, costs around $5 billion annually.[7] Public officials and traffic engineers are also concerned with the necessity for developing more adequate traffic control programs and devices to reduce the heavy accident rate associated with automobiles, which the National Safety Council estimated would account in 1956 for an economic loss of approximately $5 billion.[8]

The $33.8 billion Federal road-aid plan which became effective in July 1956 was designed to provide 41,000 miles of new or improved roads, with about half the funds scheduled for urban roads. The program was initially planned for completion in 13 years, but rising costs and other problems may postpone completion. Passenger cars are expected to number 100 million by 1975, compared with 54 million in 1955, with mileage driven expanding about 35 percent. The increase in highway mileage under the new program would be much less proportionately, compared with the 2.5 million miles of public surfaced roads in 1955. As The New York Times pointed out, "the immensity of the roadbuilding needs can be gaged by noting that since 1946 only 53,000 miles of lanes have been added to our road system, while the auto makers were turning out 200,000 miles of vehicles, bumper to bumper."

The rapidly accelerated use of automobiles, on progressively inadequate streets, roads, and highways, for conveyance to and from work, for leisure-time activities, and for recreation, as well as the expansion of trucking, has added new complications to both suburban and urban living. The clogged roads have reduced the value of the shorter work schedules and have increased travel costs. Despite these disadvantages, the worker prefers the car to public transportation, which, though cheaper, frequently offers poor service, uncertain schedules, and excessive crowding. The value of more flexible use of leisure and the greater freedom to choose pursuits are evidently regarded by most of the population as advantages outweighing annoyances accompanying car ownership and use.

In some respects, the motor car has replaced apparel and other consumer goods as a demonstration of "conspicuous consumption." Manufacturers provide glamorous vehicles with swank fittings, powerful engines, and a variety of equipment that sometimes add less to efficient transportation than to display. The American market for the small car is expanding and there are indications that American manufacturers are looking toward a coming market, but they have not announced plans for mass production of a small, economy car.[9]

One final observation seems pertinent. The extensive ownership of automobiles may be symbolic of an equalizing process apparent in this country. The distinction between economic levels in the ownership of tangibles is diminishing. This is true in homeownership, in household equipment, in apparel, and in automobiles. Certainly the automobile has aided wage earners and others in narrowly circumscribed environments in breaking down the barriers of community and class by giving them opportunities for travel, wide-ranging recreation, and broadened acquaintance and outlook. The automobile has also made possible a new freedom and range of choice of places of residence and types of work.

Footnotes

[1] The quoted matter in the first two paragraphs is from J. Frederic Dewhurst and Associates, *America's Needs and Resources, A New Survey* (New York, The Twentieth Century Fund, 1955), p. 283, citing H. P. Maxim, *Horseless Carriage Days* (New York, Harper, 1937); *Motor*, October 1905, p. 37, and May 1909, p. 33; and Editorial, *Engineering News Record*, May 16, 1912, pp. 103, 937.

[2] *Cost of Living in American Towns*, Board of Trade of Great Britain (London, 1911), p. 103.

[3] *41st Annual Report on the Statistics of Labor, 1910*, Massachusetts Bureau of Statistics (Boston, 1911), p. 233.

[4] *Automotive News*, October 8, 1956, p. 37, quoting from *Rambler Magazine*, 1905.

[5] *Family Expenditures in Selected Cities, 1935–36*, Vol. VI: *Travel and Transportation*, U.S. Bureau of Labor Statistics Bulletin 648, p. 3.

[6] Faith M. Williams and Alice C. Hanson, *Money Disbursements of Wage Earners and Clerical Workers, 1934–36, Summary Volume*, U.S. Bureau of Labor Statistics Bulletin 638, p. 41.

[7] *The New York Times*, January 28, 1957.

[8] This estimate, which appeared in *Accident Facts, 1957 Edition* (pp. 13 and 41), is somewhat lower than the $6.5 billion annual economic loss attributed to automobile accidents by the Association of Casualty and Surety Companies (in *The New York Times* issue of January 28, 1957).

[9] After this chapter had been set in type, it was reported that the three major auto producers were likely to include a so-called "compact" car in their 1960 model lines. (See Why Smaller Cars Are Coming, in *Business Week*, January 17, 1959, p. 29.)

CHAPTER IX

Time for Living

> *A well-balanced preservation of the faculties of man requires that he give himself periodically to physical and intellectual exercises essentially distinct from work.*
> —Carle C. Zimmerman and Merle E. Frampton.

Perhaps no single feature of the worker's level of living in the United States better illustrates its spectacular improvement during the last half century than the expansion and profitable utilization of his leisure time. Since 1900, technological advances and the mechanization of industry have made possible the 8-hour day, the long weekend, and the vacation with pay.

Workers generally have eagerly taken advantage of their added leisure time to improve their surroundings, extend their education, develop their hobbies, participate in community affairs, enjoy sports, and generally fulfill their cultural desires. Some of them, on the other hand, have turned into "moonlighters," getting a second job, usually part-time, to increase their income.

CHANGES IN WORKING TIME

The Workweek

In 1900, the 10-hour day, 6-day week was not uncommon. And such important continuous process industries as steel manufacturing operated day and night, with the 24 hours divided between two shifts.

Agitation for the 8-hour day, which unions had begun late in the 19th century, continued throughout the first decade of the 20th century. The argument that, with a 10-hour day, accumulated fatigue, and often boredom, reduced the workers' efficiency and lowered their output seemed to be the most pertinent and effective, especially in respect to the continuous-operation industries. However, rising productivity was probably the prime factor that made the 8-hour day possible. Also, it eventually became recognized generally that workers occupied for the most part with strenuous toil or rest from it were not good customers for the products of

SMALL FRY ON PLEASURE BENT—Joy is for children, be it on weekly excursion to some distant picnic spot, or daily in the pool in their own backyard. Over the past 50 years, a big gain for city workers' children has been the accessibility of recreational facilities.

their efforts. In 1926, when Henry Ford announced the 5-day week for his company, he said:

> The industry of this country could not long exist if factories generally went back to the 10-hour day, because the people would not have the time to consume the goods produced. For instance, a workman would have little use for an automobile if he had to be in the shops from dawn to dusk. And that would react in countless directions, for the automobile, by enabling people to get about quickly and easily, gives them a chance to find out what is going on in the world—which leads them to a larger life that requires more food, more and better goods, more books, more music—more of everything.[1]

These various influences combined to effect a gradual reduction in scheduled hours. By 1929, the 8-hour day was prevalent in manufacturing, mining, and railroading, but the workweek usually was spread over 6 days. The trend toward a 5-day week had been developing rapidly in the 1920's in some industries, particularly men's clothing and the building trades. But in 1931 a Department of Labor survey showed that in United States industries as a whole only 6 percent of the employees were enjoying a 2-day weekend.

By the time of the depression of the 1930's, the 8-hour day was quite widely accepted as the standard among industries, with the apparent exception of the steel mills. During the depression, the workday and the workweek were shortened, often as a device for spreading work; but, as the economy recovered, it appeared that the 8-hour day was optimum for most of industry. A workweek of five 8-hour days became widespread with the passage of the Fair Labor Standards Act of 1938, requiring the payment of premium rates for work exceeding 40 hours a week in employment subject to the act.

During World War II, of course, work schedules were lengthened—commonly to 6 days of 8 or 9 hours—to meet war production needs. Since then, weekly hours of factory production workers have averaged about 40, although they rose somewhat during the Korean conflict and turned downward during the economic recessions of 1948–49, 1953–54, and 1957–58.

Vacations

Along with the general establishment of shorter working hours, the movement for paid vacations for workers gained favor, although progress was slow. As late as 1920, a survey of 63 manufacturing concerns showed that 36 did not give vacations to workers paid on an hourly, daily, or piecework basis. Five allowed vacations without pay, 1 gave vacations with half pay, and only 11 provided vacation time with full pay. Interviews with those employers granting paid vacations showed in general that they regarded vacations as a good investment because employees returned in better health and spirits and with greater enthusiasm for the job. Another survey of 624 manufacturing plants made in the same year showed that white-collar employees fared better than factory workers. Eighty-five percent of the plants granted paid vacations to clerical workers, but only 18 percent to wage earners. At the time of these surveys, emphasis on the wage rate, rather than supplementary benefits, characterized the bargaining demands of unions representing wage earners. In the period during and following World War II, fringe benefits, including paid vacations, more and more became major subjects of collective bargaining. Nearly 85 percent of about 1,500 collective bargaining agreements examined by the Bureau of Labor Statistics in 1948–49 stipulated 2 or more weeks as the maximum vacation time; over 30 percent specified a maximum of more than 2 weeks, usually for longer-service employees.

By 1957, according to a similar study, 86 percent of the agreements (as contrasted with about 30 percent 9 years earlier) called for more than 2 weeks, with 20 percent providing 4 weeks.

Retirement

The amount of leisure time spent in retirement has also risen appreciably. In 1900, a man 60 years old could expect to live until he was 74, and to retire at age 71. In 1950, he could anticipate living until he reached 75, but he would probably retire at the age of 69. Much of the 3 additional years in retirement could be credited to the development of old-age insurance under the social security system and to the prevalence of private pension schemes which gave workers economic security to retire before they were forced to do so by illness or disability. In 1955, some 47 million nonfarm workers were employed in jobs covered by old-age and survivors insurance in a typical quarter, and over 7 million were covered by collectively bargained pension plans.

Increase in Free Time

Thus, during our century the workers' gains in free time for living are momentous. Workers now work not far from 20 hours less each week than their grandfathers did at the century's beginning. In addition, they have 2 full days free as a rule and, if they must work on Saturday or Sunday, they are usually paid at premium rates or get equivalent time off on other days. Furthermore, they are generally eligible for paid vacations and several paid holidays. Finally, instead of having to work until no longer able to do so, workers can now retire while active; and, living longer, they have added years of leisure in retirement.

Workers' families, too, have gained free time. Women are now more often employed outside their homes, but they spend less time at their household chores than their mothers or grandmothers, and children begin work at a much later age. (For fuller discussion, see chapter IV.)

Looking ahead toward the possible further shortening of working hours in the new age of automation and atomic energy, many unions have tried to ascertain the wishes of their membership on the scheduling of leisure time. For example, the Oil, Chemical, and Atomic Workers in 1957 asked members whether they would prefer shorter daily hours, fewer workdays per week, occasional 3-day weekends, longer vacations, or a combination of these alternatives. Most members who replied favored an extra day off weekly. The main reason given was that cutting the hours of work per day would not help as much as an extra day off, because so many workers spend considerable time traveling to and from work daily. There was sentiment expressed also for a 4-day week with Wednesdays off to shop. Most men, said one union member, "never go shopping because they are so busy weekends fishing, working on the car, around the yard, and so forth."

INCREASING VARIETY OF LEISURE-TIME ACTIVITIES

Naturally, the workers of 50 years ago had to be content with much more modest opportunities for entertainment and recreation than their grandchildren, who have the advantages not only of far more free time and more buying power but also of more mobility and more varied attractions. Comparison is difficult because of the astonishing variety of choices open to the worker and also because it is almost impossible to measure the amount and quality of leisure-time activities which workers' families enjoy, even at a particular point in time. Moreover, statistics on the subject are much more comprehensive now than then. At best we can outline only the main activities and trace the most pronounced trends.

Today, American workers devote a sizable share of their leisure time to sports, both as participants and as spectators, and to other outdoor activities, many of which were the exclusive province of the "idle rich" in 1900. Moreover, much of the workers' leisure time is absorbed by the movies, radio, and television—all mediums of entertainment which were virtually undreamed of in 1900. Yet they have time to spare for furthering their education, participating in civic affairs, entertaining friends, reading which goes far beyond the "escapist" detective thriller or western story, engaging in "do-it-yourself" projects, and traveling on weekends or during the annual vacation.

American workers in 1900 exhibited a much more restricted pattern of leisure-time activities.

Entertainment

In the early years of the century, in many neighborhoods, the music hall variety show was the popular form of entertainment. Unions, mutual aid societies, and clubs also provided a friendly and relaxed atmosphere. Church-sponsored suppers, picnics, and social "get togethers" were favorite pastimes. The neighborhood saloon, though much condemned for other reasons, in many communities provided a place for conversation and entertainment.

Inexpensive amusement was found in billiard halls, bowling alleys, shooting galleries, and skating rinks. Trolley-car rides into the country and occasional excursions to the seashore or other resorts were popular. Many families had pianos, accordions, player pianos, or phonographs, and music was a key attraction at social gatherings. The Sunday band concerts in the park were also a popular form of diversion.

These organizational, ceremonial, home-centered, and kindred forms of entertainment were generally the only ones workers and their families could afford. In fact, they were the only ones that were available in most communities.

The first decade of the century saw the spectacular rise of the motion picture. It was preceded by the penny arcade "peep show"; then came the nickelodeon, offering short historical and travel topics and occasionally comedy; gradually there developed feature pictures with plot and story. By 1908, there were approximately 800 to 1,000 nickelodeons in New York City alone. Workers stopped on the way home from work for a 15-minute show and children pleaded for nickels to go to the "flickers."

In those early days also, vaudeville, which developed out of the less refined entertainment of the music hall variety show, offered music, plays, and comedy. Burlesque, which arose as a lower cost variety of vaudeville, has served, nevertheless, to provide the entertainment world with such top stars as Will Rogers, Bert Lahr, Phil Silvers, and Fanny Brice.

One of the most colorful of all entertainment media was the circus, which reached its apex under Barnum and Bailey and the Ringling Brothers. But despite its strong appeal, the circus has been losing ground since 1930, and today, even in some large communities, the traveling circus—like the "nickel beer"— is becoming only a nostalgic memory.

GOOD MUSIC FOR ALL—The band of earlier days supplied background music to social gossip and a stroll in the park. The highly developed public address system of modern days holds silent a much larger audience indoors.

Sports

Baseball by 1900 had become an integral part of American life. The improvement of transportation brought larger numbers of fans from all parts of the surrounding area to the ball park. Personal interest in teams and players, coupled with hero worship of colorful individuals like Babe Ruth and Ty Cobb, was highlighted by radio broadcasts which gave millions of enthusiasts an opportunity to follow the game play by play, and intensified the desire to see the action in person.

Football and basketball also became popular sports. Originally high school and college sports events patronized largely by students and alumni, both games are now played professionally as well and rival baseball in attendance by the general public.

An upswing in sports participation, as distinguished from spectator attendance, was in line with emphasis on "active" leisure. Hunting, fishing, boating, and camping boomed. Nonteam sports like golf and tennis attracted increasing numbers of devotees from lower income groups. Swimming has approached the status of a universal pastime. Public pools have been established in the city proper and cooperatively owned community swimming pools are scattered through suburban areas. Amateur baseball leagues of varied sponsorship, drawing participants from a broad cross section of the population, abound.

These trends appear to be competing with the older industrial recreation programs which flourished in the period between the two world wars. A Labor Department study of 51 companies in 1913 showed that 53 percent maintained recreation programs. Another study in 1916–17 showed that 152 of 431 establishments reporting, or 35 percent, had facilities for indoor recreation such as poolrooms, gymnasiums, clubhouses. Slightly over half provided for social gatherings, lectures, and music for employees. Fifty percent provided some outdoor recreation.

Industrial recreation probably reached its peak in the depression years and declined somewhat in relative importance thereafter with the movement to the suburbs and the attendant lure of other pursuits. But the bowling league, the company baseball team, and the annual company outing attest to the continued existence of recreation associated with employment. Some industrial concerns maintain elaborate recreational programs characterized by vigorous employee participation.

Travel

It was not until after World War I that the automobile began to play an important role in shaping the spare-time activities of workers. (See chapter VIII for transportation developments.)

Rapidly increasing numbers of workers began to discover recreational uses of the automobile. Short drives to cool off on a hot summer evening, the Sunday trip into the country, and the vacation tour rapidly replaced or supplemented such forms of recreational activity as trolley rides, strolling in the park, or bicycling. Many homes accepted tourists as overnight guests. Tourist cabins and roadside restaurants began to spring up, foreshadowing the spectacular motel boom of the current decade. The motorized holiday began to assume large proportions during the 1920's; surveys in several States indicated that over 50 percent of all automobile use was for social and recreational purposes.

Public Recreation Facilities

At the turn of the century, many large cities had begun to provide public playgrounds, and the movement gained rapid headway after 1906, when the National Recreation Association was organized. By 1912, supervised public playground activities were being directed by over 5,000 paid supervisors, and this number grew rapidly to almost 60,000 by 1950. During the depression years of the 1930's, community recreation facilities were extended considerably under government auspices, and thousands of camps, picnicking grounds, trails, swimming pools, tennis courts, and recreation buildings were constructed. The growth in the number of selected facilities and personnel in municipal recreation from 1920 to 1950, shown in the following tabulation, attests to the vigor with which American communities met the expanding demand for leisure-time play facilities.

Facilities and personnel	1920	1930	1940	1950
Baseball diamonds		4,322	3,904	5,502
Bathing beaches	260	457	572	780
Golf courses		312	387	454
Handball courts			2,737	1,953
Ice skating areas			2,912	3,274
Outdoor playgrounds	4,293	7,316	9,921	14,747
Recreation buildings	300	642	1,750	2,987
Indoor recreation centers		1,963	3,986	6,630
Stadiums			261	504
Swimming pools	359	1,042	1,200	1,616
Tennis courts		8,422	12,075	13,085
Toboggan slides		221	314	268
Paid leaders	10,218	24,949	[1] 24,533	58,029
Volunteer leaders		8,216	12,890	52,982

[1] Excludes leaders paid with Federal emergency funds.

SOURCE: Reports to the National Recreation Association, as published in America's Needs and Resources: A New Survey, by J. Frederick Dewhurst and Associates (New York, The Twentieth Century Fund, 1955).

Keeping pace with the development of playground areas was the creation of public parks in most large cities. By 1902, almost

800 cities had made a beginning at providing parks where urban dwellers could enjoy the "rural, sylvan, and natural scenery." City planners rapidly expanded municipal park acreage and facilities throughout the country. By 1950, an estimated 700,000 acres of park lands were in use in urban areas, and additional acres of forest preserves and recreation areas were within easy access to city dwellers. The National Park Service in 1956 operated 26 national parks comprising nearly 11 million acres of land and 4 recreation areas totaling over 2 million acres. In addition, there were over 2,000 State parks embracing over 5 million acres.

In spite of this remarkable development of recreational facilities, millions of urban and suburban children still do not have adequate play areas, and adult demand for time on municipal golf courses and tennis courts cannot be satisfied. Public beaches are crowded and highways are choked with cars. Partly offsetting these inadequacies, the worker's home, once again, has become an important recreational center. As suburban communities continue their spectacular development, interest and active participation in community and church affairs take a growing share of the worker's leisure time. Furthermore, growing suburban communities are devoting more attention to planning for adequate recreational facilities and park lands.

Workers and Community Affairs. There are many signs of growing wage-earner participation in community affairs. For example, the AFL-CIO has established a community services program with a national staff, 125 full-time community workers, and 25,000 trained counselors—volunteers who advise workers on their personal problems. This activity benefits not only union members and their families, but other members of the community as well, particularly in meeting special health, welfare, educational, and recreational needs. Moreover, it has helped to promote a greater sense of civic awareness and citizenship responsibility on the part of wage earners. Recently a union official declared that "trade unionists are on social agency boards that run the gamut of the Boy Scouts and the Girl Scouts right up to the board of directors of the American Red Cross."[2] Another pointed out that union members are participating in such volunteer activities as raising funds for service agencies in their communities, contributing labor to building hospitals and fire stations, and aiding disaster relief.

Various unions have been operating rest homes, summer camps, and musical programs and otherwise taking measures to meet the recreational and related needs of members and their families. In recent years, one of the best-known union efforts in the entertainment field has been the New York Philharmonic's tour of steel towns under the sponsorship of the United Steelworkers of America.

The United Automobile Workers recently sponsored a choral group in the Detroit area as a community activity open to all residents of the area with the requisite talent. It was emphasized that the choral group would provide an outlet for increased leisure. The male chorus of the Homestead Steel Works—an organization composed mainly of plant workers—has achieved considerable fame, having appeared on national TV and radio networks.

Radio, Television, and Music

Radio arrived as a public feature of the American scene in 1920. Receiving sets began as a do-it-yourself hobby, first with crystal and earphones, then with tubes, coils, condensers, and battery. Many an amateur radio builder experienced the thrill of hearing the first crackle and sputterings of a far distant station through his homemade creation. By 1927, although the industry was still experimenting both with reception and transmission, 732 broadcasting stations were in existence and the first network broadcast of a symphony had been made. About 30 percent of American homes had radios, compared with 40 percent owning phonographs, which with pianos had long provided musical entertainment in the home.

The manufacture of relatively inexpensive radio receivers in the following years made radio available to all, and in the early 1940's, when wartime restrictions and production for military use prevented further expansion, about 4 out of every 5 American homes had radio service. After World War II, it was an unusual household that did not have at least one radio in the home, and many had one in the family car as well. Roughly a third of the programs offered to radio listeners in the early postwar years included mysteries, situation comedies, and drama. Variety shows represented over 20 percent of listening time; music, 20 percent; news and commentators, 20 percent; and audience participation and quiz programs, the balance.

In the late 1920's, the radio threatened the phonograph with virtual extinction, and cut deeply into expenditures for pianos and other musical instruments. A study made by Business Week, comparing the distribution of the "recreation dollar" in 1919 and 1929, showed a startling shift to radio over the 10-year period, and a corresponding decrease in the proportion allotted to phonographs and musical instruments.

The subsequent development of the electric phonograph, in part as an adjunct to radio, and the stimulation of interest in music by radio broadcasts of popular, familiar, and classical compositions, revived the use of the record player. After the advent of longer playing records in 1948, Americans looked for better and better equipment to get the utmost in musical fidelity from an ever-expanding selection of popular and classical recordings. By 1957, almost all major works of musical art had been superbly recorded and record manufacturers were turning to suitable nonmusical materials to meet the demand for new recordings.

The current interest in high-fidelity phonographs, plus increasing attendance at musical performances of all kinds, indicates the growing importance of music in leisure pursuits. In 1953, Newsweek indicated that "hi-fi" had become "big business" and predicted that annual sales would rise from $70 million to $300 million. Sales of records were expected to rise from $225 million to $300 million.

These advances in radio and record players may also have intensified the interest in playing a musical instrument. The number of music stores increased slightly between 1948 and 1954, and such large numbers of teen-agers have wanted to play in a high school band that nearly all but the smallest schools have bands or orchestras nowadays.

Television burst upon the American scene in 1948. Prewar experimentation with receivers and telecasting, and continued small-scale development after the war, achieved a high degree of technical proficiency which made mass production of sets and large-scale broadcasting possible. In 1948, nearly 1 million receivers were produced and the broadcasting stations in operation increased from 17 to 50. In 1949, 3 million sets were produced and 97 stations were operating on a regular program basis. In 1956, an estimated 39 million sets were in use, three-quarters of all American households had at least one, and network broadcasts were carried by about 500 TV stations. TV viewing had become a major attraction.

The predominance of television as a means of occupying leisure time was clearly shown by a 1-week survey of how people spent their time in 1957. An estimated 75 million (out of a total sampled population of 123 million people over 12 years of age) averaged approximately 19 hours per person during the week in front of the TV set. Radio came next, with 69 million listeners averaging 14 hours per person for the week. Newspapers occupied 100 million for an average of 4 hours. Magazines were read by 37 million, who averaged a little over 4½ hours. Sixty-one million saw movies during the week, with the average time of 4 hours being closer to two movies (or a double feature) than to one.

In the first years of television, the elaborate variety show held first place in program preference, but outstanding sports events were also popular. In the following years, variety shows, comedy, drama, and news ranked high on network schedules and the showing of full-length movies became a standard feature. An increasing amount of time devoted to public events allowed millions of workers to witness national political conventions, Presidential inaugurations, and congressional investigating bodies in action. The use of television by candidates campaigning for public office gave the voting public ample chance to study both the candidates and issues, and news commentators contributed to the educational process. Increasing attention has been given, also, to "cultural" programs, including grand opera, drama, and music. A beginning has been made, too, in the use of television for educational purposes, both by the public schools and medical schools for classroom teaching and by a few universities for adult education.

Adult Education

The worker's horizons broadened through the advance of these media of mass communication, of course, but that is only one aspect of the improvements in opportunities and facilities for education of the worker and his family that have taken place in the last half century. More children go to school for a longer time, and the level of education of the population generally has risen remarkably. These improvements are due in large part to improvements in school facilities.

By 1900, the American free public school system was well established, and stood as a glowing accomplishment of those in the 19th century who struggled to achieve a public, State-supported school system, free from sectarian control and complete through primary and high school grades into advanced levels of education. Night schools and extension schools formed an important part of this secondary school development.

Adult instruction in the public schools, generally in the evenings, was a notable development of the period following World War I. The adult education movement had originated in the 1830's, when Boston and Louisville offered classes to adults. New York followed in 1847, first offering elementary courses and, toward the end of the century, free lectures. In 1908, almost 6,000 lectures were given on a variety of scientific and cultural subjects. The program had been characterized, a few years earlier, as follows:

> Turning from the platform to the people, we notice that young men predominate, especially when the lecture touches some practical art of electricity, photography, or lithography. If the subject is

historical or literary, the greater part of the audience will be young women, many of whom doubtless would attend the high schools if they could.[3]

The lectures flourished during the early part of the century, when immigration was heavy. As the influx slackened, attendance fell off, no doubt partially because the public schools and colleges were available to a larger percentage of the young people. Also, the establishment of vocational and commercial courses attracted many adult students who might otherwise have attended the lectures.

Illiteracy received much attention in the first quarter of this century. New York, Chicago, Philadelphia, and Boston, concerned with this problem among both foreign and native born, established courses in the fundamentals of reading and writing. The biennial survey of education of 1922–24 showed that over 336,000 adult students were enrolled in classes for native- and foreign-born illiterates. A number of the foreign born were undoubtedly literate in their native tongue but could not read or write English.

The social settlement or neighborhood houses (Hull House in Chicago, for example) were not established primarily for adult education, but they did make an appreciable contribution to the education of illiterate city workers. Countless immigrants benefited from their classes in the English language and American citizenship as well as music, literature, and science. Moreover, since they were designed primarily to supply wholesome recreation and friendship, the settlements were able to offer education in a setting more congenial than the more restrictive atmosphere of the public schools.

Along with the foregoing developments, the regular public evening schools had been growing steadily, as can be seen in the following tabulation:

Year	Cities with evening schools	Teachers	Pupils
1890	165	3,678	150,770
1900	n. a.	5,115	203,000
1910	227	9,326	374,364
1920	582	18,461	586,843
1930	664	24,071	1,038,052

SOURCE: Part-Time Secondary Schools, U. S. Office of Education Reports, Bulletin, 1932, No. 17; National Survey of Secondary Education, Monograph No. 3, U. S. Department of the Interior, 1932, p. 44.

Vocational education formed an important part of most adult programs, especially after Federal aid was made available in 1918.

Total expenditures have risen from $3 million in 1918 to $165 million in 1955. The obvious value in learning and improving a trade, accentuated by rapid changes in technology, has given rise to heavy demand for vocational courses.

In recent years, there has been a noticeable increase in attendance by hobby enthusiasts. Amateur woodworkers and camera fans now attend vocational classes side by side with would-be "professionals." Housewives, too, are resorting to vocational courses for efficiency in such homemaking arts as fancy cooking, sewing, and home decoration. Even bridge, dancing, and flower arrangement appear in some curriculums.

The changing character and growing importance of adult education is apparent in the National Education Association's concern with it. In 1921, the NEA formed a separate adult education department to deal with the education of immigrants. This was extended, in 1927, to include all adults, and, in 1945, it became a separate division known as the Adult Education Service. In 1951, the Adult Education Association was established. It absorbed the membership of the Carnegie Foundation's American Association for Adult Education and the Adult Education Service of the National Education Association.

A recent study shows that 3 million adults were enrolled in public school courses in the 1952-53 academic year. Over 6,000 school districts had such courses. Some States, e.g., California, are particularly active in this respect and, in the larger urban areas, offer an amazingly varied number of courses to adults.

Another facet of adult education is the university extension course, aimed at carrying adults beyond the levels attainable through public school night courses. The University of Wisconsin has been one of the pioneers in this field, having evolved, after considerable study and analysis, a pattern of extension work available to wage earners. The program includes correspondence courses, summer schools, extension classes, broadcasts, films, and publications. Many other universities, in varying manner, have followed the Wisconsin example. As a result, broad avenues for higher education have been opened to wage earners who could not afford regular attendance at a university. Here, too, housewives have been participating in increasing numbers, taking advantage of their leisure time to study child psychology, art appreciation, literature, and hundreds of other subjects.

The labor unions played an important role in stimulating the workers' educational movement. They took a major step in this direction in 1921 by the formation of the Workers' Education Bureau of America. This organization was designed to act as a clearinghouse for educational opportunities available to workers.

Recognition by labor unions that union leaders need training and that their members need educational opportunities for broadening their cultural background led to the establishment of education departments in a majority of national unions. These departments now carry on continuing educational programs through regional and State resident schools, sectional and city-level institutions, trade council seminars, and local union classes. Educational projects conducted through these organizations include not only labor education designed to prepare workers for active participation in union affairs, but also studies in basic economics, consumer guidance, political science, and social subjects such as intergroup relations, housing, and community service work. In 1955, unions affiliated with the American Federation of Labor and the Congress of Industrial Organizations conducted or cooperated in over 150 labor institutes, conferences, and summer schools lasting 4 days or more, and in innumerable shorter classes, courses, and lecture series. Increasingly, universities are opening their doors to such institutes and summer schools.

Skill training of workers on the job has always been an important function of management to fit workers to the particular tasks assigned to them. The increasing demand for highly skilled workers in modern production systems has accelerated the training of employees and, since World War I, private industrial initiative has greatly extended educational opportunities in industry. In large corporations, extensive training of workers and executives is undertaken in the form of corporate trade and engineering schools to supplement the practical instruction in the shops, and through cooperative arrangements with technical and vocational public schools.

Further extensions of educational benefits have been made since the last war in the form of veterans' education. The Servicemen's Readjustment Act contained provisions which made college education and other forms of training available to veterans of World War II, and the Korean GI bill of rights extended these educational advantages. Over 11 million veterans applied for these benefits up to 1955. Training received in the various military services also represents an important factor in preparing workers for the higher skills now required by modern industry.

A number of private agencies have also contributed significantly to adult education, including the settlement houses mentioned previously. One of the earlier and more notable is the Chautauqua movement which, in the words of its founder, was established to extend "the principle, now so generally accepted, that education is the privilege of all, young and old, rich and poor, that mental development is only begun in school and college and should be continued through all of life."[4] It was responsible for initiating three important elements in adult education: the summer school, the correspondence school, and guided home reading. Although Chautauqua was finally eclipsed by the increasing educational opportunities made possible through urbanization, its impact has been pronounced.

Reading

A natural accompaniment of the increased emphasis on education was the rising popularity of reading as a leisure-time activity. Despite the traditional importance of reading as a form of recreation, adequate analysis of changes in reading tastes is not feasible, since they are so elusive.

The wide use of public libraries and, especially in recent decades, the amazing success of paperbound books do, however, indicate a vigorous interest in reading. Most of the classics, now available in this form, are reaching far more people than their authors could have imagined; and contemporary books of serious content, including poetry, are in popular demand.

Hobbies

One other recreational bent is characteristic of American workers—the do-it-yourself project. Men of an industrial society with a pioneering tradition naturally fall heir to a handiness with tools. Nevertheless, in recent years, the do-it-yourself movement has become a surprising national phenomenon. The construction of radio receiving sets in the 1920's, already mentioned, and the building of hi-fi systems in the 1950's serve as illustrations.

EXPENDITURES OF WORKERS' FAMILIES

Expenditures are at best inadequate measures of leisure-time activities. Many important leisure-time activities do not affect consumer budgets directly. They are provided by governments at public cost or by private institutions financed by endowments and contributions rather than fees for services rendered. Conspicuous among these are the variety of adult education programs. Others, such as watching sunsets, or catching crayfish in the local river, or playing checkers with a neighbor, may involve little or no cost.

The four surveys of urban workers' expenditures by the Bureau of Labor Statistics since 1900 do, however, demonstrate the increasing importance of recreation, education, and reading. In 1901, families allotted, on the average, 2.7 percent of their expenditures to these activities* (table 23, below). The ratio increased to 3.7 percent in 1917-19. In the mid-1930's, in spite of the depression, employed workers were allocating 4.1 percent of their spending to leisure pursuits; by 1950, the proportion had risen to 5.8 percent. In very summary fashion, these data indicate that as real income increased over the period, wage earners were inclined to devote more to leisure-time activities.

A more revealing picture of shifts in the pattern of spending for leisure-time activities can be found in the estimates of personal consumption expenditures for all American families. (See table 24, p. 215.) In 1929, when that statistical series begins, the prosperity of the time was reflected in large expenditures for radios, phonographs, and musical instruments. Newspapers, magazines, books, and other reading materials were next in importance, with movie admissions running third. In the depression years 1933-35, the spending for both reading and recreation fell drastically, even when the fall in prices is considered, and only 10 percent of the total was for purchasing items in the radio and musical instruments group. Reading materials commanded a fourth of the total and motion pictures a fifth.

TABLE 23.—*Wage-earner and clerical-worker family expenditures for recreation, reading, and education, selected periods, 1901-50*

Item	1901 [1] Amount	1901 [1] Percent of total expenditures for current consumption	1917-19 Amount	1917-19 Percent of total expenditures for current consumption	1934-36 Amount	1934-36 Percent of total expenditures for current consumption	1950 Amount	1950 Percent of total expenditures for current consumption
Radio, television, and musical instruments			$10	0.7	$7	0.5	$67	1.7
Admissions [2]	$10	1.6	9	0.6	19	1.3	46	1.2
Reading [3]	7	1.1	11	0.8	15	1.0	34	0.9
Education [4]			7	0.5	7	0.5	17	0.4
Other [5]			14	1.1	12	0.8	63	1.6
Total	17	2.7	51	3.7	60	4.1	228	5.8

[1] Estimates based on detailed reports for 2,567 families.
[2] Movies, spectator sports, plays, and concerts.
[3] Newspapers, magazines, and rental and purchase of books other than school books.
[4] School supplies, books, tuition, music and dancing lessons, and the like.
[5] The "other" category is not entirely comparable as between 1917-19 and the subsequent periods. For example, the 1917-19 figure includes travel expenditures incident to excursions and vacations, which are classified as travel expenditures in the later surveys.

NOTE: Items may not add to totals because of rounding.
SOURCE: See tables 3, 4, 5, and 6.

*The 1901 figure is not entirely comparable with the totals for later years, mainly because it does not include expenditures for education; they are not available for that year.

TABLE 24.—*Distribution of total personal consumption expenditures for recreation and reading, selected years, 1929-55*

Item	1929	1933	1935	1940	1944	1950	1955
Total expenditures for recreation and reading:							
Amount (in millions)	$4,331	$2,202	$2,630	$3,761	$5,422	$10,768	$13,020
Percent	100.0	100.0	100.0	100.0	100.0	100.0	100.0
Admissions	21.0	26.0	25.5	24.0	28.8	16.6	13.5
Motion pictures	16.6	21.9	21.1	19.5	24.7	12.9	9.9
Theatre, opera, etc	2.9	1.8	1.7	1.9	2.6	1.6	1.8
Spectator sports	1.5	2.3	2.7	2.6	1.5	2.1	1.8
Radios, television, phonographs, and musical instruments	24.0	9.5	10.2	14.0	7.1	25.1	23.1
Commercial participant amusements	4.8	5.5	5.4	5.2	4.4	4.3	4.8
Clubs and organizations	7.0	9.4	7.5	5.4	4.4	4.4	4.5
Sport equipment, toys, etc	12.8	12.4	13.4	14.9	14.4	18.4	21.3
Reading materials	19.6	26.0	24.3	21.9	24.5	18.1	17.8
Other recreation	10.8	11.2	13.7	14.6	16.4	13.1	15.0

SOURCE: National Income, 1954, A Supplement to the Survey of Current Business, and Survey of Current Business, July 1957, table 30 (U. S. Department of Commerce, Office of Business Economics).

By 1940, recovery from the depression was marked by use of a larger part of the recreation dollar than in the depression to pay for radios, phonographs, and musical instruments, at the expense of reading, movies, and social clubs and organizations. This was short-lived, however. The effect of wartime conditions is told dramatically by the sharp drop in spending for radios and instruments. In 1944, only 7 percent of the recreation dollar went to this group of items; attendance at movies became the most popular activity, and reading was a strong second choice.

Movies reached their climax as a consumer expenditure item in World War II; thereafter, television took the lead. Addition of TV to the category of radio, phonographs, and musical instruments caused total expenditures for this group almost to triple between 1929 and 1950. By the latter year, the group commanded one-fourth of all spending for recreation and reading. Motion picture theaters lost some of their attractiveness; families often stayed at home to watch resurrected movies, plays, and variety shows on their TV sets. The proportion of recreational expenditures on movies dropped from a fourth in 1944 to less than a tenth in 1955.

Stimulated, no doubt, by TV broadcasts of sports events, higher real incomes, and the move to suburbia, the public turned toward outdoor physical activities. Homeownership contributed to the emphasis placed on outdoor activities and prompted the purchase of equipment for gardening, games, and the barbecue pit. Purchases of sporting goods and equipment, as well as toys, increased rapidly.

There remains a question as to the extent to which these changes in the distribution of aggregate spending for reading and recreation describe the urban worker's experience. The aggregate figures include spending by other urban families, farm families, and institutions.

The Bureau of Labor Statistics 1950 Survey of Consumer Expenditures shows clearly that by that year the average urban worker's family spending pattern was not very different from the average of all urban families. (See table 25, below.) Compared with all urban families, urban wage earners and clerical workers spent somewhat more of their reading, recreation, and education dollars for recreational pursuits, somewhat less for education, and about the same for reading materials. The proportion of workers' total expenditures going to these groups was about equal to the urban average: 5.8 percent compared with 5.9 percent. The differences are hardly significant. It is highly significant, however, that by 1950 the spare-time habits and expenditure patterns of urban workers differed so slightly from national norms; in 1901 they were distinctively "working class."

TABLE 25.—*Percent distribution of urban family expenditures for recreation, reading, and education, 1950*

Item [1]	All families	Workers' families
Recreation	74.3	77.1
Radio, television, and musical instruments	26.7	29.4
Admissions	18.2	20.1
Other	29.4	27.6
Reading	15.5	15.4
Education	10.2	7.5
Total	100.0	100.0

[1] For definition of items, see table 23.

SOURCE: See tables 6 and 8.

Footnotes

[1] The 5-Day Week in Ford Plants (in *Monthly Labor Review*, December 1926, p. 11).

[2] George Iles, *World's Work*, quoted in B. W. Overstreet, The Free Lecture System of New York, in *Adult Education in Action* (New York, American Association for Adult Education, 1936), p. 77.

[3] C. Hartley Grattan, *In Quest of Knowledge—A Historical Perspective on Adult Education* (New York, Association Press, 1955), p. 168.

[4] *AFL-CIO News*, September 7, 1957, p. 6.

CHAPTER X

Consumption Statistics: A Technical Comment

> *The belief in Progress, not as an ideal but as an indisputable fact, not as a task for humanity but as a law of nature, has been the working faith of the West for about a hundred and fifty years.*
> —William Ralph Inge.

In drawing on the sources of information about United States city workers and their families as consumers, previous chapters have indicated important limitations on the use of the sources for comparisons of one period with another. Even in a book with the nontechnical purpose of the present volume, readers are entitled to a summary of differences in the sources, especially those arising from changes in statistical concepts and techniques. As it happens, the very changes which impair comparability often constitute additional evidence of gains in the workers' status as consumers. Thus viewed, brief descriptions and evaluations of expenditure surveys, standard budgets, and estimates of total personal consumption expenditures for the population as a whole become an integral—if little known—part of the story, rather than a mere appendix on methods.

SURVEYS OF CONSUMER EXPENDITURES

For any study of city workers as consumers, the primary source of data is the several consumer expenditure surveys made by the U. S. Bureau of Labor Statistics* between 1888 and 1950. Although 4 of these studies—1901, 1917–19, 1934–36, and 1950—have been relied on primarily here, limited use has been made of other surveys, including an 1875 study in Massachusetts. The purposes of the several surveys were not identical—a major source of noncomparability but also a distinct reflection of the progress of workers as consumers. Other important sources of noncompara-

---

*The Bureau of Labor Statistics has operated under a variety of names and within several Federal departments during its history. It was originally established by the act of June 27, 1884, and organized in January 1885 as the Bureau of Labor within the Department of the Interior. In 1888 it was made the Department of Labor and headed by a commissioner who was not, however, a member of the President's Cabinet. In 1903 it became the Bureau of Labor in the Department of Commerce and Labor, and in 1913 was incorporated as the Bureau of Labor Statistics in the newly established Department of Labor.

bility are the populations represented, the criteria for selecting families surveyed, and the survey methods.

Laying the Foundation: 1875

The existence of general comparability among the various surveys can be attributed primarily to the use of the basic methods established in the first expenditure survey in the United States—the 1875 survey in Massachusetts—in all of the studies by the Bureau of Labor Statistics. The fact that Carroll D. Wright, chief of the Massachusetts Bureau of Statistics of Labor in 1875, became the first head of the corresponding Federal bureau and held this position from 1885 to 1905 seems to explain this fortunate circumstance. Certainly his influence on the 1888–91 and 1901 surveys is clear. Beyond that, any survey of income and expenditures, to be meaningful, must obtain the kind of basic information described in the Massachusetts report:

> Cost of living, an often-used expression, means, in its broadest sense, the relation of earnings to expenses. A complete handling of such a subject, with this comprehension, requires, first, a full investigation into the sources of income, denoting the amount received from each; second, an analysis of the total expenditure, showing the outlay for each item of necessaries or luxuries; third, a comparison between the two sides of the account, as given above, in order to show the pecuniary surplus or deficit . . . .[1]

With the exception of refinements for handling changes in family assets and liabilities, the 1875 statement might have applied to each of the subsequent surveys. Because all of the surveys provided thorough accounts, completeness and consistency have been checked severely and extensively.

Purposes of Major Surveys

Recognition of the worker's rising level of living is implicit in the stated purposes of these studies.

The 1875 study, on which table 1 (p. 35) is based, was designed "to show the actual condition of the workingman . . . and his comparative situation as regards his fellow laborers in other states and foreign countries . . . ."[2] Concern for the worker's welfare was emphasized in the report's summary:

> Our work and aim has been to hold the mirror up to the entire wage system (not with restricted application to its working in corporations), in order that it might see its own deformities, and be led to soften its visage and look with more brotherly feeling upon the laborer, who toils on and ever, and who being worthy of his hire, should receive it.[3]

In 1888, when the Bureau of Labor undertook the first nationwide expenditure survey, its purpose, in line with the legislation creating the Bureau, was to study the worker's consumption habits and living costs as elements of production costs and competition in foreign trade. (Data from this study are presented in table 2, p. 37.) Another phase of the study covered wages in these industries, both here and abroad, since advocates of higher tariffs were arguing for the "protection" of workers from "cheap" labor in competing countries. The extent to which the surveys emphasized the worker's role as a producer, rather than as a consumer, is suggested in the Sixth Annual Report of the Commissioner of Labor, which presented the results:

> An essential element in the cost of production and in the efficiency of the labor employed is the cost of living. In connection, therefore, with the facts gathered by the agents of the Department relating to the cost of production, earnings, and efficiency of labor, there has been collected a vast amount of information pertaining to the cost of living of the men engaged . . .[4]

The 1901 study, which is the basis for table 3 (p. 40), reflected an interest in workers' consumption patterns per se. Thus the Bureau sought to obtain a representative sample of all industrial wage earners. Two principal reasons were cited for this survey: The passage of time (more than a decade) since the preceding study indicated the need for more recent data, and expenditure data were needed to derive weights for combining retail food prices, collected concurrently but covering the preceding decade, into a retail food price index.

The 1917–19 survey had similar aims, but it was designed also to serve other objectives. (See table 4, p. 42, for results of this survey.) Royal Meeker, Commissioner of Labor Statistics at the time, indicated that the survey had the purposes—

> . . . (1) of determining the quantities and cost of all important items of family consumption in all the more important industrial centers in the United States, (2) of applying the accepted dietary standards for determining whether the families studied were obtaining a sufficient number of calories and sufficient variety in their diets to maintain their members in health, (3) of working out, if possible, standards—similar to the recognized dietary standards—for clothing, housing, fuel, housefurnishings, education, amusement, medical care, insurance and perhaps some other items which have been heretofore blanketed and lost under the term "miscellaneous," (4) of formulating eventually tentative standard budgets to be used by wage adjustment boards in determining minimum and fair wage awards, (5) of enabling the Bureau of Labor Statistics to compute a cost of living index number that will show variations in total family expenses in the same way as the retail food price index shows variations in the cost of the family food budget.[5]

This quotation indicates the first use of one of the studies to derive a list of items representing both the kinds and quantities of things bought by workers' families for constructing a "cost of living" index. The subsequent discussion of standard budgets (p. 232) indicates how the Bureau drew on the 1917–19 study for its standard budget studies.

The 1934–36 survey of income and expenditures, presented in table 5 (p. 44), was designed primarily to revise the cost of living index; the spending patterns of wage earners and clerical workers living in large cities had changed substantially since 1917–19. It was conducted concurrently with a study of consumer purchases, made by the Bureau in cooperation with four other Federal agencies. The latter study undertook to reflect consumption of all segments of the population, both urban and rural. The attempt was in line with the new and sharp awareness of the importance of consumption data for analytical and policy-making purposes which were very different and much broader than those of the earlier studies. The Bureau's recognition of these developments in economic analysis and theory, as well as of other uses of expenditure survey data, is shown by the summary report of the 1934–36 study:

> In addition [to its use for index revision], it has supplied valuable data about the kind of living available to the families of employed wage earners and clerical workers in large cities, as defined by the sources of their incomes, the kinds of goods and services they buy in a year, and the kind of dwellings in which they live.
>
> The material, supplying as it does the largest body of available data on the entire range of items for which moderate-income families in large cities spend, will be of great value to businessmen wishing to estimate the demand for specific products among urban families at the income levels in which these groups are found. It will also be of value to legislators and other students of taxation problems, to labor leaders and employers in connection with wage adjustments, to welfare workers planning family budgets and relief allowances, and to students of consumption problems interested in the more theoretical aspects of the subject.[6]

In its 1950 study (tables 6, 8, and 9, chapter II), the Bureau sought to determine current expenditure patterns of workers' families for purposes of revising the index (which had meanwhile been renamed the Consumer Price Index) and also to obtain comparable data for all urban consumers. Thus the survey included all levels of income, all occupational groups, and "single consumers," i. e., unrelated individuals functioning as consumer units, in addition to families. This provided not only the basis for comparing wage-earner and clerical-worker family expenditure patterns with those of other economic groups but also a wealth of material for use in other types of consumption analyses.

Purposes of Other Surveys

Among the more interesting and unusual of the other expenditure surveys used in this book was the study of wages, food prices, rents, and living conditions among industrial workers in 1909, conducted by the British Board of Trade. Like our government's 1888-91 survey, the study's primary purpose was a comparison of the cost of living in various countries. Data were obtained from over 8,000 workers in 28 cities, located mostly in the area east of the Mississippi, which was considered sufficiently industrialized and urbanized to be comparable with England and Wales. In addition to the overall averages, separate data were published for each city and for major nationality groups.

The study of consumer purchases in 1935-36 was conducted under the auspices of 5 cooperating Federal agencies—the National Resources Committee, the Central Statistical Board, the Works Progress Administration, the Bureau of Home Economics of the U. S. Department of Agriculture, and the Bureau of Labor Statistics. This study provided, for the first time, "an extensive and comparable body of data on the spending habits of the various major groups of American consumers,"[7] reflecting the new emphasis on the role of consumption in the Nation's economy. It yielded a battery of reports which remain unique statistically. They provide reliable estimates* for both urban and rural consumer groups, based on a national sample of sufficient size to permit cross-classification by the significant characteristics which are essential to the analysis of consumer behavior.

Two nationwide surveys were made during World War II, in 1941-42 and in 1944, with the former including rural consumers. Both were designed primarily to obtain nationwide data required for tax, rationing, and other wartime economic policy purposes. Accordingly, relatively small samples could be used to obtain reliable national averages.

The impact of World War II on consumption patterns led to fears that the weights used in the Consumer Price Index (then based on the 1934-36 survey) were no longer representative. Accordingly, the Bureau of Labor Statistics made expenditure surveys in several cities during the years 1947-49, which demonstrated the need for index revision. The 91-city expenditure survey in 1950 was designed, as previously indicated, to provide the basis for a complete revision of the index. However, the Korean hostilities necessitated index adjustments before the comprehen-

---

*Statisticians call any figure obtained from a sample of a large population an "estimate," in distinction from data collected from all members of the population as in a census, which are known technically as "parameters."

sive revision could be completed. Therefore, the relatively small 1947-49 surveys were used in making immediate improvements to the index. Subsequent analysis of the 1950 survey data established the substantial validity of this interim adjustment.

Populations Represented*

Differences in purposes and, to a lesser extent, advances in knowledge of sampling created significant differences in the populations represented in these surveys.

In the earlier expenditure surveys, the purposes dictated that the coverage be confined to workers: In 1888-91, those employed in 9 major industries protected by the tariff; in 1901, workers in principal industrial centers (those employed in services and trade and transportation as well as manufacturing); in 1917-19, workers in 92 urban places located in 42 States; and in 1934-36, wage earners and clerical workers in 42 large cities.

In all these surveys, two stages of sampling were employed. Urban centers in effect served as primary sampling points, largely because industries usually were located in cities. In the second stage in sampling, individual workers were chosen from the payrolls of particular companies. Precise information about some of the earlier sampling procedures is now lacking, but experimental and somewhat informal methods are apparent, for example, from the quotation given below (p. 225) regarding the 1875 Massachusetts survey.

Because the total population was to be sampled in the 1935-36 study of consumer purchases, the individual consumer units were drawn from city directories.** Newly developed area sampling techniques were applied in the World War II and subsequent expenditure surveys. In the Bureau's surveys, the areas were blocks or their equivalent, so stratified as to obtain a sample representative of the population.

The sample for the 1950 study was much larger than for the wartime surveys, in order to obtain usable data for individual cities and classes of cities. The sample was also designed to permit extensive cross-classification by important family characteristics that influence expenditures significantly. These include not only income and family type and size but also such characteristics of the family head as age, sex, race, occupation, and education.

---

*In the subsequent discussion of populations represented and eligibility differences in the various surveys, indebtedness is acknowledged for access to the following monograph scheduled for publication in 1959 by the Wharton School of Finance and Commerce: Helen Humes Lamale, Methodology of the Survey of Consumer Expenditures in 1950, Appendix B, Summaries of Nationwide Expenditure Surveys, 1888-1950. Selections from and interpretations of the facts are, of course, the author's responsibility.

**Except for New York City and Chicago, where samples were selected from real property inventory lists. Area sampling techniques were employed for villages and farms.

Criteria for Selection of Families

Survey eligibility rules (i. e., the standards used in determining whether to include a family in the survey) also affect the representativeness of the data and comparability between surveys. As the purposes shifted to the derivation of price index structure and the construction of standard budgets, eligibility rules were required to assure that the survey would yield data for families which could be deemed "normal."* Sometimes this was achieved by tabulating data separately for the normal families, as in 1901. In other cases, e. g., 1917–19 and 1934–36, data were collected only from wage-earner and clerical-worker families. The concept of normality has varied considerably; so have the sets of rules designed to define "workers" or "wage earners," as the case may be.

In both 1888–91 and 1901, the normal family was defined as a husband at work, a wife, no more than 5 children and none over age 14, and no other dependents living with the family. In 1901, salaried workers receiving more than $1,200 were ineligible, but no eligibility ceiling was placed on earnings of wage earners. Families with roomers and boarders were not classified as normal, although data for such families were obtained and published. In 1917–19, families were eligible only if they included at least 1 child who was not a boarder or a lodger. The family could have up to 3 lodgers, but families with income from boarders were not eligible. "Slum" and "charity" families were excluded, as were families unable to speak English and those living in the United States less than 5 years.

With the Nation plagued by unemployment and underemployment when the 1934–36 expenditure study was planned, a new eligibility requirement was deemed necessary: At least one wage earner or clerical worker in the family must have been employed as much as 1,008 hours spread over a period of 36 weeks. Families receiving either direct or work relief were excluded.** The result was that the group surveyed had a significantly higher average income than did all urban wage-earner and clerical-worker families. In all probability, too, that group was better off relative to other groups in the economy than sample families had been in other surveys. The traditional eligibility rules were somewhat relaxed; married couples with no children and 2-person families with one parent absent were eligible. The family could have the

---
*To provide norms in the statistical sense; i. e., families of size and composition so near the average that their expenditure patterns could be used as the basis for learning how much the expenditure patterns of less common types of families differed from the "norm."
**If the aim had been to represent simply the 1934–36 situation, such families might have been included, but the fact that revision of the index of prices of goods and services purchased by wage earners and clerical workers was the major objective made it important to obtain data which would be reasonably representative of such workers over a period of years.

equivalent of two full-time roomers or boarders (i. e., roomers or boarders present for a total of up to 104 weeks). All native-born families of two or more were eligible for the 1935-36 study of consumer purchases, with a few inconsequential restrictions.

In 1941-42, only the institutional population* was excluded, so that the sample for the first time included single consumers in proportion to their importance numerically in the total population. (The 1935-36 study had included some single consumers, but they were asked for income information in only 4 cities and for expenditure data in only 2 of the 4.) In both 1944 and 1950, the sample was designed to represent the entire urban noninstitutional population. Eligibility rules, therefore, eliminated very few consumer units.**

Varying representation of Negroes in the earlier surveys introduced an indeterminate statistical bias which affects historical comparisons. Very little is known about the extent to which Negroes were included in the 1888-91 and 1901 studies, but relatively few were then employed in the industries from which the samples were drawn.

The principal report on the 1917-19 survey included data from few if any Negro families. For those areas where Negroes were a sizable segment of the population, the data were tabulated and published separately. The data for white and Negro families were not combined for this volume because of lack of knowledge of the sampling design of that study and the consequent danger of constructing invalid or misleading averages for urban workers as a whole. Accordingly, average incomes and expenditures shown in table 4 of this volume are somewhat higher than if data for Negro families had been included.

Likewise, there is reason to believe that Negroes were underrepresented in the two surveys of the mid-thirties, except in areas where they comprised a substantial portion of the total population. In the 1941 and subsequent surveys, however, Negroes were included in proportion to their number in the total covered population.

Several of the expenditure surveys provided separate data for groups whose characteristics differed somewhat from those of the survey group as a whole. These are shown in table 26 (p. 226), which, although designed for another purpose, is useful in this connection. The groups most nearly comparable with the 1917-19

---

*Inmates of institutions, residents of military camps, posts, and reservations, etc.

**Probably the most important exclusion was that of families which existed only part of the survey year. The principal example would be a couple who married during the year, living as members of other families prior to marriage. In deriving Consumer Price Index weights, only data from the wage-earner and clerical-worker families were used. This procedure excluded single consumers, the self-employed, and other occupational groups not classified as wage earners or clerical workers, and all families with incomes of $10,000 or more after taxes.

and 1934–36 wage-earner and clerical-worker samples include the "normal" families in 1901, urban families of 2 or more in 1935–36, 1941–42, and 1944, and the wage-earner and clerical-worker families of 2 or more in 1950.

Survey Methods

Much of our ability to use the various studies in this type of analysis stems from the uniformity of basic survey methods. All of the Bureau's surveys—like the 1875 Massachusetts study—emphasized obtaining data on total incomes and expenditures of families or consumer units. In the 1934–36 study, this was expanded to include an equally comprehensive inquiry into changes in family assets and liabilities during the survey year. Previously, the difference between income and expenditures had been arbitrarily assigned as savings or debt, as the case might be. The same survey marked the first explicit recognition that families might report income, expenditures, or changes in savings—or indeed all three—erroneously.*

From the beginning, data have been obtained for a full year, although not always a calendar year. Likewise, since experience proved that personal inquiry by a trained interviewer elicited more complete and accurate information than other methods, this technique was built into each survey.

The Massachusetts study includes a piquant paragraph on this point:

> In every case, in the following returns, the entire earnings and the entire expenses are given. This desirable uniformity has been secured . . . by direct personal inquiry. The agent, upon arriving in a place selected for investigation, and, knowing its prominent or peculiar industries, visited the mill, workshop, wharf, public works, or foundry, as the case might be. Accosting the first workman at hand, a statement of what was desired was made; in case of compliance, a time was fixed, convenient to workingmen, at which to supply the desired figures and information; in case of inability or want of inclination, application was made to one and another of the workmen, and at other establishments, until the desired number was secured. Visits by day were made in order that the locality and the immediate surroundings of the houses could be examined, and visits in the evening were required, for then the workmen could refer to their account-books and bills, and find the items of

---

*This led to initiating use of the "balancing difference," i. e., calculation of the difference between total receipts and total disbursements as reported by the consumer unit, with the difference calculated as a percentage of the larger figure. In 1934–36, schedules with differences larger than 5 percent were not used. In subsequent surveys, higher differences were accepted. By 1950, this measure was used to "point the finger" at schedules which required a very rigorous examination, but no schedule was rejected automatically. The change in approach represented increasing awareness that automatic disqualification tempted field supervisors and interviewers to "force" schedules into balance by leading respondents to alter their original reports.

TABLE 26.—Total personal consumption expenditures per capita and average expenditures for current consumption per family member,[1] selected years, 1901–56

[In current dollars]

Year	Source and other identification [2]	Food	Rent	House-furnish-ings	House-hold opera-tion	Fuel, light, and refrigera-tion	Clothing	Transportation Public	Transportation Private	Medical care	Personal care	Recrea-tion [3]	Other goods and services [4]
1901	BLS—2,567 normal families	62	19	5	(3)	8	20	(3)	(3)	4	(3)	4	13
1901	BLS—11,156 normal families	68	28	(3)	(3)	9	20	(3)	(3)	9	(3)	(3)	31
1909	Dewhurst	81	61	15	17	15	41	9	7	9	3	13	35
1914	Dewhurst	90	63	15	16	17	41	11	11	9	3	14	35
1917–19	Dewhurst	112	38	13	8	15	49	5	3	13	3	10	7
1919	BLS—12,096 families of 3 or more	178	77	31	26	21	81	14	33	20	6	27	49
1921	Dewhurst	128	89	26	25	24	75	16	29	14	6	25	40
1923	Dewhurst	144	95	37	29	28	85	16	42	20	8	29	43
1925	Dewhurst	155	99	36	31	24	81	17	49	22	8	31	49
1927	Dewhurst	154	95	36	33	26	83	18	49	23	9	33	53
1929	Dewhurst	6 162	6 94	37	36	25	81	18	43	25	9	39	6 58
1929	Commerce	145	37	37	36	25	84	15	48	24	9	39	43
1930	Commerce	132	36	29	33	25	72	13	51	23	8	37	32
1931	Commerce	108	34	25	27	23	60	11	40	21	8	31	29
1932	Commerce	83	30	18	21	21	44	9	32	17	7	23	24
1933	Commerce	78	26	17	19	20	39	8	25	16	5	21	29
1934	Commerce	87	25	19	21	22	48	9	26	17	6	22	40
1934–36	BLS—14,469 families of 2 or more	7 141	54	17	16	30	44	11	30	16	8	17	10
1935	Commerce	96	25	22	23	22	51	9	35	18	6	24	45
1935–36	NRC—18,496 families of 2 or more	7 155	8 65	15	23	29	44	6	33	19	9	23	10
1935–36	NRC—42,876 consumer units, including rural	7 117	9 57	11	42	(9)	42	7	30	18	8	21	10
1936	Commerce	107	26	27	25	23	55	10	41	19	7	27	53
1937	Commerce	115	28	30	28	24	57	10	43	21	7	29	58
1938	Commerce	109	30	26	26	23	56	10	36	21	7	28	55
1939	Commerce	110	31	29	28	24	59	10	41	22	8	29	57
1940	Commerce	116	31	32	29	26	61	10	47	23	8	31	59
1941	BLS—1,012 families of 2 or more	7 208	9 124	35	36	(9)	82	16	66	31	15	42	19
1941	BLS—1,220 urban consumer units	202	95	35	36	34	82	16	66	32	15	44	30
1941	BLS—Agriculture, 2,963 consumer units, including rural	150	61	28	26	27	62	10	52	25	11	30	32

226

Year	Source								
1941	Commerce	133	39	33	32	27	71	11	55	25	9	35	66
1942	Commerce	158	38	35	37	29	85	15	29	28	10	39	74
1943	Commerce	180	36	35	42	30	103	20	23	31	12	42	82
1944	BLS—1,713 urban consumer units	*208*	*26*	*8 102*	*41*	*37*	*126*	*18*	*31*	*44*	*19*	*35*	*36*
1944	BLS—1,408 urban families of 2 or more	*278*	*26*	*9 140*	*43*	*(9)*	*128*	*19*	*31*	*44*	*19*	*35*	*37*
1944	Commerce	197	38	36	49	32	114	21	25	35	14	45	90
1945	Commerce	221	44	35	54	34	129	22	33	38	15	50	100
1946	Commerce	262	68	34	57	35	142	23	68	44	15	65	106
1947	Commerce	293	81	36	64	39	144	22	90	48	16	70	111
1948	Commerce	313	84	39	67	43	147	23	102	50	16	72	111
1949	Commerce	307	77	43	67	41	136	22	118	52	15	73	110
1950	Commerce	317	86	47	70	45	133	23	138	55	16	79	115
1950	BLS—12,489 urban consumer units	*377*	*87*	*8 76*	*59*	*53*	*146*	*22*	*148*	*66*	*28*	*75*	*63*
1950	BLS—10,791 urban families of 2 or more	*370*	*88*	*8 68*	*58*	*52*	*144*	*21*	*148*	*65*	*28*	*75*	*61*
1950	BLS—7,007 urban wage-earner and clerical-worker families of 2 or more	*354*	*82*	*8 68*	*46*	*48*	*133*	*20*	*139*	*59*	*27*	*67*	*58*
1951	Commerce	355	85	50	74	47	139	23	132	57	16	80	120
1952	Commerce	368	82	53	76	48	143	23	133	60	17	82	126
1953	Commerce	374	83	56	80	50	138	23	154	64	17	84	131
1954	Commerce	378	81	58	79	52	135	22	152	66	18	86	131
1955	Commerce	389	88	59	84	55	139	22	182	69	19	92	136
1956	Commerce	408	90	59	89	58	144	22	168	72	21	97	141

[1] Personal consumption expenditures per capita calculated by dividing aggregate expenditures to nearest billion dollars by total U. S. population to nearest hundred thousand; expenditures for current consumption per family member calculated by dividing average expenditures per family by average family size to 1 decimal place as determined during respective expenditure surveys. For personal consumption expenditures, the data are from a time series prepared and published for 1909–29 by Dewhurst and Associates and from 1929 forward and published by the U. S. Department of Commerce (see sources). For expenditures for current consumption, data are from various cross section expenditure surveys conducted by the Bureau of Labor Statistics, on occasion in cooperation with agencies of the U. S. Department of Agriculture (see sources).

[2] Sources are given more fully in source note below. Other identification supplied where necessary to identify series or sample segment from a study where more than 1 selection is or could be used. Data collected only from urban samples except as indicated. "Consumer units" include "single consumer" as well as families of 2 or more.

[3] Recreation includes reading and education expenditures in all of the expenditure surveys, except the one for 1901.

[4] Other goods and services include principally alcoholic beverages (except as noted otherwise) and tobacco in the expenditure surveys.

[5] Included in other goods and services.

[6] Dewhurst data for 1929 based on same amount of detail as for 1927 and earlier years because of noncomparability with Commerce series for food, rent, and "other goods and services." For other consumption groups, very minor differences in classification exist.

[7] Includes expenditures for alcoholic beverages.

[8] Total housing expenditures, i. e., includes costs of homeownership as well as rent.

[9] Rent includes total housing expenditures plus fuel, light, and refrigeration.

NOTE: Items may not add to totals because of rounding.

SOURCE: (a) Time Series: 1909–29—J. Frederic Dewhurst and Associates, America's Needs and Resources: A New Survey (The Twentieth Century Fund, 1955) appendix table 4-4, pp. 965–963; 1929–56—U. S. Department of Commerce, Survey of Current Business, National Income Supplement (1954 ed.) and July 1957 issue, table 30. (b) Cross Section Studies: 1901, 1917–19, 1934–36, and 1950—see tables 3–6, ch. II; 1935–36, National Resources Committee, Consumer Expenditures in the United States, Estimates for 1935–36; 1941—Family Spending and Saving in Wartime, U. S. Bureau of Labor Statistics Bulletin 822; 1944—Monthly Labor Review, January 1946, pp. 1–5.

expenditure of their cost of living. As a matter of fact, our returns would have been materially smaller in number, or wanting in completeness, but for these evening visits made after work was done. The rooms were inspected and their pleasant or unpleasant features noted. The children were at home, and the physical appearance and dress of the family were observed.[8]

The discretion earlier vested in the agent in selecting the samples of plants and especially of individuals has declined progressively; in the more recent studies this potential bias in selecting the sample has been eliminated.* The techniques of interview—multiple visits, strong encouragement to utilize written records, and use of home surroundings to stimulate accurate recall of expenditure data—remain cardinal principles.

Although they reflect successive refinements, both the schedules used to record the data and the more important summary tabulations bear a strong resemblance throughout the surveys. The 1950 survey schedule, of course, dwarfs that used in 1901, because many of the varied goods and services bought by the worker's family in 1950 were unknown and even more of them were beyond the worker's means, perhaps beyond his fondest dreams, early in this century.

PERSONAL CONSUMPTION EXPENDITURES

Summary use has been made in other chapters of the estimates of total personal consumption expenditures, a continuing series in the estimates of national income and product, or national economic accounts, compiled by the Department of Commerce. That series and the periodic BLS surveys of family incomes and expenditures supplement each other significantly. The continuing Commerce series indicates changes in consumer expenditures between the infrequent expenditure surveys. The BLS expenditure surveys, on the other hand, provide checks on the validity and reliability of estimates for the various components of the annual series. They can also be used to improve those estimates.

Adjustments for Noncomparability

Paradoxically, the two sets of figures, although supplementary, are essentially noncomparable. The reasons for the noncomparability, and the adjustments required to make them reasonably comparable, call for brief discussion.

Like the other series in the national accounts, the Commerce estimates of personal income and personal consumption expendi-

---

*The "field agents" who obtained the basic data in the 1875 survey were undoubtedly well instructed under the tuition of such an outstanding statistician and administrator as Carroll D. Wright and they seem, too, to have been, as a rule, inspired by Mr. Wright's keen devotion to the ideals of accuracy and objectivity.

tures are aggregates designed to embrace the entire economy; they therefore reflect incomes and expenditures of all segments of the population, both urban and rural. The expenditure series includes expenditures by nonprofit institutions (such as churches and health, welfare, and charitable organizations) for goods and services usually purchased by the ultimate consumer. It also includes expenditures for goods consumed by personnel of the armed services, which affect the food and clothing components in particular. The treatment of income in kind especially affects homeowner costs, because both personal income and housing expenditures include an appropriate allocation for the net rental value of homes occupied by the owners. (Value of food raised for home consumption has little significance, of course, in studies of urban consumption.) The aggregates, moreover, are essentially a carefully constructed mosaic, pieced together skillfully and carefully from a variety of sources.

The BLS expenditure data, on the other hand, have represented the total urban population in some of the more recent studies, but earlier surveys were more likely to include only city workers. In most of the surveys, it was found that the consumer units had little nonmonetary income and reported only money receipts and disbursements. These units were included in samples designed to be representative and, in the last 25 years, so drawn that the sampling error was a known factor.

Thus the BLS surveys permit greater assurance of consistency for estimates of urban family expenditures than does the Commerce series, which was designed for another purpose and for which data from a variety of sources must be combined.

Despite these differences, both sets of statistics can be used to cast additional light on the welfare of the American worker. By careful adjustments, some of the noncomparability can be eliminated, and much of the residual difference can be explained (but not measured).

In computing the figures shown in table 26 (p. 226), both the Commerce aggregates, stated in billions of dollars, and the BLS data, expressed as average expenditures per family or consumer unit, were converted to per capita figures. Using the per capita basis as a common denominator eliminated the effects of the increase in population from the Commerce series, and partly erased the effects of differences in family size from the BLS data.

For years prior to 1929, when the Commerce series begins, personal consumption expenditures were derived from those assembled by Dewhurst and Associates in their studies for the Twentieth Century Fund. For 1929, both are shown, since they cannot be satisfactorily linked because of certain noncomparabilities, which affect chiefly food, rent, and "other goods and services." (See table footnotes for explanation.)

The Dewhurst and Commerce aggregates were reclassified on the basis of the consumption groups used for the Consumer Price Index. Those series which had no counterpart in the expenditure surveys, e. g., food and clothing for military personnel, were omitted. In the case of housing, only rent expenditures were used because this seemed less misleading than to attempt adjustment of the Commerce homeownership expenditure data, which are completely noncomparable with the BLS treatment of these costs.

Some major sources of noncomparability could not be eliminated or adjusted. With a few obvious exceptions, the Commerce series could not be adjusted to separate expenditures by the rural population from those of the urban, nor could institutional expenditures be eliminated. Similarly, in the years prior to World War II, when the BLS surveys relate solely to wage-earner and clerical-worker families, it was impossible to segregate the Commerce data on expenditures by single consumers and other groups in the urban population. Nor could the shifting urban-rural composition of the population, which affects the Commerce series, be taken into account.

Comparison With Expenditure Surveys

The various differences between the per capita expenditure averages and the expenditures per family member impair comparisons of levels of expenditure at a given time. Trends shown by the respective averages in table 26 can, however, be compared, although the inclusion of the rural population and of institutional expenditures in the personal consumption expenditures series makes it an imperfect indicator of trends of expenditures per family member for urban families and especially for city workers' families. Trend comparisons are valid even though the two measures do not cover precisely the same time periods in the early years.

Price changes, of course, are reflected in both sets of data, and the dollar figures cannot be used to measure the trend of actual consumption of goods and services. Nevertheless, even a casual inspection of the Commerce data shows fluctuations in consumption not evident from the occasional surveys of family spending.

Trend comparisons indicate a remarkable narrowing of the gap between city workers and other groups. The 1909 per capita personal consumption expenditures were from 2 to 3 times the 1901 per family member expenditures of city workers, with the exception of food, where they were only about one-third higher. The difference was still very great at the end of World War I. Expenditures for food were only $112 per family member in 1917–19, in contrast to $178 per capita in 1919, and private transportation costs per capita were 11 times as much as per family member. The 1919 figures reflect price advances which occurred after the BLS conducted its World War I expenditure survey (in which 75 percent of the reports covered the year ended in July 1918 and none covered a year ending later than February 1919).* Nevertheless, the price increases can account for only a small part of the extreme differences.

By 1950, spending per family member by city workers for many groups of consumption items equaled or exceeded per capita expenditures by the population as a whole. The outstanding exception was in respect to "other goods and services," and much of that difference stemmed from the more comprehensive coverage of the Commerce series for that group.**

Estimating 1956 Family Expenditures

The personal consumption expenditure series can also be used to project current expenditure patterns of urban consumers and, with less reliability, those of city workers and their families. Such projections are useful because there has been no general expenditure survey since 1950. Consumption patterns are, of course, affected by changes in income levels and in price levels, as well as by other factors. Since the various forces are reflected in the Commerce personal consumption expenditure series, their trends are reasonable approximations of changes in the expenditures of all urban consumer units.†

The procedure is mathematically simple. From table 26, the 1956 average expenditure per capita for each consumption group was calculated as a ratio of the 1950 expenditure for the group. Applying these ratios to the corresponding average expenditures of all urban consumer units in 1950 results in the estimated average expenditures and patterns shown in table 27. These estimates appear to be conservative in comparison with the results of alternative estimating procedures.

---

*Consumer prices in 1919 were 15 percent higher than in 1918 and 35 percent above their 1917 levels.

**The BLS "other goods and services" group includes chiefly tobacco and alcoholic beverages; see footnote 4, table 26.

†In fact, they are acceptable, but in diminishing degree, for estimating expenditures of urban families of 2 or more, urban wage-earner and clerical-worker families of 2 or more (but not with the accuracy necessary in any revision of the Consumer Price Index weights), urban single consumers, and wage-earner and clerical-worker single consumers, as well as corresponding segments of the rural population.

TABLE 27.—*Consumption expenditures of all urban consumer units, 1950 averages and 1956 estimates*

Consumption group	1950 average expenditures	Estimated 1956 expenditures Amount	Percent of total expenditures for current consumption
Food	$1,130	$1,454	31.3
Housing	438	[1] 538	11.6
Fuel, light, and refrigeration	158	204	4.4
Household operation	178	226	4.9
Furnishings and equipment	261	273	5.9
Clothing	437	473	10.2
Transportation:			
Private	443	539	11.6
Public	67	64	1.4
Medical care	197	258	5.5
Personal care	85	112	2.4
Recreation, reading, and education	226	278	6.0
Other goods and services	188	230	4.9
Total expenditures for current consumption	$3,808	$4,649	100.0

[1] Housing was estimated in several ways, because of noncomparability of Commerce aggregates with BLS expenditure survey data. The estimate used, $538, was obtained by applying the rent ratio (1.255) to the rent segment of the 1950 survey data and the average of the ratios for other groups (1.202) to the homeowner expenditure segment. If the latter were used for the entire housing group, the estimates would be lower by $6; if the rent ratio were used, higher by $12. Other alternatives yield a maximum of $560, with $538 as the minimum.

NOTE: Items do not equal total because of rounding.

STANDARD BUDGETS AS INDICATORS OF PROGRESS

Other data which have been used in this volume to supplement the family expenditure surveys are standard budgets relating to particular kinds of families. Makers of standard budgets, in striving to define a standard of living, are often likely to describe a way of living somewhat higher than the contemporary level. Scientific standards, for example of diet, usually are somewhat higher than have been attained by many families in the group for whom the budget is designed. Such standards, however, do not depart radically from what is accepted as feasible. For consumption goods and services for which standards have not been evolved, the budget designer relies primarily on the actual levels of living attained by families most nearly like the "budget family." As will be indicated below, the post-World War II budgets of the BLS embodied in the City Worker's Family Budget represented a closer approach to objective realization of a budget, with the subordination of subjective elements, than had theretofore been attempted.

As we shift from use of consumer expenditure surveys as mileposts of consumer gains to a necessarily sketchy review of the role of standard budgets as progress indicators, another Meeker statement provides an apt introduction:

> ... not only do we have the cost but we have the quantity, in most instances, of all important items of the family budget. The quantity bought is absolutely essential for working out standard budgets. Expenditures stated merely in sums of money are useless for the determination of the standard of living or of the quantitative change in the cost of this standard of living.[9]

In effect, Meeker signaled the end of the pioneer phase of budget construction, when budgets had been developed directly from money expenditure data usually obtained from studies conducted for that specific purpose. Such budgets were valid only for the place where the study was conducted and only as long as prices remained fairly stable. The big price inflation during World War I emphasized this deficiency. Differences in the impact of inflation among cities, perhaps exaggerated by the situation in shipbuilding centers, underscored the need for emphasis on physical quantities.

Conceptual Advances*

The incorporation of objective standards, particularly of nutrition and housing, characterized all but the very earliest budget studies, which were often sponsored by charitable organizations. In line with the "subsistence" concept inherited from abroad and still influential in both sociological and economic thinking in the early years of the current century, such organizations were primarily concerned that recipients of assistance should obtain sufficient food, shelter, clothing, and medical care to maintain health.

The subsistence approach was influenced by the "iron law of wages" and the "wages fund doctrine," which imposed rigid limits on the workers' potential as well as actual betterment.** American workers, and gradually the economists, of this century reacted even more strongly than their predecessors against the essentially pessimistic implications of these ideas. Accordingly, a "living wage" concept found widening acceptance through the first 30 years of the century. A living wage was defined as sufficient to provide not only the food, shelter, clothing, and medical care necessary for health and decency, but also an additional margin for "comfort." And standard budgets, as distinguished from "assistance" or "subsistence" budgets, tended progressively to define standards somewhat higher than the contemporary levels of living among workers.

---

*This treatment of concepts of income adequacy was suggested, and is more completely set forth, by Helen Humes Lamale, in Changes in Concepts of Income Adequacy Over the Last Century (in Papers and Proceedings of the Seventieth Annual Meeting, American Economic Review, Volume XLVIII, No. 2, May 1958).

**Those concepts were not abandoned by John Stuart Mill until 1869 (see W. J. Ashley's 1909 edition of Mill's Principles of Political Economy, pp. 991–993). Similar ideas survived, however, even in America.

The long depression of the 1930's, with chronic unemployment on a scale never before encountered in this country, created a temporary demand for budgets geared to "emergency" and "maintenance of health and decency" (at minimal levels) concepts. As the economy recovered, earlier humanitarian and reform impulses in support of social betterment were reinforced by recognition of the necessity for a conscious, deliberate policy of emphasizing consumption, rather than depending on the "automatic" forces of the market to maintain high-level production and employment.

The comparatively recent development of a concept of income "adequacy" in budget making is, in fact, influenced by the national policy of maintaining an expanding economy, with high-level consumption regarded as inseparable from the maintenance of high-level production. Nowadays, primary interest in budget development attaches to providing tools to measure the adequacy of self-supporting families' incomes. Even the "assistance" budgets are based on standards which would have been adjudged luxurious by earlier generations.

Contemporary crosscurrents lessened interest in the use of budgets as a basis for appraising wage levels. Such forces as manpower and material shortages in World War II, the postwar inflation, and the 1948–49 downturn, with the decline of capital goods spending, were accompanied by rapid shifts of emphasis in the area of wage income. Workers were primarily concerned with maintaining the buying power of wages in the face of advancing prices. A more general recognition that real earnings were limited by the amount of output available for consumption led to widespread interest in the linking of wages to productivity, for example by "improvement factors."

For some groups of workers, however, the concept of the standard budget as a measure of "adequacy" has remained useful. New distortions of economic rewards, often particularly serious in the lower ranges of salaried employees, were created by the uneven pressures of wartime and postwar inflation, and some of these still remain.

Budget Studies

The foregoing discussion of the changing concepts and uses of standard budgets provides a backdrop for a summary view of important budgets. The 22 budgets shown in table 28 (p. 236) were selected to provide a representative cross section of budgets compiled during the 20th century. Exclusion of certain budgets carries no implications regarding their validity or reliability. Where choices among budgets for different cities were necessary, broad geographic coverage and the presentation of budgets for a given city at different times were the criteria for selection.

Average dollar figures for the total budget and its major components are given for their general interest. However, since the purchasing power of the dollar varied widely during the half century, only percentages of total goods and services required for food, rent, fuel and light, clothing, health, and "all other goods and services" are shown. As in the expenditure surveys, the percentages yield more meaningful comparisons. They are also useful for comparisons with the percentages of family expenditures for roughly comparable groups of goods and services, as shown in the tables in chapter II. The total budget costs should not, however, be compared with total expenditures for current consumption. In addition to the goods and services which comprise the bulk of each budget, it includes additional costs—principally personal taxes, life insurance, and occupational expense—that are usually excluded from the expenditure figures. These costs are shown separately in table 28, and their relationship to the total budget is indicated.

The budgets for which costs are shown in different cities illustrate an important secondary purpose of some of the budgets, namely comparisons of differences in the cost of living in different places. Such comparisons are valid only in terms of equivalent levels of living;* a given standard budget, of course, defines such a level. Because of the technical difficulties, scope, and cost of these studies, comparisons of place-to-place differences in the cost of living have been left largely to the Federal Government.

In the earliest studies, the standards were inferred directly from the expenditure data, which, however, included substantial detail as to quantities involved. The New York, Chicago, and Philadelphia budgets through 1914, for example, were based primarily on data obtained by expenditure surveys of varying scope, tailored specifically for this purpose.

The first budgets in this country to be expressed in quantities of goods and services for which prices were obtained to determine budget costs were those for southern and Fall River cotton-mill workers. The Bureau of Labor Statistics made this basic contribution to budget methodology as one phase of an exhaustive investigation of the condition of women and child workers, ordered by Congress in 1907. They were also the first budgets to define explicitly two living levels ("minimum" and "fair") simultaneously.

---

*The concept of equivalent levels of living permits minor differences from place to place in the lists of goods and services included in the budget because of differences in climate, in availability of goods or services, or in other factors, provided the different lists yield the satisfaction specified or implied by the definition of level or standard of living.

TABLE 28.—Selected standard family budgets in the United States, 1903–56

Short title of budget [1]	Time period covered	Family size	Total cost of goods and services	Percent distribution of the cost of goods and services									Other budget costs [3]		Total budget
				Total	Food	Housing			Clothing	Health [2]	All other goods and services	Amount	Percent of total budget	
						Rent	Fuel and light							
1. New York City Wage Earners	1903–05	5.6	$803.90	100.0	45.2	20.2	5.3	11.0	2.1	16.2	$32.35	3.9	$836.25
2. New York City Workingmen	1907		782.00	100.0	45.9	21.5	5.2	14.6	2.8	10.0	29.00	3.6	811.00
3. Southern Cotton-Mill Workers:													
Minimum	1908	5.0	408.26	100.0	60.5	11.0	12.0	14.4	0	2.1	0	0	408.26
Fair	1908	5.0	582.54	100.0	49.2	7.7	8.4	19.4	2.8	12.5	18.20	3.0	600.74
4. Cotton-Mill Workers of Fall River, Mass.:													
Minimum	1908–09	5.0	484.41	100.0	56.8	16.1	8.8	16.5	0	1.8	0	0	484.41
Fair [4]	1908–09	5.0	713.44	100.0	43.6	18.5	6.0	19.2	1.6	11.1	18.55	2.5	731.99
Fair [5]	1908–09	5.0	672.40	100.0	46.3	13.5	6.4	20.3	1.7	11.8	18.55	2.7	690.95
5. Chicago Stockyards Families	1909–10	5.3	765.10	100.0	48.0	15.7	4.7	13.1	1.2	17.3	34.90	4.4	800.00
6. Philadelphia Textile Mill Families	1913–14	5.0	943.94	100.0	40.3	19.1	5.4	16.7	2.8	15.7	126.00	11.8	1,069.94
	March 1918	5.0	1,411.00	100.0	41.5	14.7	4.5	22.4	2.9	14.0	192.00	12.0	1,603.00
7. New York Factory Commission:													
New York City	1914	3.3	840.83	100.0	38.7	23.8	2.3	16.7	2.6	15.9	35.60	4.1	876.43
Buffalo	1914	3.3	772.43	100.0	38.1	16.3	5.4	19.0	3.0	18.2	35.60	4.6	772.43
8. Philadelphia Workingmen	Autumn 1918	3.0	1,580.60	100.0	42.5	15.2	4.7	18.9	2.7	16.1	56.19	3.4	1,636.79
	November 1919	5.0	1,741.25	100.0	39.4	17.2	4.8	19.9	2.7	16.0	61.89	3.4	1,803.14
	August 1920	5.0	1,920.07	100.0	36.2	17.5	5.1	22.9	2.7	15.7	68.25	3.4	1,988.32
	March 1921	5.0	1,682.86	100.0	33.7	21.4	6.2	19.4	2.6	16.7	59.82	3.4	1,742.68
	March 1923	5.0	1,790.63	100.0	30.0	24.8	5.8	19.8	2.7	17.0	63.65	3.4	1,854.28
9. Dallas Normal Family	April 1917	5.0		[6]100.0	44.5	15.2	[7]9.6	12.6	3.9	14.2	(⁵)		1,081.72
10. Seattle-Tacoma Transit Workers	October 1917	5.0	1,375.60	100.0	38.8	13.4	6.9	21.2	4.3	15.4	130.00	8.6	1,505.60
11. Pacific Coast Workers	October 1917	5.0	1,377.40	100.0	39.3	17.4	3.9	20.9	5.4	13.1	99.00	6.7	1,476.40
12. New York Minimum Comfort	June 1918	5.0	1,595.50	100.0	40.1	13.8	4.7	19.6	3.8	18.0	165.00	9.4	1,760.50
13. Washington, D. C. Federal Workers	July–August 1919	5.0	2,142.47	100.0	36.1	14.0	6.0	24.0	3.7	16.2	120.00	5.3	2,232.47
14. NICB, Fall River, Mass:													
Minimum	October 1919	5.0	1,226.16	100.0	46.7	9.5	5.7	19.9	2.5	15.7	41.60	3.3	1,267.76
More liberal	October 1919	5.0	1,511.50	100.0	41.9	12.0	5.6	21.3	2.2	17.0	62.40	4.0	1,573.90
15. Coal-mine Workers	December 1919	5.0	1,935.14	100.0	40.7	11.2	3.6	23.5	4.1	16.9	308.80	13.8	[9]2,243.94

236

16. Labor Bureau, New York City	November 1920	5.0	(5)	100.0	33.2	16.6	2.6	20.1	(10)	27.5	(10)		2,632.68
17. Heller Committee, San Francisco:												
Clerks	1929	5.0	2,354.31	100.0	31.4	20.4	4.5	18.8	3.1	21.8	130.00	5.2	2,484.31
Wage earners	1929	5.0	1,861.48	100.0	35.7	19.3	4.6	16.0	4.0	20.4	65.00	3.4	1,926.48
18. WPA Maintenance Budget	March 1935	4.0	1,211.68	100.0	37.0	18.3	8.2	13.2	4.3	19.0	48.94	3.9	1,260.62
Atlanta	March 1935		1,213.82	100.0	38.2	20.3	7.0	12.0	4.4	18.1	54.40	4.3	1,268.22
Boston	March 1935		1,306.37	100.0	35.9	20.2	8.4	12.5	4.2	18.8	46.40	3.4	1,352.77
Chicago	March 1935	4.0	1,307.90	100.0	35.3	18.4	8.5	12.7	4.4	20.7	48.21	3.6	1,356.11
New York	March 1935	4.0	1,328.73	100.0	36.0	22.6	8.1	11.1	4.2	18.0	46.40	3.4	1,375.13
San Francisco	March 1935	4.0	1,343.47	100.0	34.3	20.1	8.5	13.3	4.8	19.0	46.40	3.3	1,389.87
Washington, D. C	March 1935	4.0	1,368.14	100.0	34.9	25.0	7.0	11.3	4.3	17.5	46.40	3.3	1,414.54
19. BLS City Worker's Family Budget:												
Atlanta	June 1947	4.0	2,853.00	100.0	36.6	[11] 20.9	(11)	14.5	5.4	22.6	297.00	9.4	3,150.00
Boston	June 1947	4.0	2,981.00	100.0	35.7	[11] 20.9	(11)	14.1	5.5	23.8	329.00	9.9	3,310.00
Buffalo	June 1947	4.0	2,810.00	100.0	37.1	[11] 18.6	(11)	15.4	5.1	23.8	285.00	9.2	3,095.00
Chicago	June 1947	4.0	2,965.00	100.0	35.6	[11] 22.6	(11)	15.2	5.0	21.6	317.00	9.7	3,282.00
Denver	June 1947	4.0	2,870.00	100.0	36.3	[11] 19.9	(11)	15.1	5.5	23.2	298.00	9.4	3,168.00
Kansas City	June 1947	4.0	2,739.00	100.0	37.3	[11] 18.1	(11)	15.0	5.5	24.1	271.00	9.0	3,010.00
New York City	June 1947	4.0	3,019.00	100.0	36.4	[11] 22.0	(11)	15.7	5.5	20.6	328.00	9.8	3,347.00
San Francisco	June 1947	4.0	2,964.00	100.0	35.7	[11] 18.8	(11)	15.1	6.9	23.5	353.00	10.6	3,317.00
Seattle	June 1947	4.0	3,054.00	100.0	35.8	[11] 20.0	(11)	15.0	6.4	22.8	334.00	9.9	3,388.00
Washington, D. C	June 1947	4.0	3,111.00	100.0	33.4	[11] 24.3	(11)	14.9	5.9	21.5	347.00	10.0	3,458.00
20. BLS City Worker's Family Budget:												
Atlanta	October 1951	4.0	3,844.00	100.0	35.9	[11] 24.3	(11)	(12)	(12)	[12] 39.8	471.00	10.9	4,315.00
Boston	October 1951	4.0	3,753.00	100.0	36.1	[11] 21.3	(11)	(12)	(12)	[12] 42.6	464.00	11.0	4,217.00
Buffalo	October 1951	4.0	3,674.00	100.0	36.0	[11] 21.1	(11)	(12)	(12)	[12] 42.9	453.00	11.0	4,127.00
Chicago	October 1951	4.0	3,745.00	100.0	36.1	[11] 22.0	(11)	(12)	(12)	[12] 41.9	440.00	10.5	4,185.00
Denver	October 1951	4.0	3,748.00	100.0	35.5	[11] 22.9	(11)	(12)	(12)	[12] 41.6	451.00	10.7	4,199.00
Kansas City	October 1951	4.0	3,558.00	100.0	36.7	[11] 19.2	(11)	(12)	(12)	[12] 44.1	402.00	10.2	3,960.00
New York City	October 1951	4.0	3,639.00	100.0	37.6	[11] 19.8	(11)	(12)	(12)	[12] 42.6	444.00	10.9	4,083.00
San Francisco	October 1951	4.0	3,779.00	100.0	35.8	[11] 21.1	(11)	(12)	(12)	[12] 43.1	484.00	11.4	4,263.00
Seattle	October 1951	4.0	3,823.00	100.0	35.9	[11] 21.0	(11)	(12)	(12)	[12] 43.1	457.00	10.7	4,280.00
Washington, D. C	October 1951	4.0	3,965.00	100.0	34.1	[11] 26.1	(11)	(12)	(12)	[12] 39.8	489.00	11.0	4,454.00
21. New York City Family Budget Standard	1954	4.0	3,728.40	100.0	38.3	18.1	2.7	11.8	7.0	22.1	493.48	11.7	4,221.88

See footnotes at end of table.

237

TABLE 28.—Selected standard family budgets in the United States, 1903–56—Continued

| Short title of budget [1] | Time period covered | Family size | Total cost of goods and services | Percent distribution of the cost of goods and services ||||||| Other budget costs [3] || Total budget |
| | | | | Total | Food | Housing || Clothing | Health [2] | All other goods and services | Amount | Percent of total budget | |
						Rent	Fuel and light						
22. Heller Committee, San Francisco:													
Salaried workers	1956	4.0	7,017.79	100.0	31.1	16.0	1.8	9.7	7.3	34.1	1,351.18	16.2	8,368.97
Renting wage earners	1956	4.0	4,771.68	100.0	35.1	14.7	2.4	9.7	9.1	29.0	820.91	14.7	5,592.59
Homeowning wage earners	1956	4.0	5,038.75	100.0	33.2	[13] 18.1	1.9	9.2	8.7	28.9	810.92	13.9	5,849.67

[1] For full title of budget or study, see sources.
[2] Medical and dental care except as noted.
[3] Includes such items as personal taxes, life insurance, and occupational expenses.
[4] English, Irish, and French Canadian families.
[5] Portuguese, Polish, and Italian families.
[6] Percentages are based on total budget cost.
[7] Includes water, ice, laundry, and phone.
[8] "Other budget costs" are included in "all other goods and services."
[9] Total increased by $100 to agree with text and table IV in report.
[10] "Health" and "other budget costs" are included in "all other goods and services."
[11] "Fuel and light" included in "rent."
[12] "Clothing" and "health" included in "all other goods and services." The estimated budget cost for 1951 for clothing, housefurnishings, medical care, personal care, household operation, and other groups combined were based on prices of a relatively small sample list of items, which did not yield separate estimates within a satisfactory degree of accuracy for these groups.
[13] Homeownership costs.

NOTE: Items may not add to totals because of rounding.

SOURCES: 1. Louise B. More, Wage-Earners' Budgets: A Study of Standards and Cost of Living in New York City (New York, H. Holt and Co., 1907). 2. Robert C. Chapin, The Standard of Living Among Workingmen's Families in New York City, 1907 (New York, Russell Sage Foundation, Charities Publication Committee, 1909). 3 and 4. U. S. Bureau of Labor, Report on Condition of Woman and Child Wage-Earners in the United States, Volume XVI, Family Budgets of Typical Cotton-Mill Workers (Washington, 61st Cong., 2d sess., Senate Doc. 645, 1911). 5. J. C. Kennedy, Wages and Family Budgets in the Chicago Stockyards District, with Wage Statistics from Other Industries Employing Unskilled Labor (Chicago, University of Chicago Press, 1914). 6. Esther Louise Little and William Joseph Cotton, Budgets of Families and individuals of Kensington, Philadelphia (Lancaster, Pa., New Era Printing Co., 1920). 7. State of New York, Fourth Report of the Factory Investigating Commission, 1915, Volume IV (Albany, J. B. Lyon Co., 1915). 8. Bureau of Municipal Research of Philadelphia, Workingmen's Standard of Living in Philadelphia (New York, The Macmillan Co., 1919) and Citizens' Business (the Bureau's bulletin), Sept. 9, 1920, Apr. 7, 1921, and Apr. 5, 1923. 9. Dallas, Tex., Wage Commission, Report of the Survey Committee to the Dallas Wage Commission (Dallas, 1917). 10, 11, and 12. Standards of Living, A Compilation of Budgetary Studies (Washington, Bureau of Applied Economics, Inc., 1920). 13. U. S. Bureau of Labor Statistics, Tentative Quantity and Cost Budget Necessary to Maintain a Family of Five in Washington, D. C., 1919 (Washington, 1919; also published in source for item 10). 14. National Industrial Conference Board, The Cost of Living Among Wage-Earners, Fall River, Mass., October 1919, Research Report 22 (Boston, 1919; also published in source for item 10). 15. William F. Ogburn, Budget for Bituminous Coal Mine Workers, 1920 (published in source for item 10). 16. Labor Bureau, Inc., Cost of Living in New York City in November 1920, based on the BLS budget in item 13 (in MLR, Feb. 1921). 17. Heller Committee for Research in Social Economics, Quantity and Cost Budgets (Berkeley, University of California, 1929). 18. Works Progress Administration, Intercity Differences in Costs of Living in March 1935, 59 Cities, Research Monograph XII, by Margaret Loomis Stecker (Washington, 1937). 19. U. S. Bureau of Labor Statistics, Workers' Budgets in the United States: City Families and Single Persons, 1946 and 1947, Bulletin 927 (Washington, 1948). 20. U. S. Bureau of Labor Statistics, City Worker's Family Budget for October 1951 (in Monthly Labor Review, May 1952, pp. 520–522). 21. Welfare and Health Council of New York City, A Family Budget Standard (New York, 1955). 22. Heller Committee for Research in Social Economics, Quantity and Cost Budgets for Two Income Levels (Berkeley, University of California, 1956).

Whereas the earlier budgets were affected to a marked degree by the "subsistence" concept of income adequacy, the inflationary effects of World War I accentuated the demand for budgets defining levels of living which would meet the "living wage" concept. Thus, governmental and quasi-governmental agencies in the Pacific Northwest, Philadelphia, and New York City commissioned the formulation of budgets which would provide a basis for setting wages of transit workers or salaries of city employees at levels adequate to provide what became known as "minimum comfort."

In 1919, the Joint Reclassification Committee of Congress requested the Bureau of Labor Statistics to prepare a budget for Government employees in Washington, D. C. Although the Bureau did not price this budget (known as the "tentative quantity" budget) elsewhere, the quantities set forth therein were priced in a number of coal mining communities in 1920 for the U. S. Bituminous Coal Commission and by the Labor Bureau, Inc., an organization that often represented employees.

Special interest attaches to the budgets published in 1919 and 1920 by the National Industrial Conference Board. Although only the Fall River budgets are shown in the table, such budgets were compiled for a number of cities regarded as important industrial centers. The Board prepared budgets at two levels, which were designated as describing "minimum" and "more liberal" standards of living. These marked a major effort in the budget field conducted by private industry.

Except for sporadic pricing of the BLS "tentative quantity" budget during the 1920's, only one major budget study throws light on levels of living in this period.* The 1929 budgets of the Heller Committee for Research in Social Economics of the University of California give one of the few objective pictures of the workers' status as consumers just before the depression of the thirties. These budgets grew out of earlier work requested by the California State Civil Service Commission. The Heller budgets have been prepared and priced periodically in San Francisco for more than 30 years, usually for two groups of workers—wage earners and the group originally designated as "clerks," more recently as "salaried workers."

In the thirties, when the Federal Government was seeking reemployment for as many workers as possible, the Works Progress Administration formulated a "maintenance" budget, which was described as being above the "minimum subsistence level" but

---

*Although no quantitative measurement defining the relationship between levels and standards of living at any given time has been accepted generally, the two are of course closely if intangibly related. Although it is primarily concerned with changes in levels of living between the mid-thirties and 1950, an illuminating discussion is provided by Faith M. Williams, in Standards and Levels of Living of City-Worker Families, (in Monthly Labor Review, September 1956, pp. 1015–1023).

which did not approach "the content of what may be considered a satisfactory American standard of living."[10] An "emergency" budget comprised estimates derived by cutting even the maintenance budget for emergency conditions "with least harm to individuals and the social group."[11] Such uses of the general concept of the standard budget were no doubt effective in dealing with depression problems but represented a reversion to subsistence concepts.

In its 1946 and 1947 City Worker's Family Budget, the Bureau of Labor Statistics broke new ground. That budget did not depend upon subjective judgments nor did it have the limitations of being designed specifically for wage fixing or other administrative purposes. Objectively determined standards of adequacy (for example, from the scientific study of diets) and, in the absence of conclusive scientific data, the informed judgments of experts were extensively incorporated in the budget. Actual consumer preferences were also widely utilized, that is, "standards that are revealed by the ways in which people actually spend their money . . . . The point selected for measurement is in general the point where the struggle for 'more and more' things gives way to the desire for 'better and better' quality." Thus wrote the official under whose authority the budget was initiated. "Actually," he continued, "this budget is primarily a new tool in the kit of the research worker."[12]

"The point selected for measurement" in the City Worker's Family Budget, the Bureau publication on the subject went on to say, was determined in the following way:

> The definition of the budget recognizes that in the actual experience of families there is a scale which ranks various consumption patterns in an ascending order from mere subsistence to plenitude in every respect. The budget level described here is at a point on this scale below which deficiencies exist in one or more aspects of family consumption.
>
> * * * * *
>
> To find the dividing point it is necessary to use some indicator of group judgment that marks the place in the scale below which reduction meets greater and greater resistance; above which expansions become more and more limited. The chief indicator of group judgment which was used in deriving this budget was the manner in which families increase their consumption as their purchasing power increases. As purchasing power increases [at each successively higher level on the income scale], the consumption level expands and more goods and better quality goods enter into the pattern of living. As purchasing power decreases, the consumption level contracts, fewer goods are purchased, and the quality of the goods purchased is reduced. As the consumption level approaches the dividing point in the judgment of society, families resist further

decreases with increasing stubbornness. As purchasing power increases, consumption levels above the dividing point expand at slower and slower rates.[13]

The Bureau for a time priced the budget periodically in the 34 large cities in which price data were then collected for the Consumer Price Index. So rapid, however, were changes in types of consumer choices and in standards, particularly of food, housing, and medical care, that the pricing of the budget was discontinued after October 1951.

The resulting void has been filled in small part by the New York City family budget standard and the Heller Committee budgets for San Francisco. Both utilize postwar standards and quantity data developed from postwar expenditure surveys (chiefly the 1950 BLS survey) by objective methods generally similar to those used in the City Worker's Family Budget. The price and quantity data relate only to these two cities. The Heller Committee has also made a significant innovation—the development of a separate budget for homeowning wage earners, an increasingly numerous group.

The evidence of the standard budgets substantiates the various other indications of the worker's progress as consumer. The transformation of the purposes of the budget framers is itself indicative. Moreover, the importance of food allocations, as in the "level of living" surveys, fell quite sharply; allowances for health and for residual items, largely a margin beyond the basic necessities, rose from usually almost negligible sums in the earlier budgets to around a third of the total in later budgets. The content of a recent budget is incomparably superior to the content of an earlier budget.

The standard budgets, a significant phase of the Nation's growing concern for social betterment and economic equity, thus corroborate the diversified evidence of attainment by city workers of successively higher levels of well-being. With workers free to seek the realization of today's ideals, who can doubt that those standards will be transformed, as in the past, into tomorrow's levels of living?

Footnotes

[1] Commonwealth of Massachusetts, *Sixth Annual Report on the Statistics of Labor*, Part IV, *Condition of Workingmen's Families* (Boston, Wright & Potter, State Printers, 1875), p. 354.

[2] *Ibid.*, p. 192.

[3] *Ibid.*, p. 450.

[4] *Cost of Production: Iron, Steel, Coal, etc.*, Sixth Annual Report of the Commissioner of Labor (Washington, 1891), p. 605.

[5] Royal Meeker, What is the American Standard of Living? (in *Monthly Labor Review*, July 1919, p. 2).

[6] Faith M. Williams and Alice C. Hanson, *Money Disbursements of Wage Earners and Clerical Workers, 1934–36, Summary Volume*, U.S. Bureau of Labor Statistics Bulletin 638 (Washington, 1941), p. vii.

[7] *Consumer Expenditures in the United States, Estimates for 1935–36* (Washington, National Resources Committee, 1939), p. 3.

[8] *Sixth Annual Report on the Statistics of Labor, op. cit.*, p. 219.

[9] Royal Meeker, *op. cit.*, p. 3.

[10] *Intercity Differences in Cost of Living in March 1935, 59 cities*, Works Progress Administration Research Monograph XII, p. xiv.

[11] Dorothy S. Brady, Family Budgets: A Historical Survey, in *Workers' Budgets in the United States: City Families and Single Persons, 1946 and 1947*, U.S. Bureau of Labor Statistics Bulletin 927, p. 44.

[12] A. Ford Hinrichs, The Budget in Perspective, in BLS Bulletin 927, *op. cit.*, p. 2. (Mr. Hinrichs was Acting Commissioner of Labor Statistics when the project which culminated in the City Worker's Family Budget was initiated.)

[13] Lester S. Kellogg and Dorothy S. Brady, The City Worker's Family Budget, in BLS Bulletin 927, *op. cit.*, p. 9.

REFERENCES

The following publications were used in preparing this volume:

Public Documents

Dallas, Texas. Wage Commission. *Report of the Survey Committee to the Dallas Wage Commission* (Dallas, 1917).

Great Britain. Board of Trade. *Cost of Living in American Towns* (London, 1911).

International Labour Office. *The Sixth International Conference of Labour Statisticians, Montreal, 4 to 12 August 1947*, Studies and Reports, New Series, No. 7, Pt. 4 (Geneva, 1948).

Massachusetts, Commonwealth of. *6th Annual Report on the Statistics of Labor*, Pt. IV: *Condition of Workingmen's Families*, Public Document 31 (Boston, Wright & Potter, State Printers, 1875).

—— Bureau of Statistics. *41st Annual Report on the Statistics of Labor, 1910* (Boston, 1911).

New York City. Housing Authority. *19th Annual Report* (New York, 1952).

—— Welfare and Health Council. *A Family Budget Standard* (New York, 1955).

New York, State of. *4th Report of the Factory Investigating Commission, 1915*, Vol. IV (Albany, J. B. Lyon Co., 1915).

Philadelphia. Bureau of Municipal Research. *Workingmen's Standard of Living in Philadelphia* (New York, The Macmillan Co., 1919).

United Nations. *Report on International Definition and Measurement of Standards and Levels of Living*, Sales No., 1954, IV, 5 (New York, Columbia University Press, International Documents Service, 1954).

—— Statistical Office. *Statistical Yearbook, 1956* (New York, United Nations, 1956).

United States:

Anthracite Coal Strike Commission. *Report to the President on the Anthracite Coal Strike of May–October, 1902* (Washington, 1903). Also printed in *Bulletin of the Department of Labor*, No. 46, May 1903.

Board of Governors of the Federal Reserve System. *Consumer Installment Credit*, Pt. 1, Vol. 1, *Growth and Import* (Washington, 1957).

Bureau of Labor Standards. *State Workmen's Compensation Laws*, Bull. 161 (Revised) (Washington, 1957).

Bureau of Labor Statistics and Predecessor Agencies. *American Labor and the American Spirit*, by Witt Bowden, Bull. 1145 (Washington, 1954).

—— *Analysis of Health and Insurance Plans Under Collective Bargaining, Late 1955*, by Evan Keith Rowe and Dorothy Kittner Greene, Bull. 1221 (Washington, 1957).

—— *Case Study Data on Productivity and Factory Performance: Men's Bib Overalls and Men's Work Jackets; Men's Work Shirts* (prepared for the Mutual Security Agency, January 1952 and December 1951, respectively), (Washington, 1951, 1952).

—— *Changes in Cost of Living in Large Cities in the United States, 1913–41*, Bull. 699 (Washington, 1941).

243

United States—Continued
—— *Child Labor in the United States*, by Hannah R. Sewall (in Bulletin of the Bureau of Labor, No. 52, May 1904).
—— *Conditions of Living Among the Poor*, by S. E. Forman (in Bulletin of the Bureau of Labor, No. 64, May 1906).
—— *Consumer Cooperatives*, Bull. 1211 (Washington, 1957).
—— *Cost of Living and Retail Prices of Food*, 18th Annual Report of the Commissioner of Labor, 1903 (Washington, 1904).
—— *Cost of Living in the United States*, Bull. 357 (Washington, 1924).
—— *Cost of Production: Iron, Steel, Coal, etc.; Textiles and Glass*, 2 volumes, 6th and 7th Annual Reports of the Commissioner of Labor, 1890 and 1891 (Washington, 1891, 1892).
—— *Employers' Welfare Work* by Elizabeth Lewis Otey, Bull. 123 (Washington, 1913).
—— *Employment and Economic Status of Older Men and Women*, Bull. 1213 (Washington, December 1956).
—— *The Exhibit of the United States Bureau of Labor at the Louisiana Purchase Exposition*, Bull. 54 (Washington, 1904).
—— *Factory Sanitation and Labor Protection*, by C. F. W. Doehring, Bull. 44 (Washington, January 1903).
—— *Family Expenditures in Selected Cities, 1935–36*, Bull. 648, 8 volumes (Washington, 1940–41).
—— *Family Income and Expenditures in Chicago, 1935–36*, Bull. 642, 2 volumes (Washington, 1939).
—— *Family Income and Expenditures in Four Urban Communities of the Pacific Northwest, 1935–36*, Bull. 649, 2 volumes (Washington, 1939 and 1940).
—— *Family Income and Expenditures in New York City, 1935–36*, Bull. 643, 2 volumes (Washington, 1939 and 1941).
—— *Family Income and Expenditures in Nine Cities of the East Central Region, 1935–36*, Bull. 644, 2 volumes (Washington, 1939 and 1941).
—— *Family Income and Expenditures in Selected New England Cities, 1935–36*, Bull. 645, 2 volumes (Washington, 1939 and 1941).
—— *Family Income and Expenditures in Selected Urban Communities of the West Central-Rocky Mountain Region, 1935–36*, Bull. 646, 2 volumes (Washington, 1939 and 1940).
—— *Family Income and Expenditures in the Southeastern Region, 1935–36*, Bull. 647, 2 volumes (Washington, 1939 and 1940).
—— *Family Income, Expenditures, and Savings in 1950*, Bull. 1097, Revised (Washington, June 1953).
—— *Family Income, Expenditures, and Savings in 1945*, Bull. 956, (Washington, 1949).
—— *Family Income, Expenditures, and Savings in 10 Cities*, Bull. 1065 (Washington, 1952).
—— *Family Spending and Saving in Wartime*, Bull. 822 (Washington, 1945).
—— *Final Report of the Industrial Commission on the Relations of Capital and Labor Employed in Manufactures and General Business*, Vol. XIX of the Commissioner's Report (Washington, 1902).
—— *Hand and Machine Labor*, 13th Annual Report of the U. S. Commissioner of Labor (Washington, 1898).
—— *The Housing of the Working People*, 8th Special Report of the Commissioner of Labor (Washington, 1895).

United States—Continued
—— *Interim Adjustment of Consumers' Price Index*, Bull. 1039 (Washington, 1951).
—— *The Italians in Chicago, A Social and Economic Study*, 9th Special Report of the Commissioner of Labor (Washington, 1897).
—— *Labor-Management Contract Provisions, 1949–50*, Bull. 1022 (Washington, 1951).
—— *Money Disbursements of Wage Earners and Clerical Workers, 1934–36, Summary Volume*, by Faith M. Williams and Alice C. Hanson, Bull. 638 (Washington, 1941).
—— *Occupational Outlook Handbook*, 1957 Edition, Bull. 1215 (Washington, 1957).
—— *Productivity of Labor in the Cotton-Garment Industry*, Bull. 662 (Done in cooperation with the Works Progress Administration and National Research Project) (Washington, 1938).
—— *Report of the Industrial Commission on the Relations of Capital and Labor Employed in Manufactures and General Business*, Vol. VII of the Commissioner's Report (Washington, 1901).
—— *Report on Condition of Woman and Child Wage-Earners in the United States*, Vol. XVI: *Family Budgets of Typical Cotton-Mill Workers* (Washington, 1911). Issued also as House Doc. 1708, 63d Cong., 3d Sess., and Senate Doc. 645, 61st Cong., 2d Sess.
—— *Report on Conditions of Employment in the Iron and Steel Industry in the United States*, Vol. I: *Wages and Hours of Labor* (Washington, 1911), Vol. III: *Working Conditions and the Relations of Employers and Employees* (Washington, 1913).
—— *The Slums of Great Cities*, 7th Special Report of the Commissioner of Labor (Washington, 1894).
—— *Tentative Quantity and Cost Budget Necessary to Maintain a Family of Five in Washington, D. C., 1919* (Washington, 1919).
—— *Wage Chronology No. 3: United States Steel Corp., Supplement No. 7—1956–57* (Reprint 2263 from *Monthly Labor Review*, Nov. 1957).
—— *Water, Gas, and Electric-Light Plants Under Private and Municipal Ownership*, 14th Annual Report of the Commissioner of Labor (Washington, 1900).
—— *Workers' Budgets in the United States: City Families and Single Persons, 1946 and 1947*, Bull 927 (Washington, 1948).
Bureau of the Census. *Census of Electrical Industries, Electric Railways* (Washington, 1922).
—— *Continuation to 1952 of Historical Statistics of the United States, 1789–1945* (Washington, 1954).
—— *Current Population Reports, Consumer Income*, Series P–60, Nos. 9, 23, 24, and 26 (Washington, 1952, 1956, and 1957).
—— *Current Population Reports, Labor Force*, Series P–50, No. 73 (Washington, April 1957).
—— *Current Population Reports, Labor Force*, Series P–57, Nos. 94 and 178 (Washington, April 1950 and May 1957).
—— *Current Population Reports, Population Characteristics*, Series P–20, Nos. 63 and 73 (Washington, 1957).
—— *Current Population Reports, Population Estimates*, Series P–25, Nos. 71, 105, 127, and 135 (Washington, 1953, 1954, 1955, and 1956).
—— *Historical Statistics of the United States, 1789–1945* (Washington, 1949).

United States—Continued
—— *Statistical Abstract of the United States: 1957*, Seventy-eighth edition (Washington, 1957).
—— *Statistics of Cities Having a Population of Over 25,000, 1902 and 1903*, Bull. 20 (Washington, 1905).
—— *United States Census of Housing: 1950—U. S. Summary, General Characteristics* (Washington, 1953).
—— *United States Census of Population: 1950*, Vol. I Ch. I (preprint) *Number of Inhabitants, U. S. Summary* (Washington, 1952).
Children's Bureau. *Child Labor Laws in the United States, Ten Questions Answered* (Washington, Department of Labor, 1942).
Commission on Industrial Relations. *Final Report and Testimony Submitted to Congress*, Vol. I (Washington, 1916).
Congress. Joint Committee on the Economic Report. *Characteristics of the Low-Income Population and Related Federal Programs, Selected Materials Assembled by the Staff of the Subcommittee on Low-Income Families* (Washington, Joint Commitee Print, 1955).
—————*Hearings, Federal Tax Policy for Economic Growth and Stability* (Washington, 1955).
—— Joint Economic Committee. *January 1958 Economic Report of the President: Hearings before the Joint Economic Committee*, 85th Cong., 2d sess., 1958.
—— Senate Committee on Finance. *Retail Prices and Wages*, Report by Nelson W. Aldrich, July 19, 1892 (52d Cong., 1st sess., Senate Report 986, Pt. 3).
————*Wholesale Prices, Wages and Transportation*, Report by Nelson W. Aldrich, March 3, 1893 (52d Cong., 2d sess., Senate Report 1394), Pt. 1.
Department of Agriculture. *Dietary Levels of Households in the United States, Household Food Consumption Survey, 1955*, Report No. 6 (Washington, March 1957).
—— *Dietary Studies in New York in 1895 and 1896*, by Wilbur O. Atwater and Charles Woods, Experiment Station Bull. No. 46 (Washington, 1898).
—— *Diets of Families of Employed Wage Earners and Clerical Workers in Cities*, Circular 507 (Washington, January 1939).
—— *Family Food Consumption in the United States, Spring 1942*, Misc. Publication 550 (Washington, 1944).
—— *Food Consumption of Households in the United States*, Report No. 1 of Household Food Consumption Survey (Washington, December 1956).
—— *Food Consumption of Urban Families in the United States*, Information Bull. 132 (Washington, 1955).
—— *Nutritive Content of City Diets*, Special Report No. 2, based on food consumption surveys of 1948–49 (Washington, October 1950).
—— *Rural Family Spending and Saving in Wartime*, Misc. Publication 520 (Washington, 1943).
—— *Trends in the Consumption of Fibers in the U. S., 1892–1948*, by Barkley Meadows, Statistical Bull. 89 (Washington, Dec. 1950).
Department of the Interior. *Abstract of Eleventh Census: 1890* (Washington, 1896).
Federal Communications Commission. *Radio and Television Broadcast Primer*, Information Bull. No. 2 (Washington, April 1956).
Federal Housing Administration. *Four Decades of Housing With a Limited Dividend Corporation* (Washington, 1939).

United States—Continued
   Federal Reserve Bank of New York. *Series of Indexes of Hourly and Weekly Earnings in Non-agricultural Industries in the United States* (New York, 1956).
   Federal Works Agency. Public Roads Administration. *Highway Statistics Summary to 1945* (Washington, 1947).
   Housing and Home Finance Agency. *1st Annual Report* (Washington, 1948).
   ——— *8th Annual Report* (Washington, 1955).
   ——— *9th Annual Report* (Washington, 1956).
   ——— *10th Annual Report* (Washington, 1957).
   Interstate Commerce Commission. *70th Annual Report* (Washington, 1957).
   National Resources Committee. *Consumer Expenditures in the United States, Estimates for 1935–36* (Washington, 1939).
   ——— *Consumer Incomes in the United States, Their Distribution in 1935–36* (Washington, 1938).
   ——— *Family Expenditures in the United States, Statistical Tables and Appendixes* (Washington, 1941).
   Office of Education. *Adult Education for Foreign Born and Native Illiterates*, Bull 36 (Washington, 1925).
   ——— *Digest of Annual Reports of the State Boards for Vocational Education to the Office of Education*, Fiscal Year Ended June 30, 1955 (Washington, 1955).
   ——— *Part-Time Secondary Schools*, Bull No. 17, National Survey of Secondary Education, Monograph No. 3 (Washington, 1932).
   President. *Economic Report of the President, January 1958* (Washington, 1958).
   President's Research Committee on Social Trends. *Recent Social Trends in the United States*, Vol. 1 (New York, McGraw-Hill Book Company, Inc., 1933).
   Public Health Service. *Careers in Industrial Health* (Washington, 1947).
   ——— *Health Manpower Chart Book*, Publication 511 (Washington, 1957).
   ——— *Preliminary Report on Volume of Dental Care, United States, July–September 1957*, from the U. S. National Health Survey, Health Statistics Series B2 (Washington, March 1958).
   ——— *Preliminary Report on Volume of Physician Visits, United States, July–September 1957*, from the U. S. National Health Survey, Health Statistics Series B1 (Washington, February 1958).
   ——— *Vital Statistics Special Reports*, Vol. 48, No. 6, *Abridged Life Tables—United States 1956* (Washington, 1958).
   Statutes at Large. Vols. 34, 42, 48, 49, 50, 52, 60, 67.
   Works Progress Administration. *Intercity Differences in Costs of Living in March 1935, 59 cities*, Research Monograph XII, by Margaret Loomis Stecker (Washington, 1937).
   ——— Division of Social Research. *Quantity Budgets for Basic Maintenance and Emergency Standards of Living* (Washington, 1936).
World Health Organization. *Constitution of the World Health Organization* (Washington, 1949).

Books

Abbott, Edith and Associates. *The Tenements of Chicago, 1908–1935* (Chicago, University of Chicago Press, 1936).

Adams, Henry. *The Education of Henry Adams, An Autobiography* (New York, Book League Edition, 1928).
Alderfer, E. B., and Michl, H. E. *Economics of American Industry* (New York, McGraw-Hill Book Co., Inc., 1942).
Amalgamated Clothing Workers of America. *The Seventh Biennial Report of the General Executive Board, 1924-26.*
American Medical Association. *Hospital Service in the United States: the 1953 Census of Hospitals* (Chicago, 1954).
Anderson, Odin W., and Feldman, Jacob J. *Family Medical Costs and Voluntary Health Insurance: A Nationwide Survey* (New York, McGraw-Hill Book Co., Inc., 1956).
Automobile Manufacturers Association. *Automobile Facts and Figures* (Detroit, 1957).
Beard, Charles and Mary. *A Basic History of the United States* (New York, The New Home Library, 1944).
Brant, Allen D. *Industrial Health Engineering* (New York, John Wiley & Sons, Inc., 1947).
Budish, J. M. and Soule, G. *The New Unionism in the Clothing Industry* (New York, Harcourt, Brace and Howe, 1920).
Bureau of Applied Economics, Inc. *Standards of Living, A Compilation of Budgetary Studies* (Washington, 1920).
Byington, Margaret F. *Homestead, the Households of a Mill Town* (New York, Russell Sage Foundation, Charities Publication Committee, 1910).
Carskadon, Thomas R., and Soule, George. *U. S. A. in New Dimensions: A Twentieth Century Fund Survey* (New York, Macmillan Co., 1957).
Chapin, Robert C. *The Standard of Living Among Workingmen's Families in New York City, 1907* (New York, Russell Sage Foundation, Charities Publication Committee, 1909).
Chotzinoff, Samuel. *A Lost Paradise* (New York, Alfred Knopf, 1955).
Commager, Henry Steele. *The American Mind, An Interpretation of American Thought and Character Since the 1880's* (New Haven, Yale University Press, 1950).
Congress of Industrial Organizations. *Proceedings, 8th Constitutional Convention* (Washington, 1946).
Cummings, Richard Osborn. *An American and His Food* (Chicago, University of Chicago Press, 1940).
Davis, Michael M. *Clinics, Hospitals and Health Centers* (New York, Harper & Brothers, 1927).
DeForest, Robert W., and Veillers, Lawrence (eds.). *The Tenement House Problem* (New York, The Macmillan Co., 1903), Vol. I.
Dewhurst, J. Frederick, and Associates. *America's Needs and Resources, A New Survey* (New York, The Twentieth Century Fund, 1955).
Douglas, Paul H. *Real Wages in the United States, 1890-1926* (Boston, Houghton Mifflin, 1930).
Douglas, Paul H., Hitchcock, Curtice N., and Atkins, Willard E. *The Worker in Modern Economic Society* (Chicago, University of Chicago Press, 1923).
Drucker, Peter F. *The New Society, the Anatomy of the Industrial Order* (New York, Harper & Brothers, 1950).
Durand, John D. *The Labor Force in the United States, 1890-1960* (New York, Social Science Research Council, 1948).
Editors of *Fortune*. *The Changing American Market* (Garden City, N. Y., Hanover House, 1955).

Falk, I. S., Klem, Margaret C., and Sinai, Nathan. *The Incidence of Illness and the Receipt and Costs of Medical Care Among Representative Families: Experiences in Twelve Consecutive Months During 1928–31*, An Abstract of a Report Published for the Committee on the Costs of Medical Care by the University of Chicago Press (Washington, 1933).

Furness, E. S. *The Position of the Laborer in a System of Nationalism* (Boston, Houghton Mifflin, 1920).

Gauss, Christian (ed.). *Democracy Today* (New York, Scott, Foresman and Company, 1917).

Goldsmith, R. W., Brady, Dorothy S., and Mendershausen, Horst. *A Study of Saving in the United States* (Princeton, N. J., Princeton University Press, 1956), Vol. III.

Grattan, C. Hartley. *In Quest of Knowledge—A Historical Perspective on Adult Education* (New York, Association Press, 1955).

Hacker, Louis M. and Kendrick, Benjamin B. *The United States Since 1865* (New York, F. S. Croft and Co., 1932).

Handlin, Oscar. *The Uprooted* (Boston, Little, Brown and Company, 1951).

Hardman, J. B. S. No Ultimatum Ends, in *Unions, Management, and the Public*, E. Wight Bakke and Clark Kerr, eds. (New York, Harcourt, Brace and Co., 1948), pp. 31–33.

Hardman, J. B. S. and Neufeld, Maurice F. (eds.). *The House of Labor, Internal Operations of American Unions* (New York, Prentice-Hall, Inc., 1951).

The Health Insurance Council. *The Extent of Voluntary Health Insurance Coverage in the United States, as of December 31, 1956* (New York, 1957).

Heller Committee for Research in Social Economics. *Quantity and Cost Budgets* (Berkeley, University of California, 1929).

——— *Quantity and Cost Budgets for Two Income Levels* (Berkeley, University of California, 1956).

Herzfeld, Elsa G. *Family Monographs, The History of Twenty-Four Families Living in the Middle West Side of New York City* (New York, The James Kempster Printing Co., 1905).

Hunter, Robert. *Tenement Conditions in Chicago* (Chicago, City Homes Association, 1901).

Kennedy, E. D. *The Automobile Industry* (New York, Reynal and Hitchcock, 1941).

Kennedy, J. C. *Wages and Family Budgets in the Chicago Stockyards District, with Wage Statistics from Other Industries Employing Unskilled Labor* (Chicago, University of Chicago Press, 1914).

Kettering, C. F., and Orth, A. *American Battle for Abundance* (Detroit, General Motors, 1947).

Lamale, Helen Humes. *Methodology of the Survey of Consumer Expenditures in 1950* (to be published by the Wharton School of the University of Pennsylvania in 1959).

Levasseur, Emile. *The American Workman*, translated by Thomas S. Adams (Baltimore, The Johns Hopkins Press, 1900).

Lewis, H. Gregg, and Douglas, Paul H. *Studies in Consumer Expenditures*, Studies in Business Administration (Chicago, University of Chicago Press, 1947).

Little, Esther Louise, and Cotton, William Joseph. *Budgets of Families and Individuals of Kensington, Philadelphia* (Lancaster, Pa., New Era Printing Co., 1920).

Mill, John Stuart. *Principles of Political Economy*, Ashley edition (New York, Longmans, Green & Co., 1909).

More, Louise Bolard. *Wage Earners' Budgets: A Study of Standards and Cost of Living in New York City* (New York, H. Holt and Company, 1907).

National Accounts Review Committee. *The National Economic Accounts of the United States: Review, Appraisal and Recommendations* (New York, National Bureau of Economic Research, Inc., 1957).

National Association of Home Builders. *Housing . . . U. S. A.* (New York, Simmons-Boardman Publishing Corporation, 1954).

National Automobile Chamber of Commerce, Inc. *Facts and Figures of the Automobile Industry* (New York, 1923).

National Commission on Adult Education Finance. *Financing Adult Education in America's Public Schools* (Washington, 1954).

National Industrial Conference Board. *Company Medical and Health Programs*, by Ethel M. Spears, Studies in Personnal Policy, No. 96 (New York, 1948).

——— *The Cost of Living Among Wage-Earners, Fall River, Mass., October 1919*, Research Report 22 (Boston, 1919).

National Safety Council. *Accident Facts, 1957 Edition* (Chicago, 1957).

Nevins, Allan. *Ford: The Times, The Man, The Company* (New York, Scribner, 1954).

Nugent, Rolf. *Consumer Credit and Economic Stability* (New York, Russell Sage Foundation, 1939).

Ogburn, William F. Budget for Bituminous Coal Mine Workers, 1920, in *Standards of Living, A Compilation of Budgetary Studies* (Washington, Bureau of Applied Economics, Inc., 1920).

Overstreet, B. W. The Free Lecture System of New York, in *Adult Education in Action*, Mary L. Ely, ed. (New York, American Association for Adult Education, 1936), pp. 76–78.

Owen, Wilfred. *The Metropolitan Transportation Problem* (Washington, Brookings Institution, 1956).

Pierson, N. G. *Principles of Economics*, translated by A. A. Wotzel (London, Macmillan and Co., Ltd., 1902).

Plumley, Margaret Lovell. *Growth of Clinics in the United States* (Chicago, Julius Rosenfeld Fund, 1932).

Pound, Arthur. *The Turning Wheel* (Garden City, N. Y., Doubleday, Doran & Company, Inc., 1934).

Price, Theodore H. The Chain Grocery Store, in *Seven Articles by Theo. H. Price* (New York, Theodore H. Price Publishing Corp. [1919?]).

Purcell, Theodore V., S. J. *The Worker Speaks His Mind on Company and Union* (Cambridge, Mass., Harvard University Press, 1953).

Study of Consumer Expenditures, Incomes and Savings: Statistical Tables, Urban U. S.—1950, tabulated by the Bureau of Labor Statistics, U. S. Department of Labor for the Wharton School of Finance and Commerce, University of Pennsylvania, 18 Vols. (University of Pennsylvania, 1956 and 1957).

Winslow, C. E. A. *The Evolution of Public Health and Its Objectives* (Cambridge, Mass., Harvard University Press, 1949).

Wood, Edith Elmer. *The Housing of the Unskilled Wage Earner* (New York, Macmillan Co., 1919).

Woytinsky, W. S. and Associates. *Employment and Wages in the United States* (New York, The Twentieth Century Fund, 1953).

Articles and Periodicals

Abbott, Grace. The Federal Government in Relation to Maternity and Infancy (in *Annals of the American Academy of Political and Social Science*, Sept. 1930, pp. 92–101).

AFL-CIO News, September 7, 1957 (Washington, American Federation of Labor and Congress of Industrial Organizations).

Altmeyer, Arthur J. The Worker's Quest for Security (in *Monthly Labor Review,* July 1950, pp. 31-37).

Automotive News, August 20 and October 8, 1956 (Detroit, Slocum Publishing Co., Inc.).

Bell, Daniel. The Impact of Advertising (in *The New Leader,* Feb. 11, 1957, pp. 9-11).

——— The Worker and His Civic Functions (in *Monthly Labor Review,* July 1950, pp. 62-69).

Bowden, Witt. Changes in Modes of Living (in *Monthly Labor Review,* July 1950, pp. 23-30).

Brooks, John Graham. The Label of the Consumer League (in *Publications of the American Economic Association,* Third Series, Vol. I, No. 1, Feb. 1900, pp. 250-258).

Burk, Marguerite C. Changing Food Patterns of the American People (in *The National Food Situation,* Aug. 2, 1955, pp. 13-22).

——— National Food Survey of the United Kingdom and Comparisons with Other British and American Food Data (in *Agricultural Economics Research,* July 1957, pp. 73-87).

Business Week, May 5, 1956 (New York, McGraw-Hill Publishing Co., Inc.).

Citizens' Business (Bulletin of the Bureau of Municipal Research of Philadelphia), Sept. 9, 1920, Apr. 7, 1921, and Apr. 5, 1923.

Clague, Ewan. *The Shifting Industrial and Occupational Composition of the Work Force During the Next Ten Years,* an Address before the AFL-CIO Conference on the Changing Character of American Industry, Washington, D. C., Jan. 16, 1958 (Washington, Bureau of Labor Statistics, 1958).

Construction, July and August 1951 (Washington, U. S. Bureau of Labor Statistics).

Cost of Living in the United States (in *Monthly Labor Review,* May 1919, pp. 147-165; June 1919, pp. 101-116; July 1919, pp. 75-114; Aug. 1919, pp. 117-119).

The Cotton Situation, CS-169, Apr. 1957 (Washington, U. S. Department of Agriculture, Agricultural Marketing Service).

Current Labor Statistics (in *Monthly Labor Review,* Dec. 1957, p. 1545).

Douglas, Paul H. The Movement of Real Wages and Its Economic Significance (in *The American Economic Review, Supplement,* Mar. 1926, pp. 17-53).

Education of Adult Working Classes (in *Monthly Labor Review,* June 1921, pp. 1301-1310).

Epstein, Albert S. The Impact of Emergencies on Labor Organizations (in *Monthly Labor Review,* Oct. 1951, pp. 388-393).

The Evening Sun, Baltimore, Jan. 4, 1954.

Brady, Dorothy S. Expenditures and Savings of City Families in 1944 (in *Monthly Labor Review,* Jan. 1946, pp. 1-5).

Extent of the 5-Day Week in American Industry, 1931 (in *Monthly Labor Review,* Sept. 1931, pp. 1-6).

Federal Reserve Bulletin, various issues reporting findings of the Surveys of Consumer Finances, conducted annually, 1946-58; also Aug. 1957 issue.

The 5-Day Week in Ford Plants (in *Monthly Labor Review,* Dec. 1926, pp. 10-14).

Gist, Noel P. Developing Patterns of Urban Decentralization (in *Social Forces,* Mar. 1952, pp. 257-266).

Goldstein, Harold. Recent Trends in and Outlook For College Enrollments (in *Monthly Labor Review,* Mar. 1956, pp. 286-291).

Good Housekeeping, October 1911.
Henderson, Harry. The Mass-Produced Suburbs: How People Live in America's Newest Towns (in *Harper's Magazine*, Nov. 1953, pp. 25–32).
High Fidelity: Next Year a $300,000,000 Industry (in *Newsweek*, Dec. 21, 1953, pp. 66–67).
Housing Research, October 1952 (Washington, Housing and Home Finance Agency).
Housing Statistics, May 1957 (Washington, Housing and Home Finance Agency).
How People Spend Their Time (in *Broadcasting Telecasting*, Sept. 16, 1957, p. 35).
Journal of the American Hospital Association: Hospitals Guide Issue, Pt. 2, Aug. 1, 1956.
A Journal of Highway Research, Vol. 23, No. 2, Apr. 1942 (Washington, Public Roads Administration).
Justice, Vol. XXXVII, No. 19, Oct. 1, 1955 (New York, International Ladies' Garment Workers' Union).
Karter, Thomas. Voluntary Agency Expenditures for Health and Welfare from Philanthropic Contributions, 1930–55 (in *Social Security Bulletin*, Feb. 1958, pp. 14–18).
Knapp, Eunice M. City Worker's Family Budget for October 1951 (in *Monthly Labor Review*, May 1952, pp. 520–522).
Kravis, Irving B. Work Time Required to Buy Food (in *Monthly Labor Review*, Nov. 1949, pp. 487–493).
Cost of Living in New York City in November 1920 (in *Monthly Labor Review*, Feb. 1921, pp. 61–66).
Ladies' Home Journal, February 1901 (Philadelphia, Curtis Publishing Co.).
Lamale, Helen Humes. Changes in Concepts of Income Adequacy Over the Last Century (in *Papers and Proceedings of the Seventieth Annual Meeting, American Economic Review*, Vol. XLVIII, No. 2, May 1958, pp. 291–299).
Lear, Walter J., M. D. Medical-Care Insurance for Industrial Workers (in *Monthly Labor Review*, Sept. 1951, pp. 251–257).
Meeker, Royal. What is the American Standard of Living? (in *Monthly Labor Review*, July 1919, pp. 1–13).
Merriam, Ida C. Social Welfare Expenditures in the United States, 1955–56 (in *Social Security Bulletin*, Oct. 1957, pp. 3–12).
Murphy, Kathryn R. Characteristics of New 1-Family Houses, 1954–56 (in *Monthly Labor Review*, May 1957, pp. 572–575).
New York Times, The, January 28, 1957.
Pinkerton, Kathrene. The College That's Tailor-made (in *Nation's Business*, Mar. 1950, Washington, Chamber of Commerce of the United States, pp. 43–44, 78–79).
A Report on Trailer Living (in *Consumer Reports*, Vol. 21, No. 3, March 1956, pp. 113–119).
Reynolds, Marcus T. The Housing of the Poor in American Cities (in *Publications of the American Economic Association*, Vol. VIII, Nos. 2 and 3, Mar. and May 1893).
Saposs, David J. Voluntarism in the American Labor Movement (in *Monthly Labor Review*, Sept. 1954, pp. 967–971).
Schiro, Bruno A. Housing Surveys in 75 Cities, 1950 and 1952 (in *Monthly Labor Review*, July 1954, pp. 744–750).
Schwellenbach, Lewis B. Work and Policies of the Department of Labor, 1913–48 (in *Monthly Labor Review*, Mar. 1948, pp. 249–254).

Smith, M. Mead. Financial Hardship Cases Handled by the Fight-Blight Fund (in *Monthly Labor Review*, Aug. 1955, pp. 882–888).
Theodore, Rose, and Gentry, John N. Paid Vacations in Major Union Contracts, 1957 (in *Monthly Labor Review*, July 1958, pp. 744–751).
The Startling Development of the Bi-Dimensional Theater (in *Current Literature*, May 1908, pp. 546–549).
Steel Labor, July 1957 (Pittsburgh, United Steelworkers of America).
Survey of Current Business, Business Statistics, 1955 supplement; National Income, *Supplement*, 1954 edition; and February and July 1957 issues (Washington, U. S. Department of Commerce, Office of Business Economics).
Time and Money Costs of Meals Using Home and Prekitchen Prepared Food, Statement from a Panel Discussion at the 31st Annual Agricultural Outlook Conference, Oct. 29, 1953 (Washington, U. S. Department of Agriculture, Bureau of Human Nutrition and Home Economics).
Union News, Feb. 18, 1957 (Norfolk, Virginia State Federation of Labor).
Union Wage Scales in Building Trades, 1957 (in *Monthly Labor Review*, February 1958, pp. 171–175).
Vacation for Factory Workers (in *Monthly Labor Review*, Aug. 1921, pp. 212–213).
Vacation with Pay for Workers (in *The Literary Digest*, Sept. 11, 1920, p. 37).
Valesh, Eva MacDonald. The Tenement House Problem in New York (in *The Arena*, Apr. 1893, pp. 580–584).
We Spend About as Much for Fun as for Running the Government (in *Business Week*, July 13, 1932, pp. 20–21).
Williams, Faith M. Standards and Levels of Living of City-Worker Families (in *Monthly Labor Review*, Sept. 1956, pp. 1015–1023).
Wolozin, Harold. Use of Instalment Credit by City-Worker Families in 1918 (in *Monthly Labor Review*, June 1957, pp. 712–716).
Zeisel, Joseph S. The Workweek in American Industry (in *Monthly Labor Review*, January 1958, pp. 23–29).

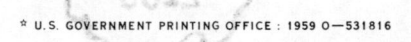

2150